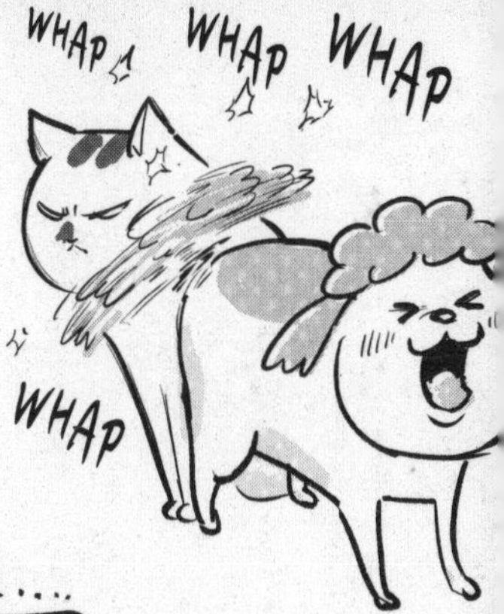
WHAP
WHAP
WHAP
WHAP
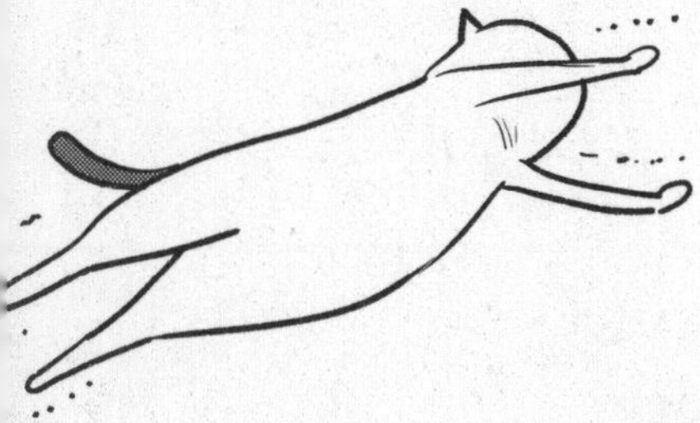
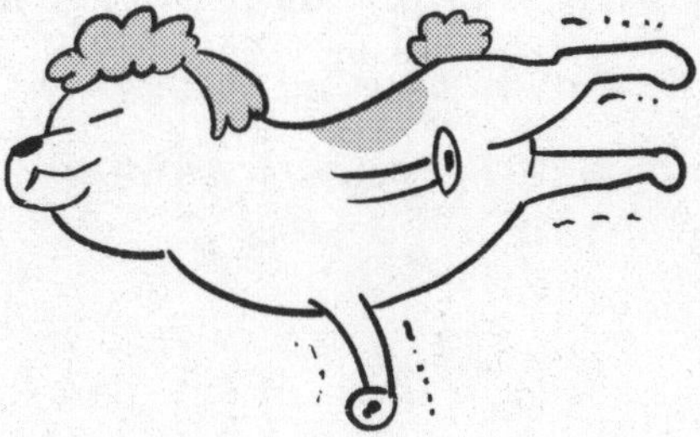
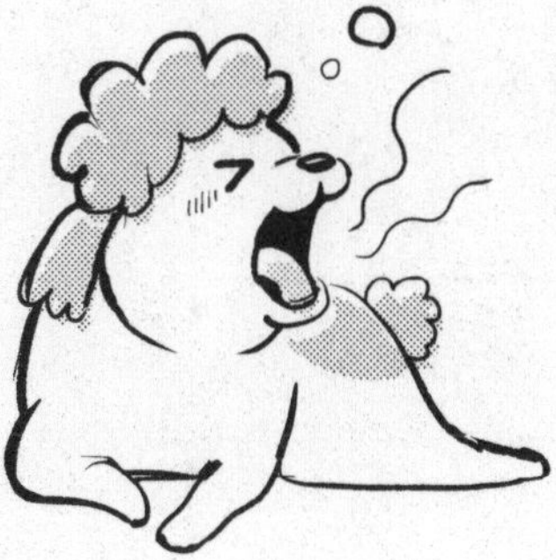
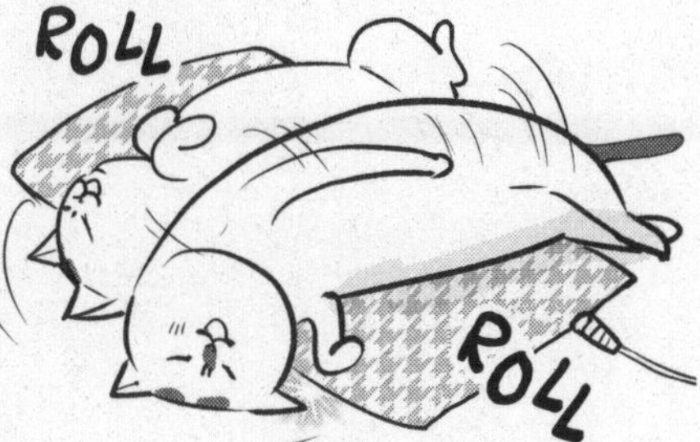
ROLL
ROLL
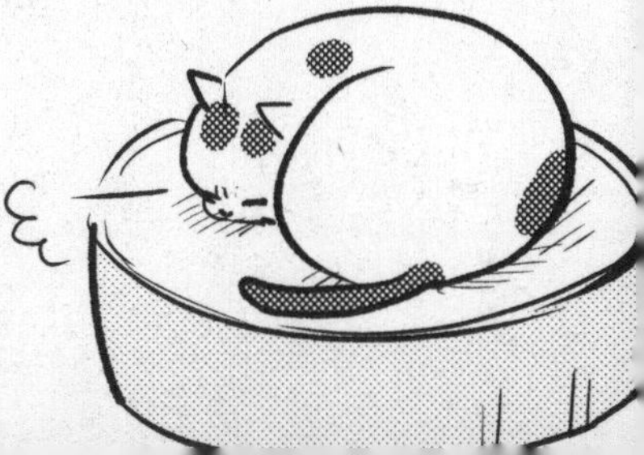
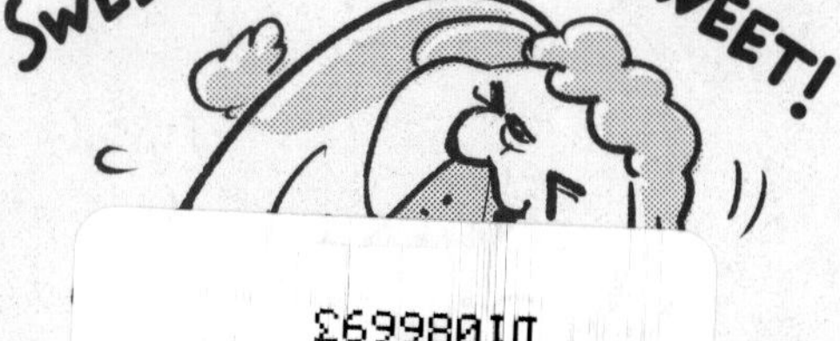
SO SWEET!
SO SWEET!

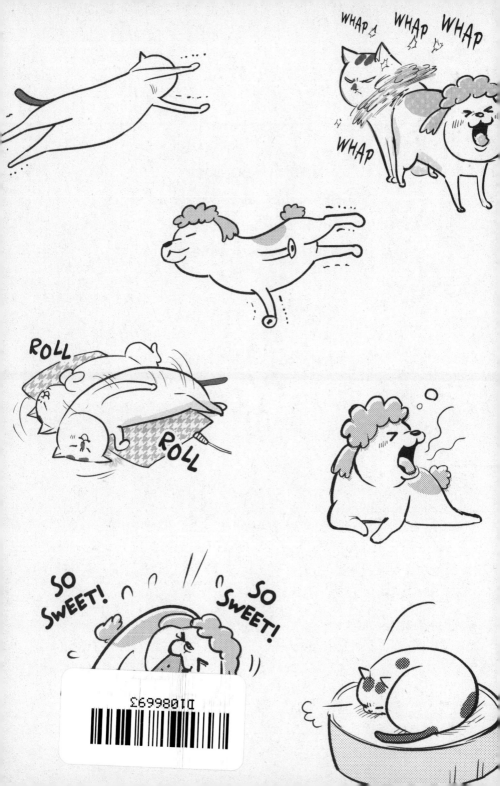

Inu and Neko with
their bellies out, plopped
down on the floor...
Reminds you of summer,
doesn't it?

Hidekichi Matsumoto

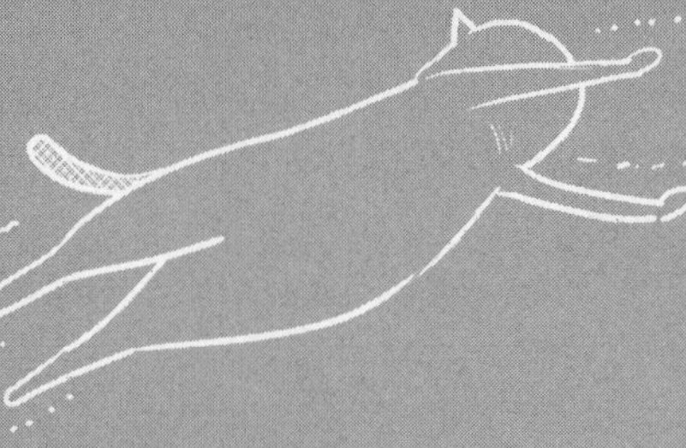

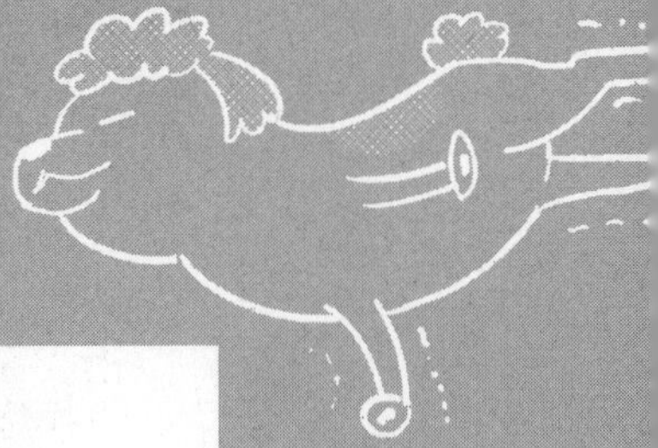

With a Dog AND a Cat, Every Day is Fun

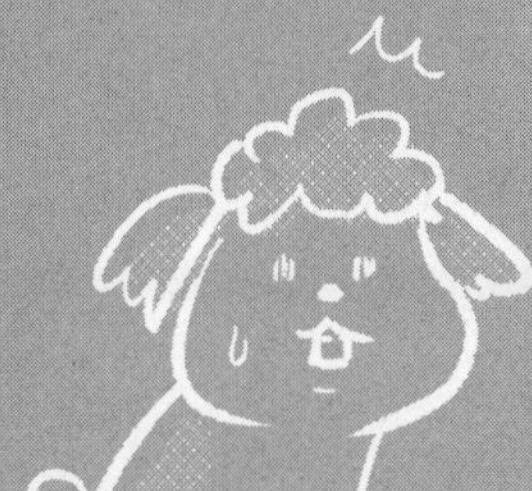

5

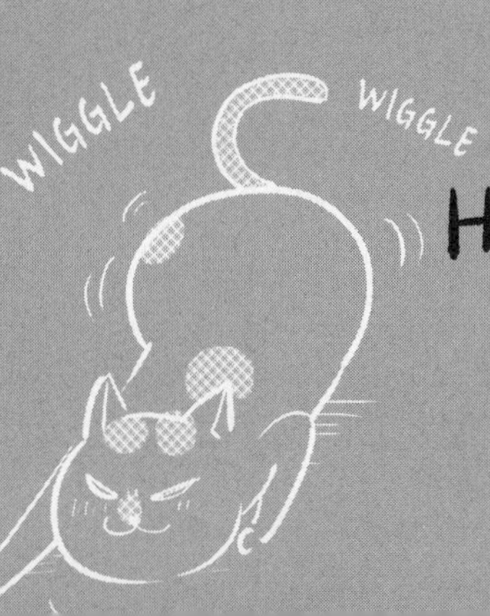
WIGGLE
WIGGLE

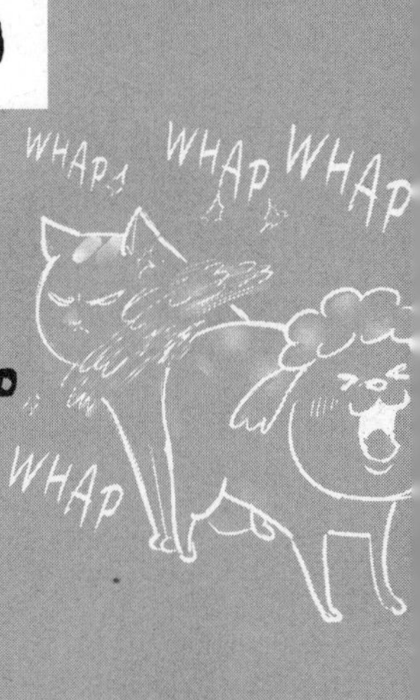
WHAP!
WHAP
WHAP
WHAP

Hidekichi Matsumoto

CAST

HIDEKICHI MATSUMOTO

Manga artist. Loves animals.

INU-KUN

Loves Neko. Even when he doesn't like something, if you sing and dance, he soon forgets about it.

NEKO-SAMA

A fearsome face. A cool customer. His passion for theft is staggering.

LEOPA

Nickname: Tokage-chan. A constant object of Neko's gaze. Has none of the cool composure you'd expect from reptiles.

DAD

Hidekichi's father. A very kind man.

MOM

Hidekichi's mother. Holds the #1 ranking in the Matsumoto household.

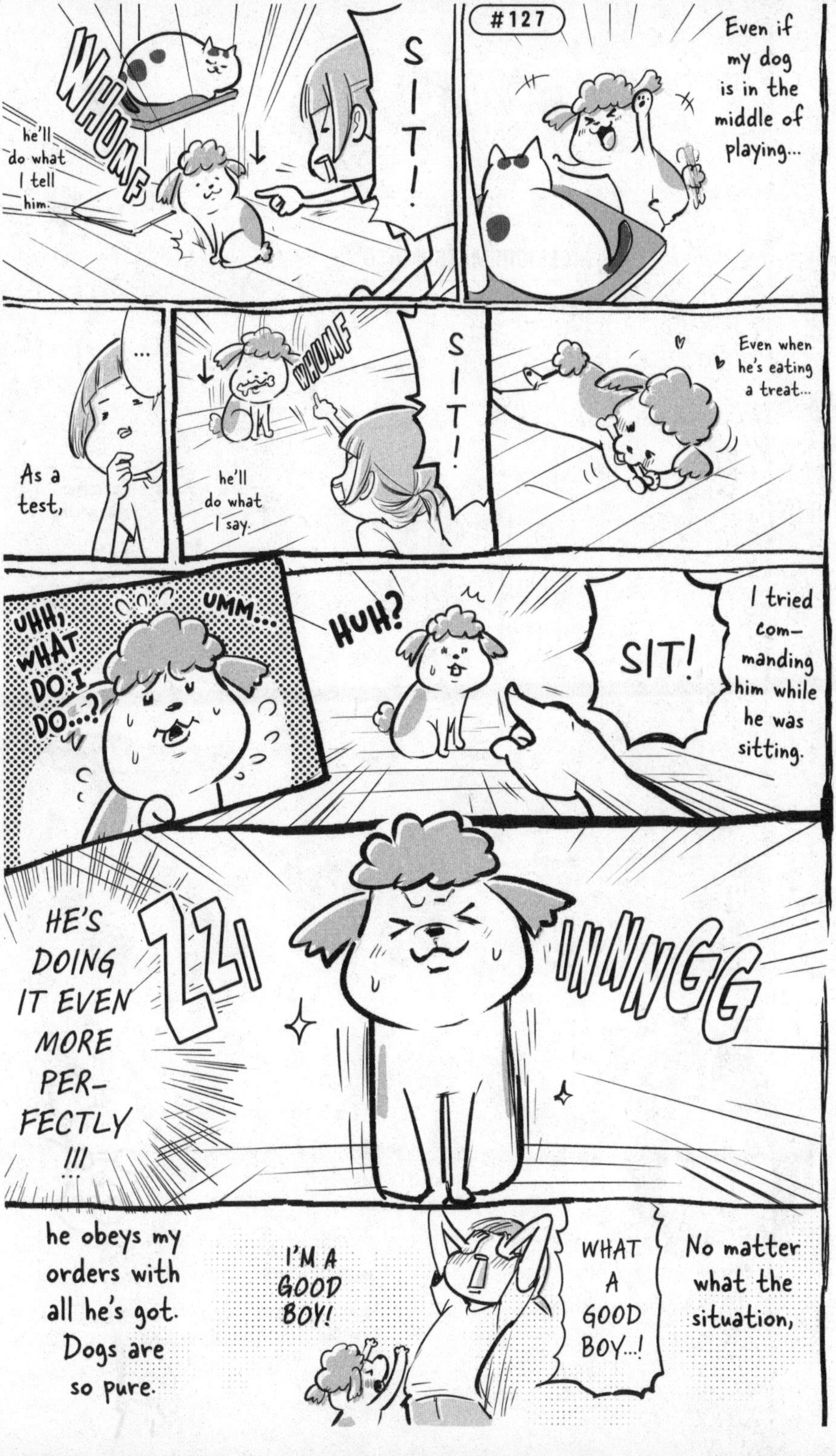
#127
Even if my dog is in the middle of playing...
SIT!
WHUMF
he'll do what I tell him.
Even when he's eating a treat...
SIT!
WHUMF
he'll do what I say.
...
As a test,
I tried commanding him while he was sitting.
SIT!
HUH?
UMM...
UHH, WHAT DO I DO...?
ZZINNNGG
HE'S DOING IT EVEN MORE PERFECTLY!!!
No matter what the situation,
WHAT A GOOD BOY...!
I'M A GOOD BOY!
he obeys my orders with all he's got. Dogs are so pure.

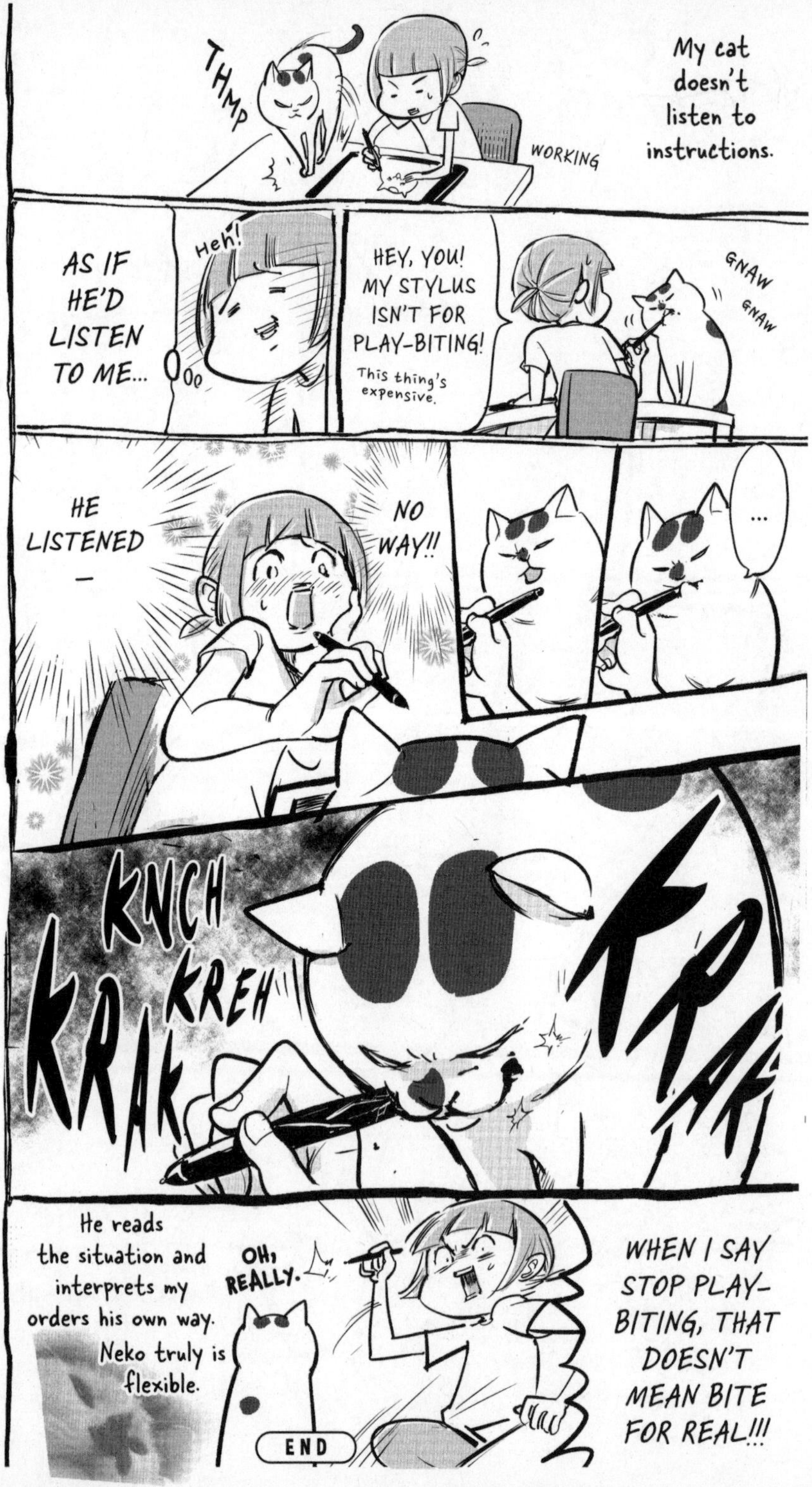
My cat doesn't listen to instructions.
WORKING
THMP
GNAW
GNAW
HEY, YOU! MY STYLUS ISN'T FOR PLAY-BITING!
This thing's expensive.
Heh!
AS IF HE'D LISTEN TO ME...
...
HE LISTENED —
NO WAY!!
KRAK
KNCH
KREH
KRAK
WHEN I SAY STOP PLAY-BITING, THAT DOESN'T MEAN BITE FOR REAL!!!
OH, REALLY.
He reads the situation and interprets my orders his own way.
Neko truly is flexible.
END

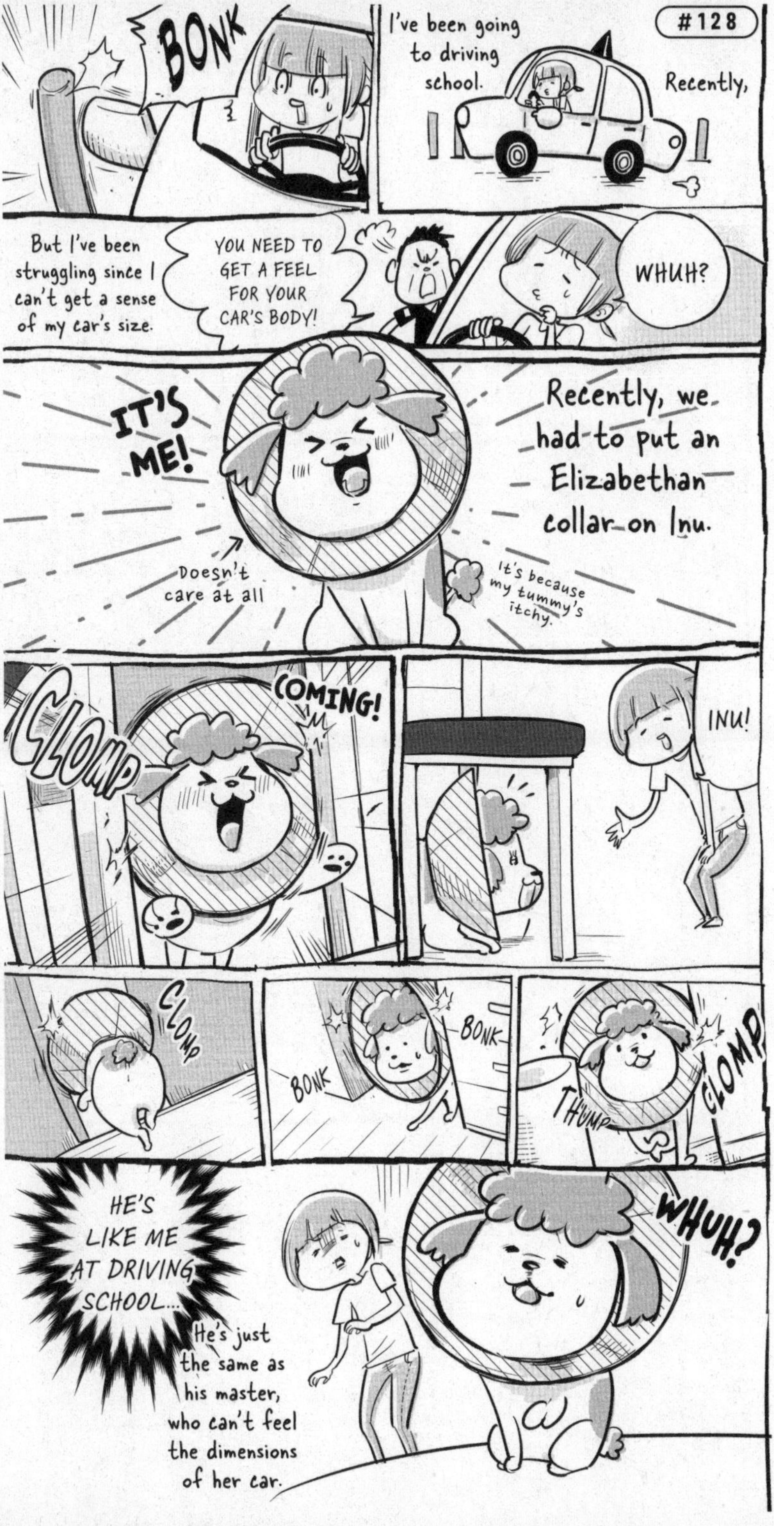
#128
Recently,
I've been going to driving school.
BONK
WHUH?
YOU NEED TO GET A FEEL FOR YOUR CAR'S BODY!
But I've been struggling since I can't get a sense of my car's size.
Recently, we had to put an Elizabethan collar on Inu.
It's because my tummy's itchy.
IT'S ME!
Doesn't care at all
INU!
COMING!
CLOMP
CLOMP
THUMP
BONK
BONK
CLOMP
WHUH?
HE'S LIKE ME AT DRIVING SCHOOL...
He's just the same as his master, who can't feel the dimensions of her car.

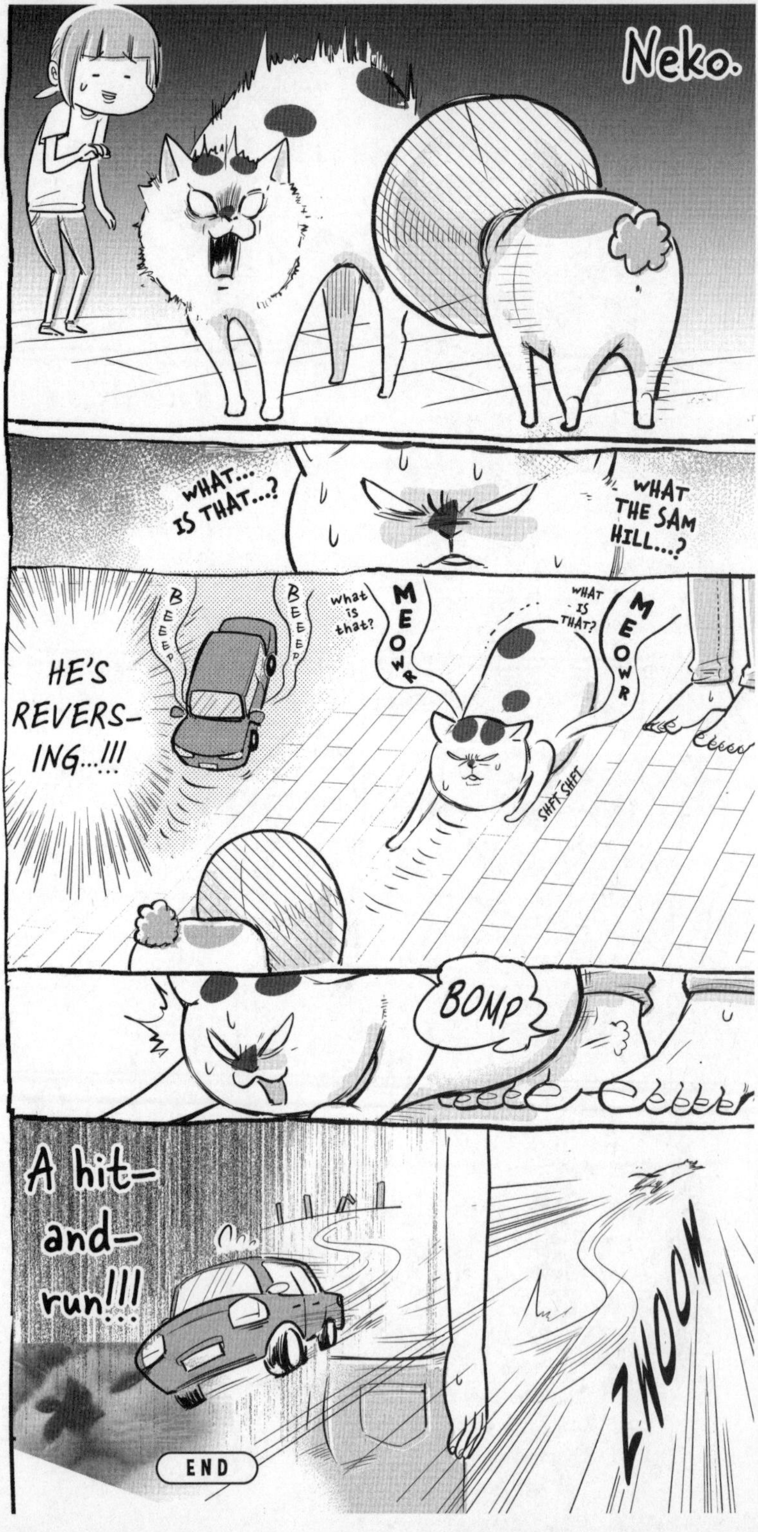
Neko.
WHAT THE SAM HILL...?
WHAT... IS THAT...?
MEOWR
WHAT IS THAT?
MEOWR
what is that?
BEEEP
BEEEP
SHFT SHFT
HE'S REVERSING...!!!
BOMP
ZHOOM
A hit-and-run!!!
END

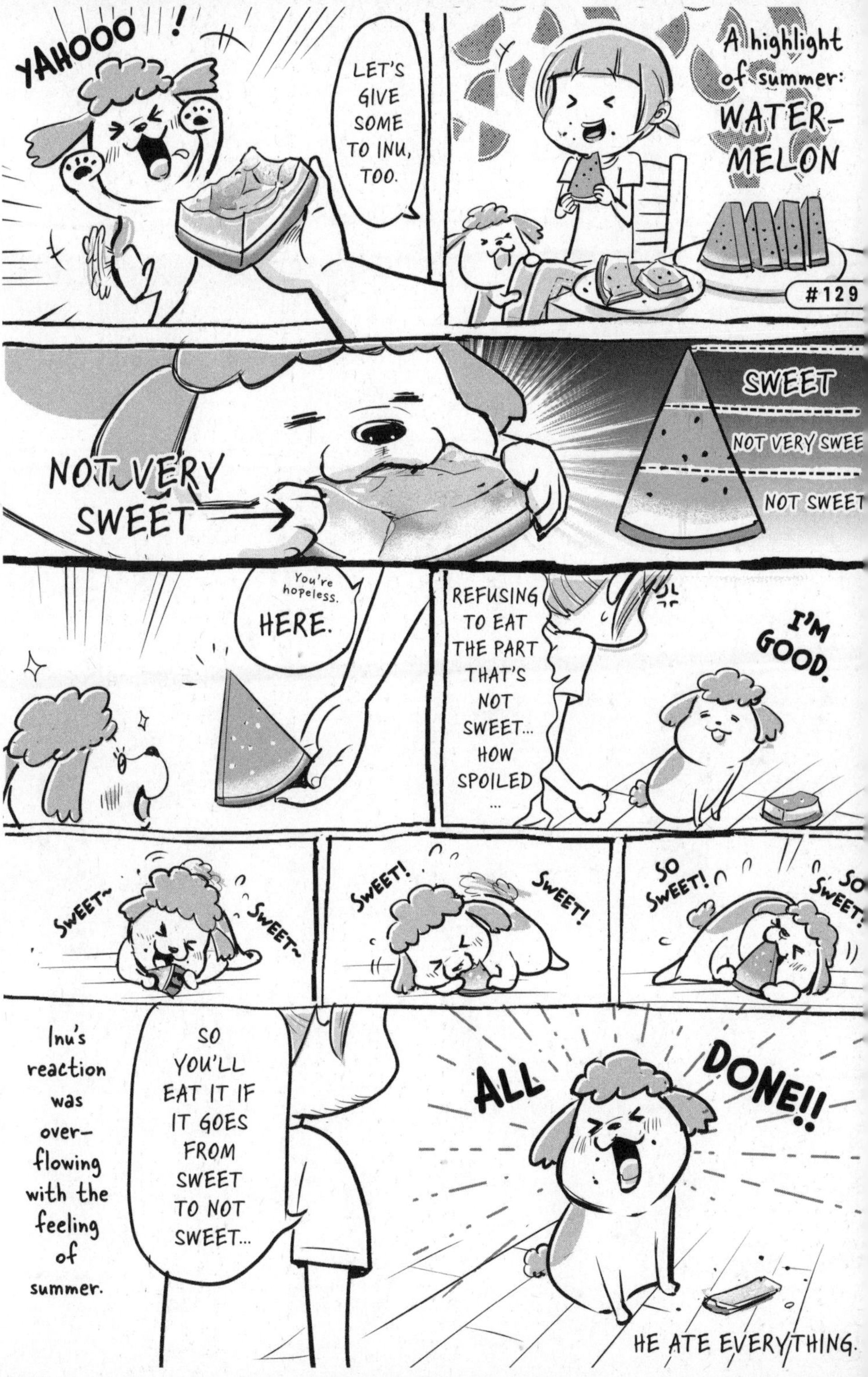
A highlight of summer: WATER-MELON
#129
LET'S GIVE SOME TO INU, TOO.
YAHOOO!
SWEET
NOT VERY SWEE
NOT SWEET
NOT VERY SWEET
I'M GOOD.
REFUSING TO EAT THE PART THAT'S NOT SWEET... HOW SPOILED ...
You're hopeless.
HERE.
SO SWEET!
SO SWEET!
SWEET!
SWEET!
SWEET~
SWEET~
ALL DONE!!
HE ATE EVERYTHING.
SO YOU'LL EAT IT IF IT GOES FROM SWEET TO NOT SWEET...
Inu's reaction was over-flowing with the feeling of summer.

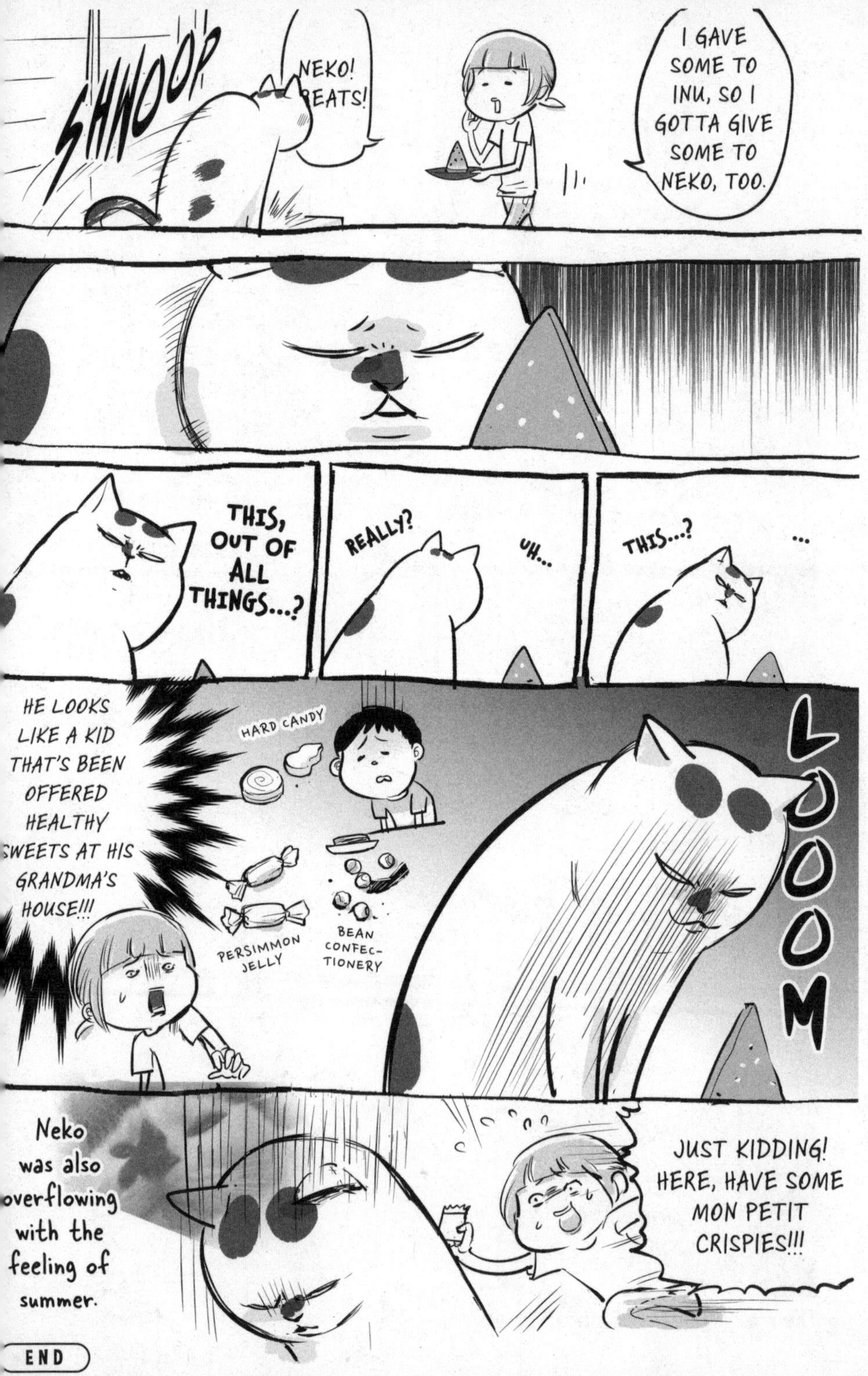
I GAVE SOME TO INU, SO I GOTTA GIVE SOME TO NEKO, TOO.
NEKO! EATS!
SHWOOP
...
THIS...?
REALLY?
UH...
THIS, OUT OF ALL THINGS...?
VOOOM
HARD CANDY
HE LOOKS LIKE A KID THAT'S BEEN OFFERED HEALTHY SWEETS AT HIS GRANDMA'S HOUSE!!!
BEAN CONFECTIONERY
PERSIMMON JELLY
JUST KIDDING! HERE, HAVE SOME MON PETIT CRISPIES!!!
Neko was also overflowing with the feeling of summer.
END

The model himself disapproves.

Newly-Drawn 4-Panel Strip

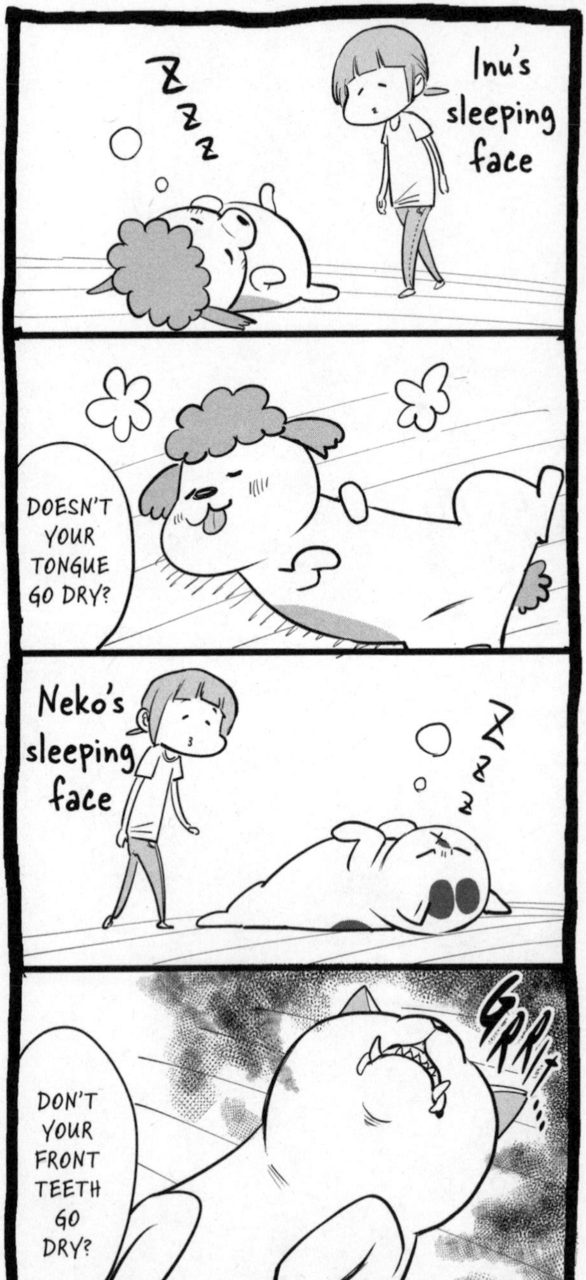
Inu's sleeping face
ZZZ
DOESN'T YOUR TONGUE GO DRY?
ZZZ
Neko's sleeping face
GRR!...
DON'T YOUR FRONT TEETH GO DRY?

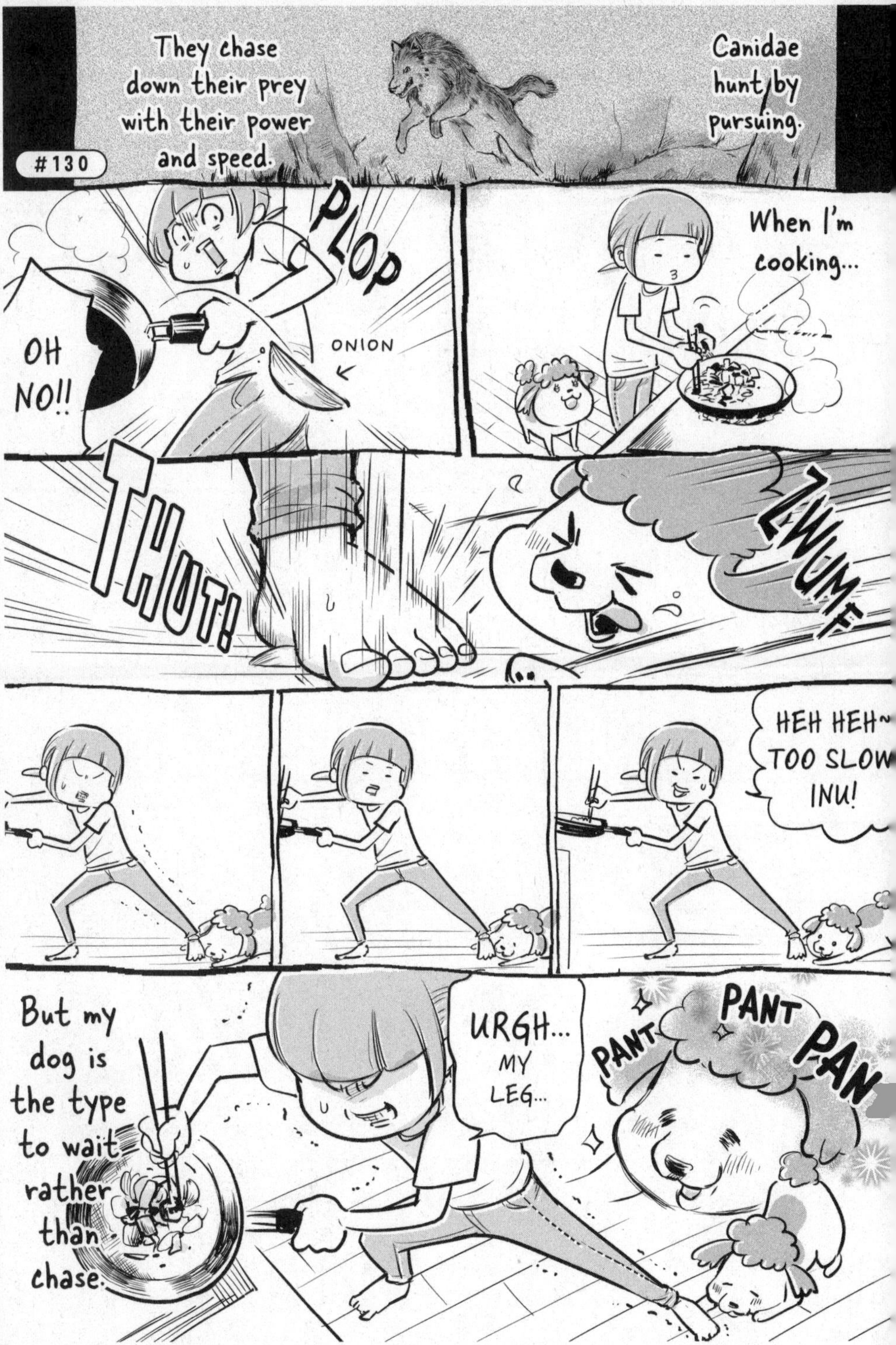

Canidae hunt by pursuing.
They chase down their prey with their power and speed.
#130
When I'm cooking...
PLOP
ONION
OH NO!!
ZWUMF
THUT!
HEH HEH~ TOO SLOW INU!
PANT
PAN
PANT
URGH... MY LEG...
But my dog is the type to wait rather than chase.

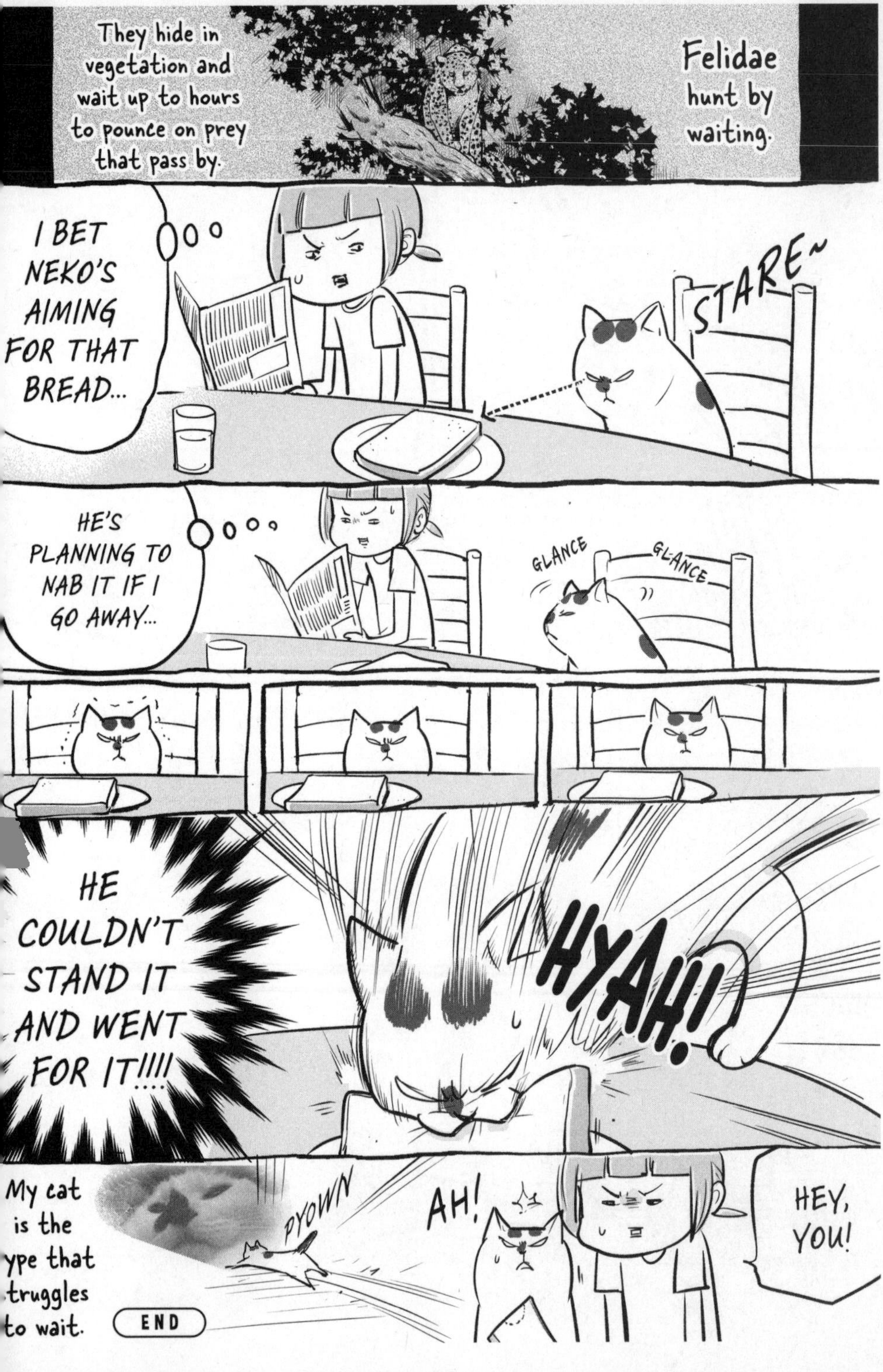
Felidae hunt by waiting.
They hide in vegetation and wait up to hours to pounce on prey that pass by.
STARE~
I BET NEKO'S AIMING FOR THAT BREAD...
GLANCE
GLANCE
HE'S PLANNING TO NAB IT IF I GO AWAY...
HYAH!!
HE COULDN'T STAND IT AND WENT FOR IT!!!!
HEY, YOU!
AH!
PYOWN
My cat is the ype that truggles to wait.
END

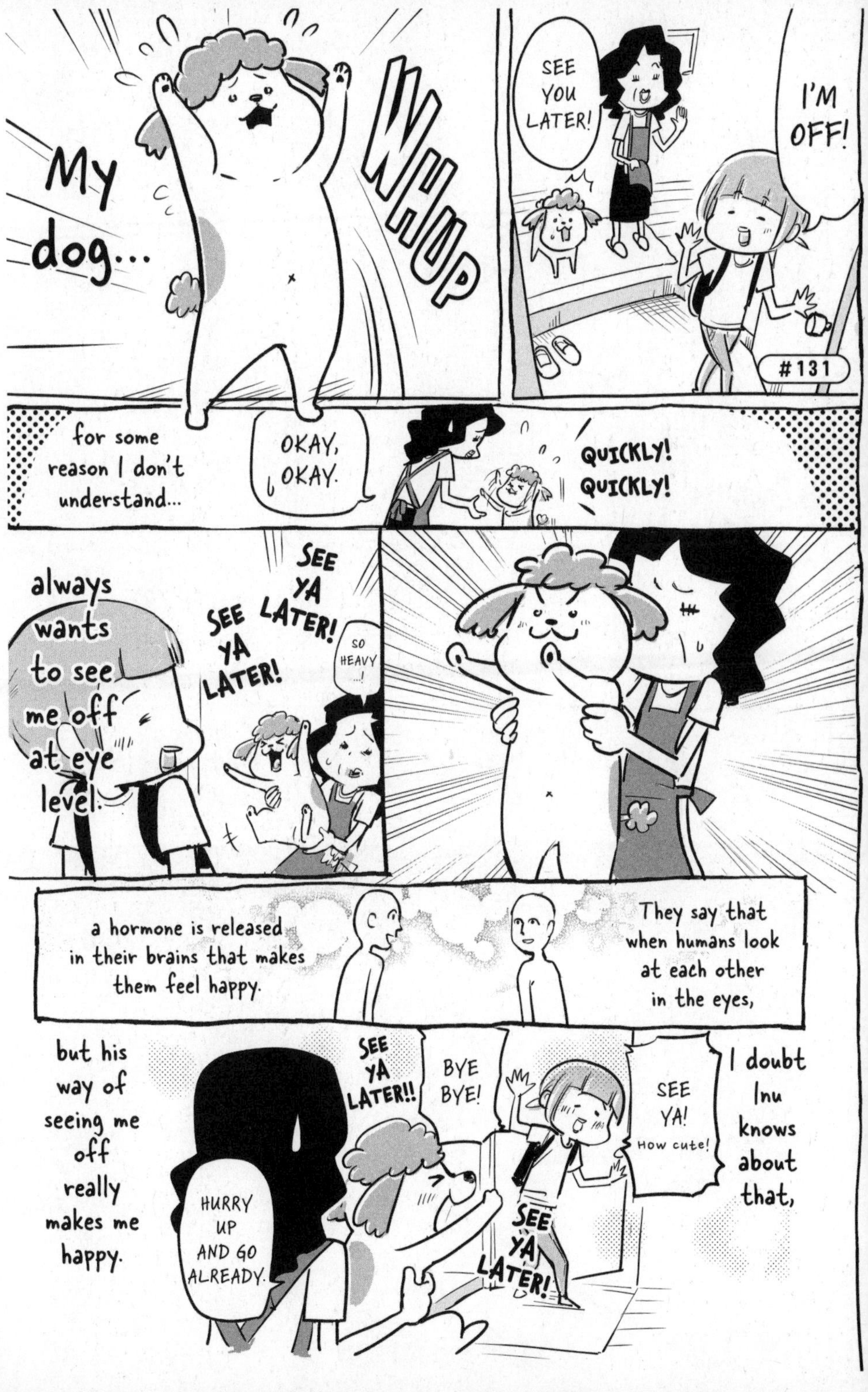
I'M OFF!
SEE YOU LATER!
#131
My dog...
WHUP
QUICKLY! QUICKLY!
OKAY, OKAY.
for some reason I don't understand...
SEE YA LATER!
SEE YA LATER!
SO HEAVY...!
always wants to see me off at eye level.
They say that when humans look at each other in the eyes,
a hormone is released in their brains that makes them feel happy.
I doubt Inu knows about that,
SEE YA! How cute!
BYE BYE!
SEE YA LATER!!
SEE YA LATER!
HURRY UP AND GO ALREADY.
but his way of seeing me off really makes me happy.

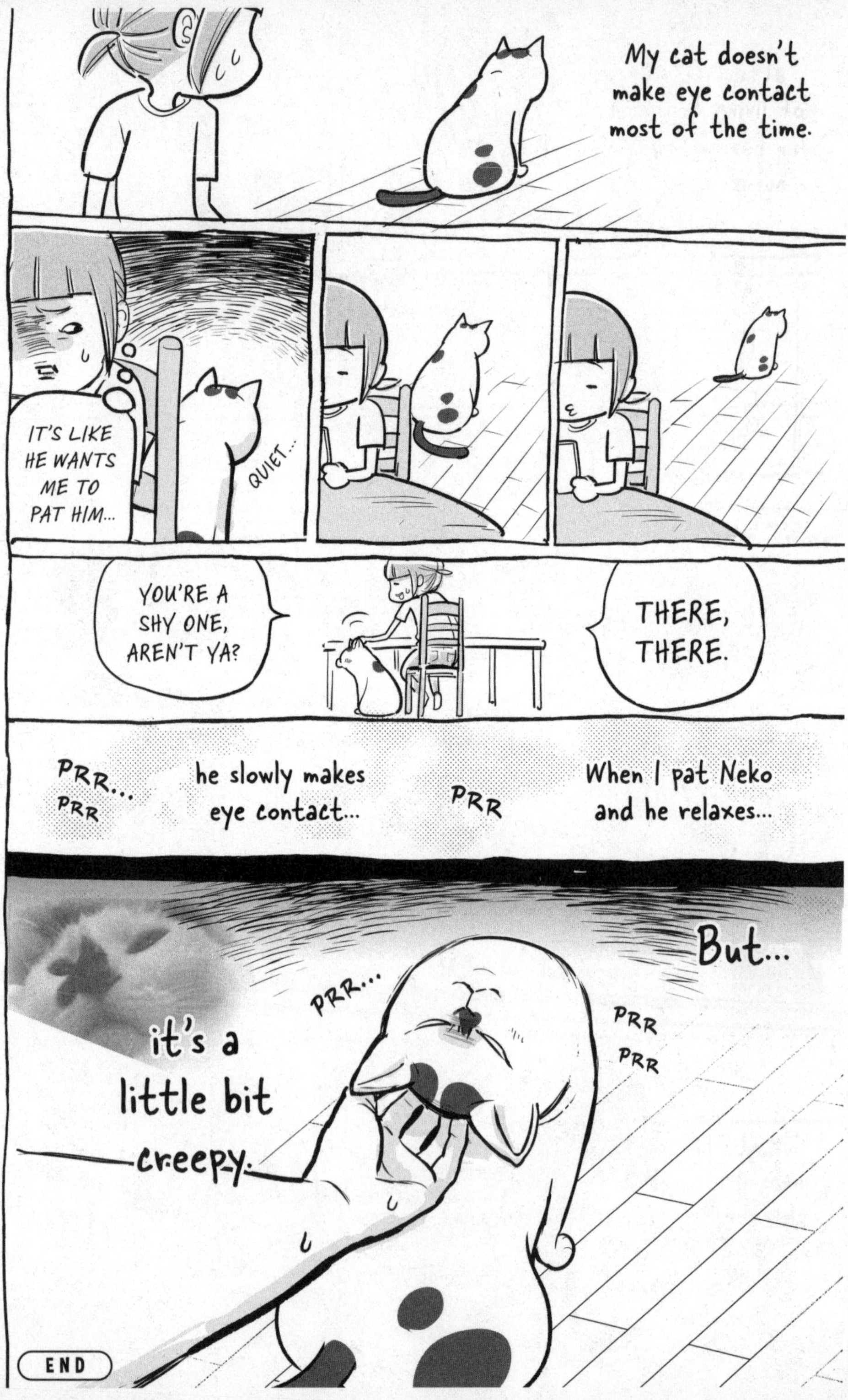

My cat doesn't make eye contact most of the time.
QUIET...
IT'S LIKE HE WANTS ME TO PAT HIM...
THERE, THERE.
YOU'RE A SHY ONE, AREN'T YA?
When I pat Neko and he relaxes...
PRR
he slowly makes eye contact...
PRR... PRR
But...
PRR PRR
PRR...
it's a little bit creepy.
END

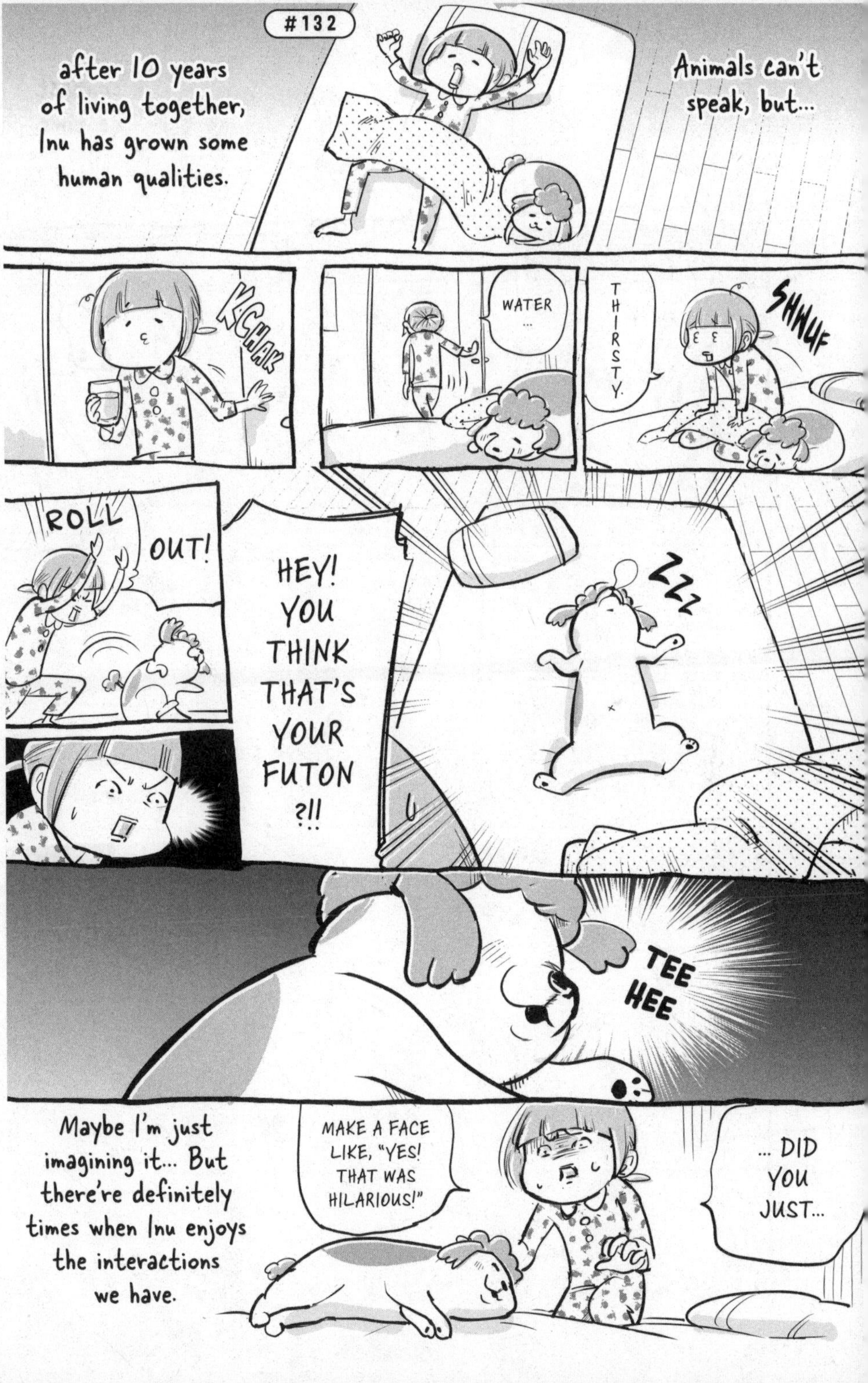
#132
Animals can't speak, but...
after 10 years of living together, Inu has grown some human qualities.
THIRSTY.
SHNUF
WATER ...
KCHAK
ZZZ
HEY! YOU THINK THAT'S YOUR FUTON ?!!
ROLL OUT!
TEE HEE
... DID YOU JUST...
MAKE A FACE LIKE, "YES! THAT WAS HILARIOUS!"
Maybe I'm just imagining it... But there're definitely times when Inu enjoys the interactions we have.

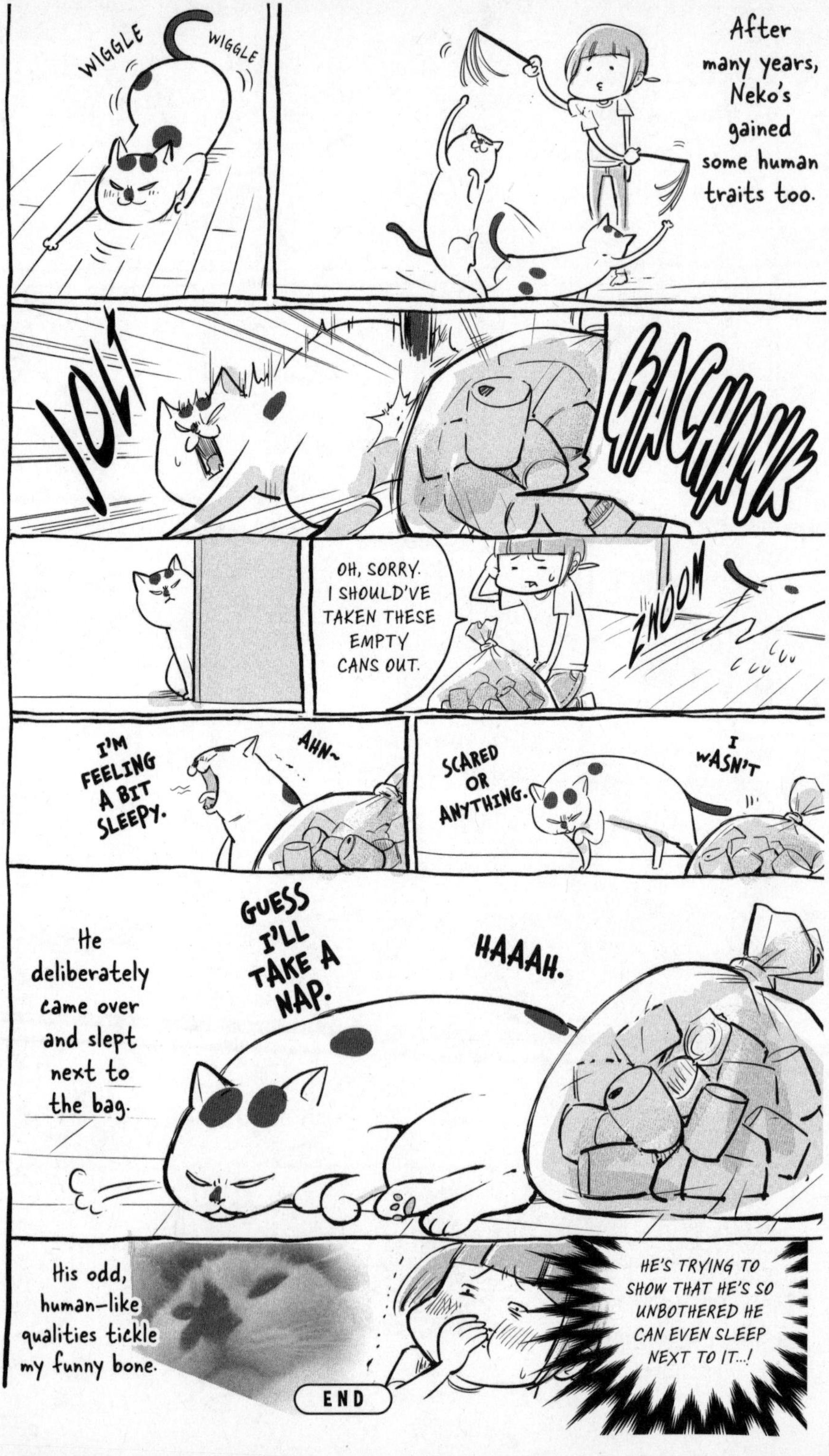
After many years, Neko's gained some human traits too.
WIGGLE
WIGGLE
GACHANK
JOLT
ZWOOM
OH, SORRY. I SHOULD'VE TAKEN THESE EMPTY CANS OUT.
I WASN'T
SCARED OR ANYTHING.
AHN~
I'M FEELING A BIT SLEEPY.
HAAAH.
GUESS I'LL TAKE A NAP.
He deliberately came over and slept next to the bag.
HE'S TRYING TO SHOW THAT HE'S SO UNBOTHERED HE CAN EVEN SLEEP NEXT TO IT...!
His odd, human-like qualities tickle my funny bone.
END

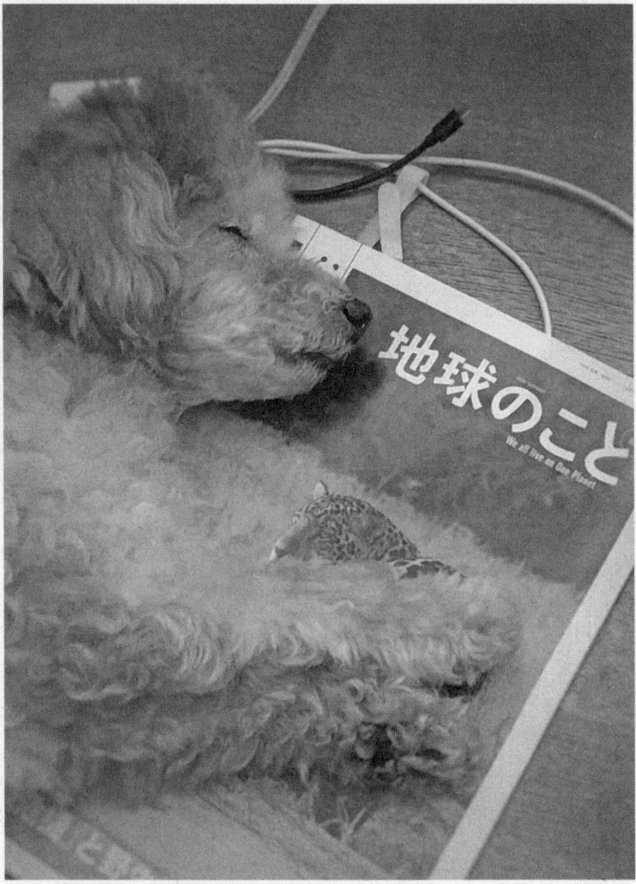
地球のこと

He's thinking about dinner.

Newly-Drawn 4-Panel Strip

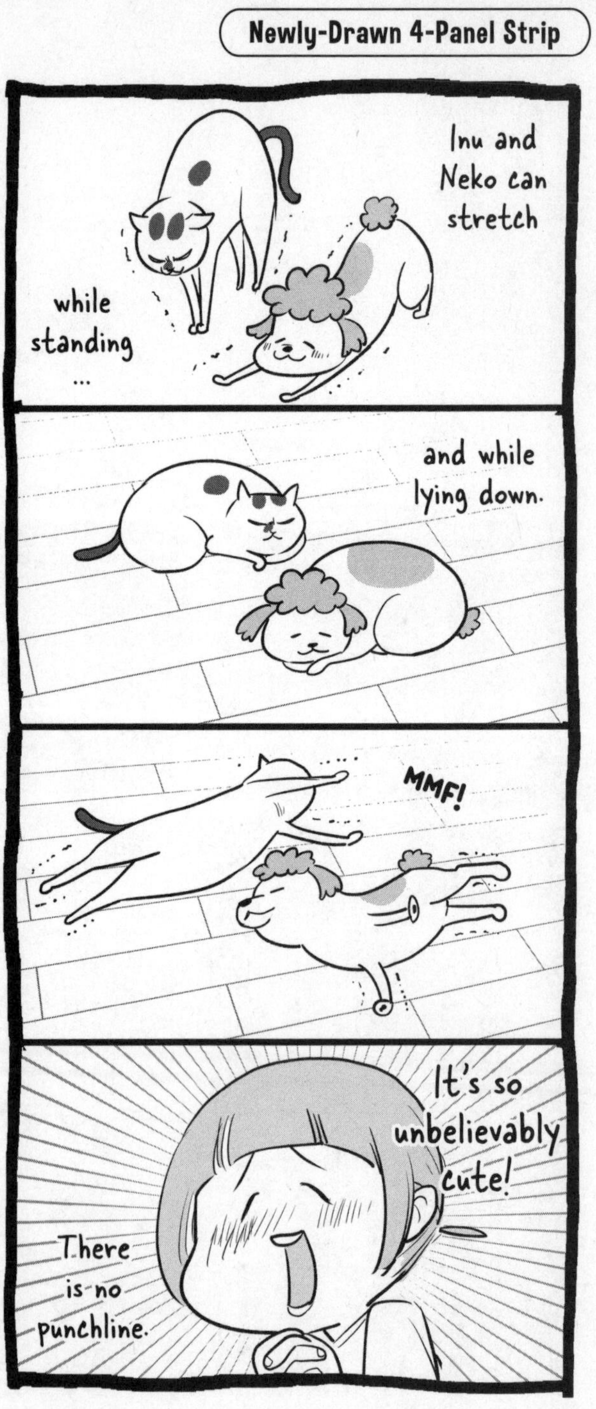
Inu and Neko can stretch
while standing ...
and while lying down.
MMF!
It's so unbelievably cute!
There is no punchline.

#133

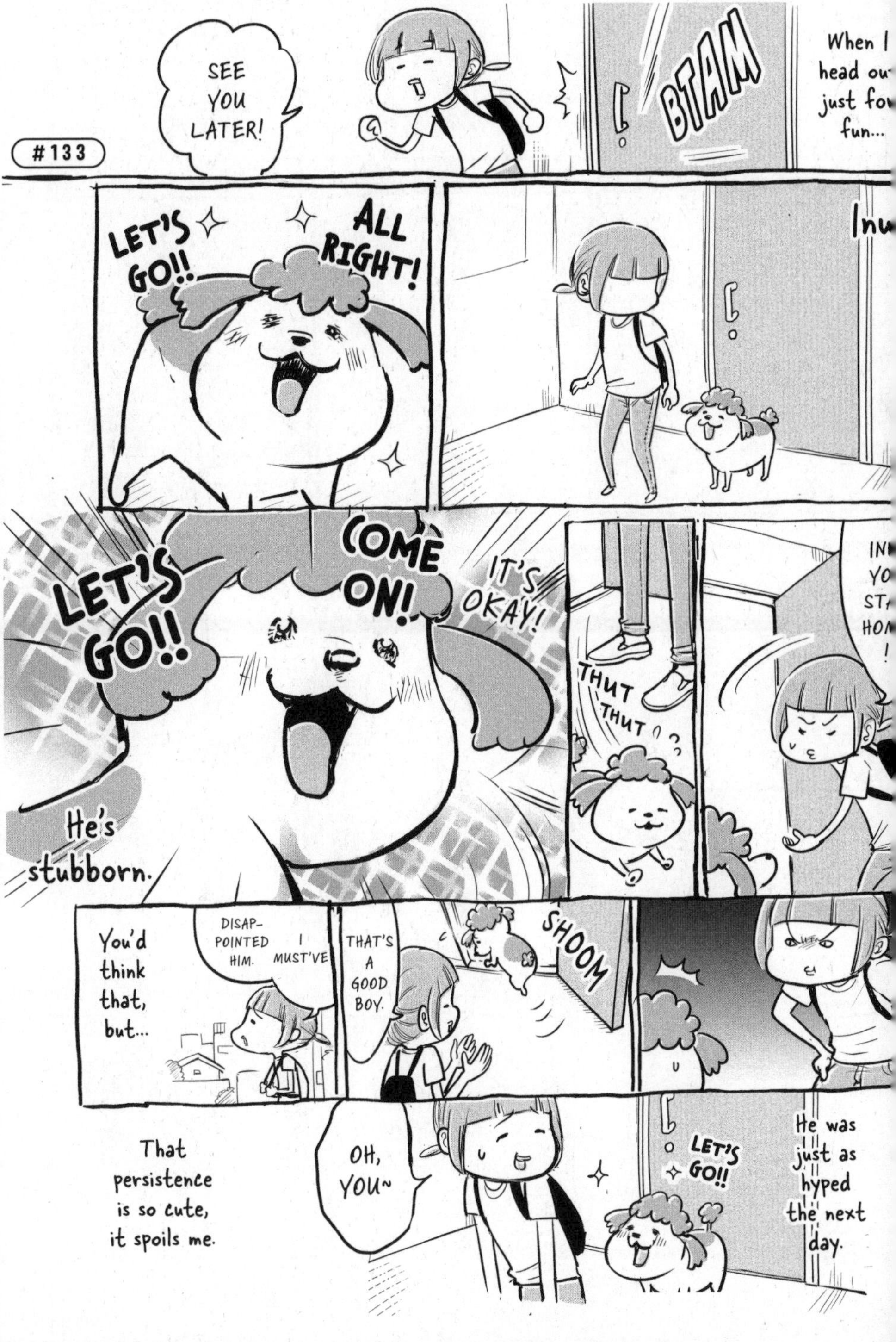
When I head ou just fo fun...
BTAM
SEE YOU LATER!
Inu
ALL RIGHT!
LET'S GO!!
IN YO ST HO !
THUT THUT
IT'S OKAY!
COME ON!
LET'S GO!!
He's stubborn.
SHOOM
THAT'S A GOOD BOY.
I MUST'VE DISAPPOINTED HIM.
You'd think that, but...
He was just as hyped the next day.
LET'S GO!!
OH, YOU~
That persistence is so cute, it spoils me.

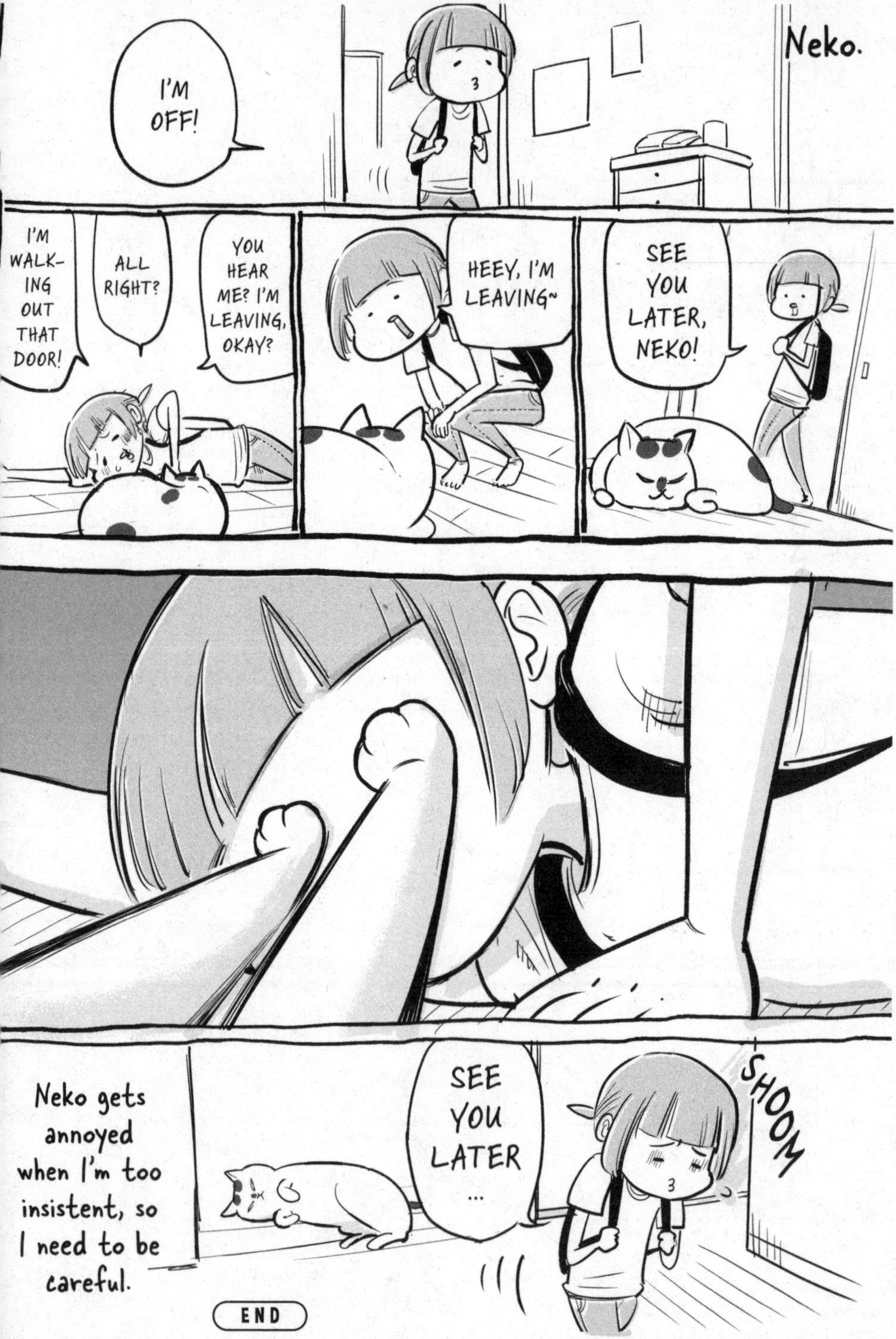
Neko.
I'M OFF!
SEE YOU LATER, NEKO!
HEEY, I'M LEAVING~
YOU HEAR ME? I'M LEAVING, OKAY?
ALL RIGHT?
I'M WALKING OUT THAT DOOR!
SHOOM
SEE YOU LATER ...
Neko gets annoyed when I'm too insistent, so I need to be careful.
END

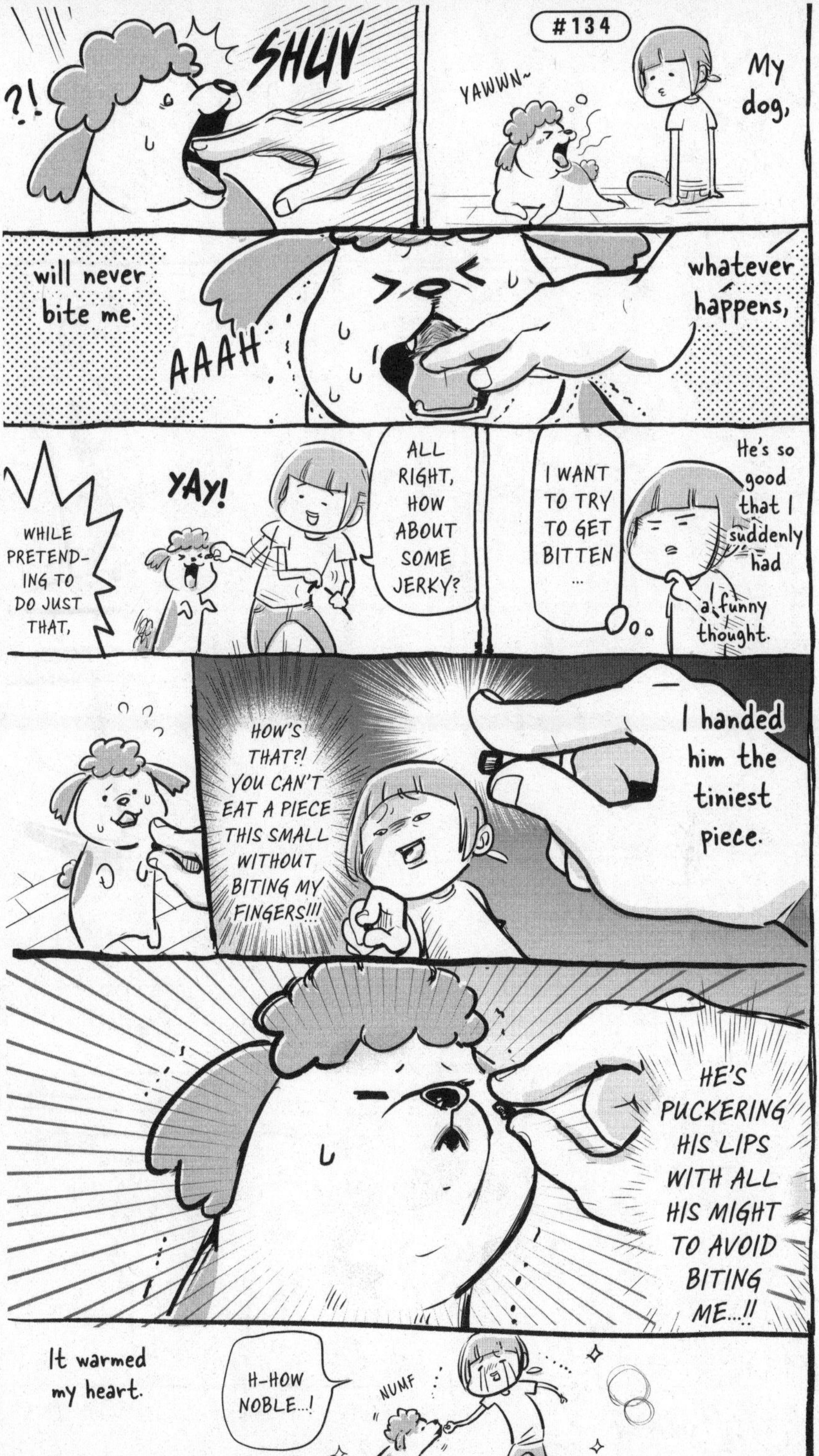
#134
My dog,
YAWWN~
?!
SHUV
whatever happens,
will never bite me.
AAAH
He's so good that I suddenly had a funny thought.
I WANT TO TRY TO GET BITTEN ...
ALL RIGHT, HOW ABOUT SOME JERKY?
YAY!
WHILE PRETENDING TO DO JUST THAT,
I handed him the tiniest piece.
HOW'S THAT?! YOU CAN'T EAT A PIECE THIS SMALL WITHOUT BITING MY FINGERS!!!
HE'S PUCKERING HIS LIPS WITH ALL HIS MIGHT TO AVOID BITING ME...!!
NUMF
H-HOW NOBLE...!
It warmed my heart.

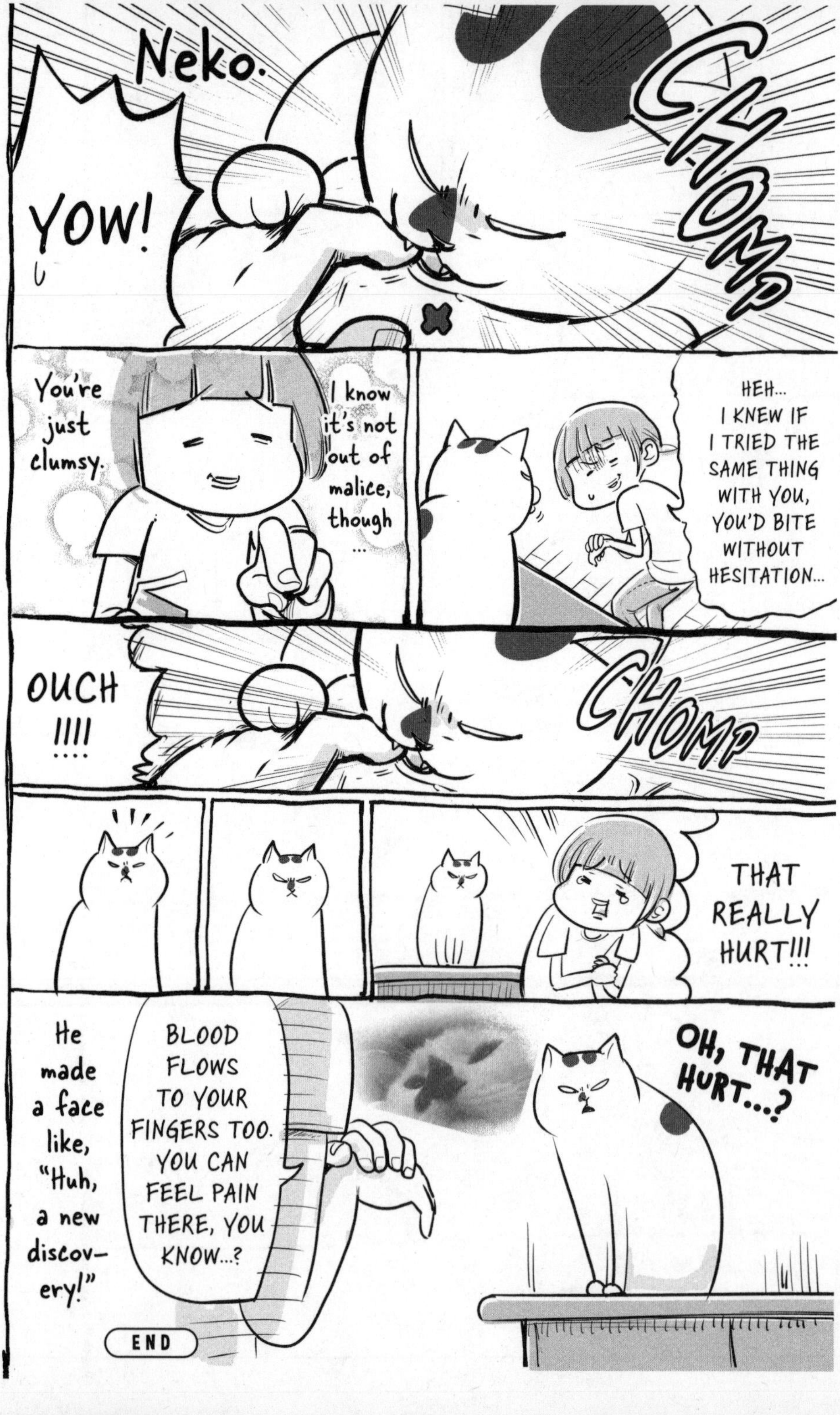
CHOMP
Neko.
YOW!
HEH... I KNEW IF I TRIED THE SAME THING WITH YOU, YOU'D BITE WITHOUT HESITATION...
I know it's not out of malice, though...
You're just clumsy.
CHOMP
OUCH!!!!
THAT REALLY HURT!!!
OH, THAT HURT...?
BLOOD FLOWS TO YOUR FINGERS TOO. YOU CAN FEEL PAIN THERE, YOU KNOW...?
He made a face like, "Huh, a new discov-ery!"
END

#135

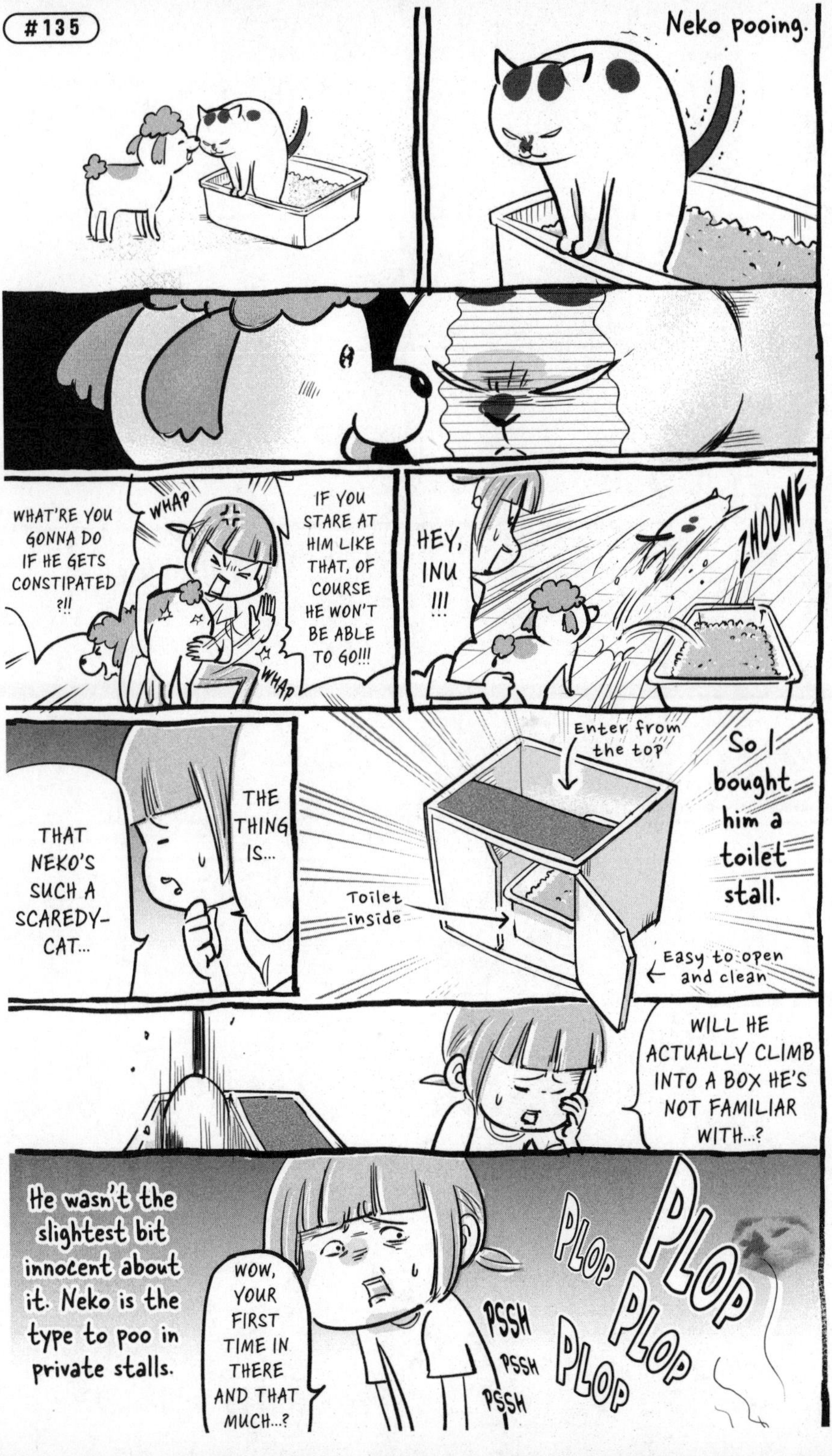
Neko pooing.
HEY, INU!!!
ZHOOMF
IF YOU STARE AT HIM LIKE THAT, OF COURSE HE WON'T BE ABLE TO GO!!!
WHAP
WHAT'RE YOU GONNA DO IF HE GETS CONSTIPATED?!!
WHAP
So I bought him a toilet stall.
Enter from the top
Toilet inside
Easy to open and clean
THE THING IS...
THAT NEKO'S SUCH A SCAREDY-CAT...
WILL HE ACTUALLY CLIMB INTO A BOX HE'S NOT FAMILIAR WITH...?
PLOP PLOP PLOP
PLOP PLOP
PSSH PSSH PSSH
WOW, YOUR FIRST TIME IN THERE AND THAT MUCH...?
He wasn't the slightest bit innocent about it. Neko is the type to poo in private stalls.

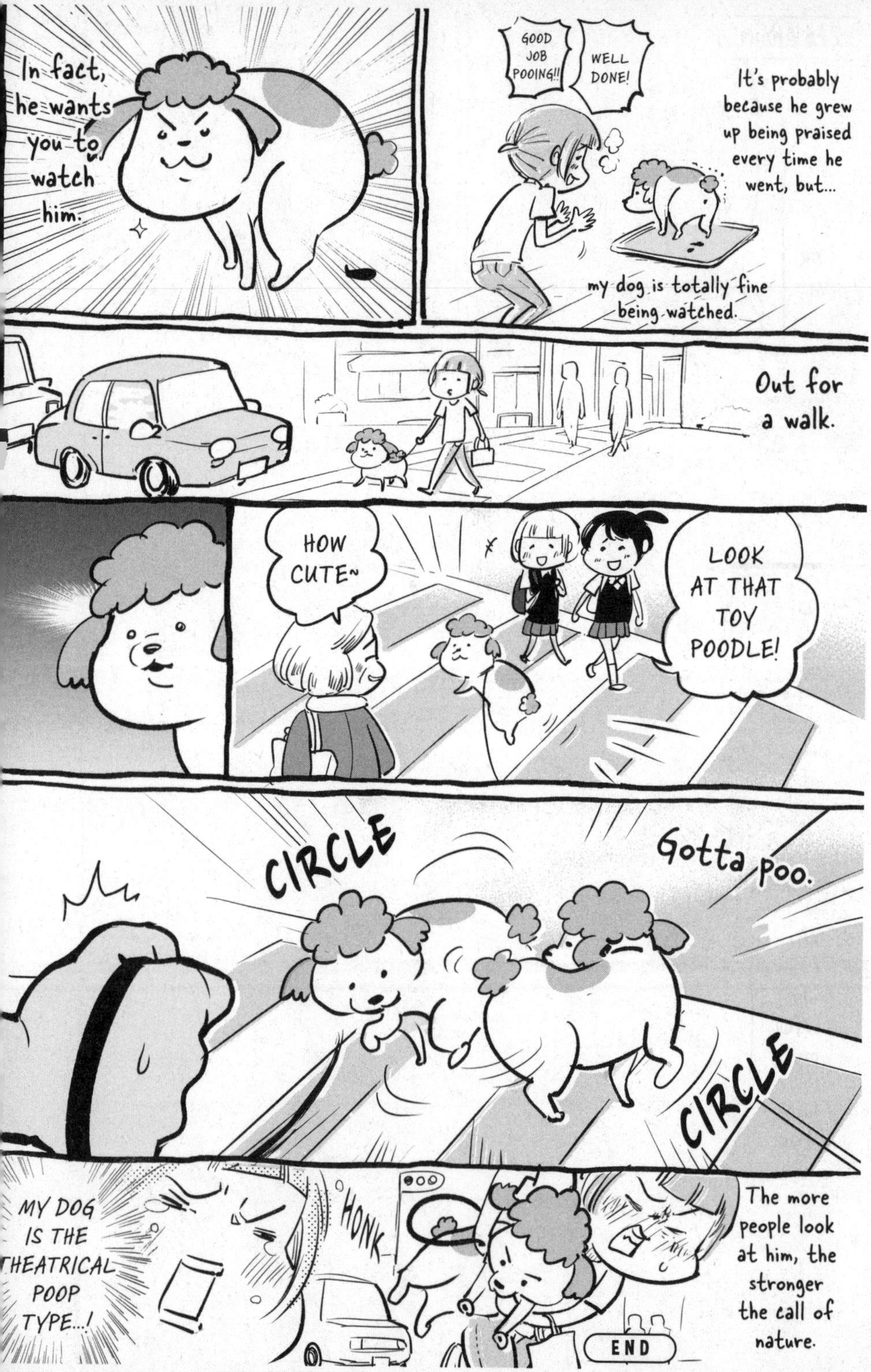
WELL DONE!
GOOD JOB POOING!!
It's probably because he grew up being praised every time he went, but...
my dog is totally fine being watched.
In fact, he wants you to watch him.
Out for a walk.
LOOK AT THAT TOY POODLE!
HOW CUTE~
Gotta poo.
CIRCLE
CIRCLE
The more people look at him, the stronger the call of nature.
HONK
MY DOG IS THE THEATRICAL POOP TYPE...!
END

More About #135 Part 1

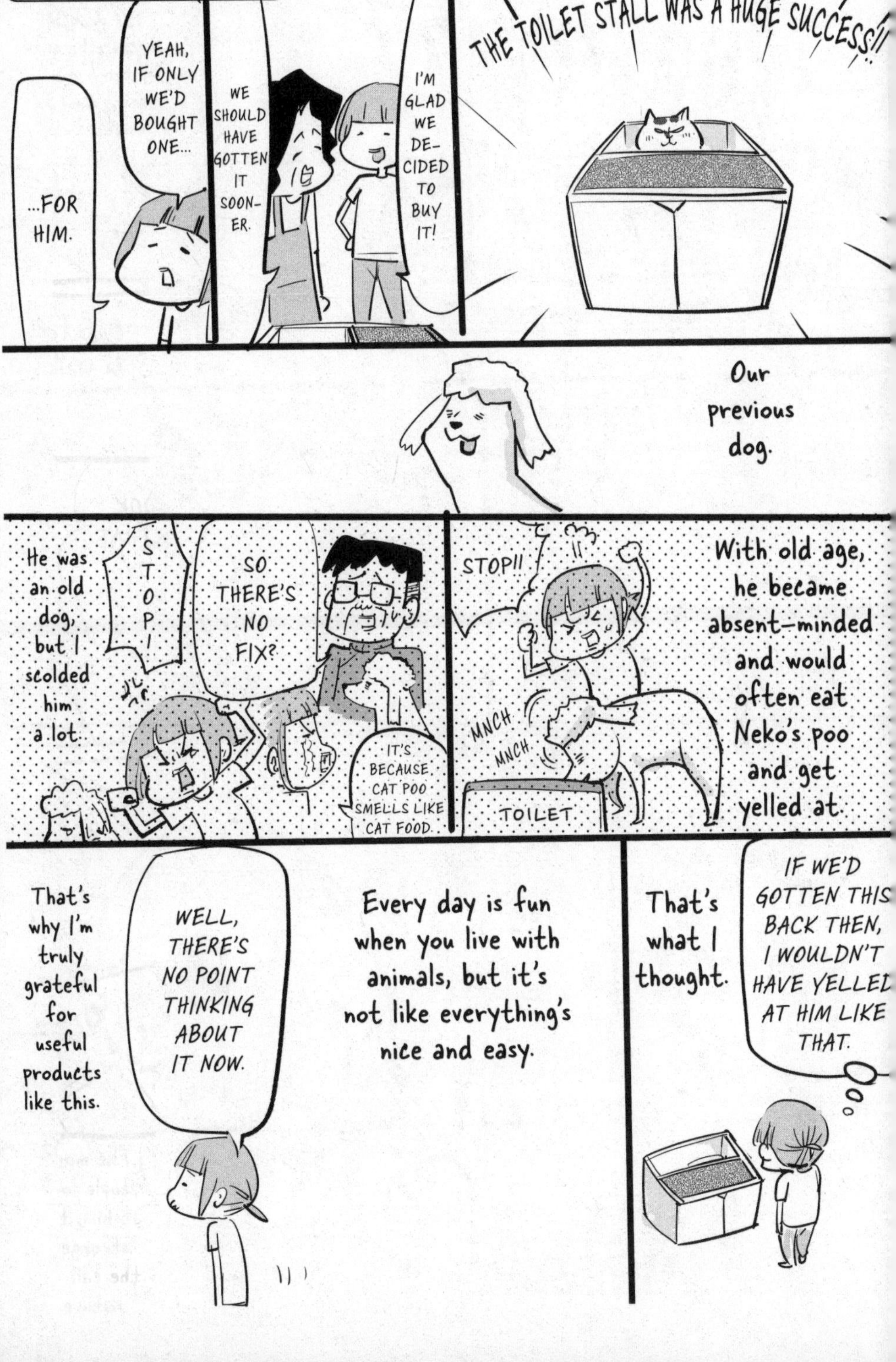

THE TOILET STALL WAS A HUGE SUCCESS!!
I'M GLAD WE DECIDED TO BUY IT!
WE SHOULD HAVE GOTTEN IT SOONER.
YEAH, IF ONLY WE'D BOUGHT ONE...
...FOR HIM.
Our previous dog.
With old age, he became absent-minded and would often eat Neko's poo and get yelled at.
STOP!!
MNCH MNCH
TOILET
SO THERE'S NO FIX?
STOP!
He was an old dog, but I scolded him a lot.
IT'S BECAUSE CAT POO SMELLS LIKE CAT FOOD.
IF WE'D GOTTEN THIS BACK THEN, I WOULDN'T HAVE YELLED AT HIM LIKE THAT.
That's what I thought.
Every day is fun when you live with animals, but it's not like everything's nice and easy.
WELL, THERE'S NO POINT THINKING ABOUT IT NOW.
That's why I'm truly grateful for useful products like this.

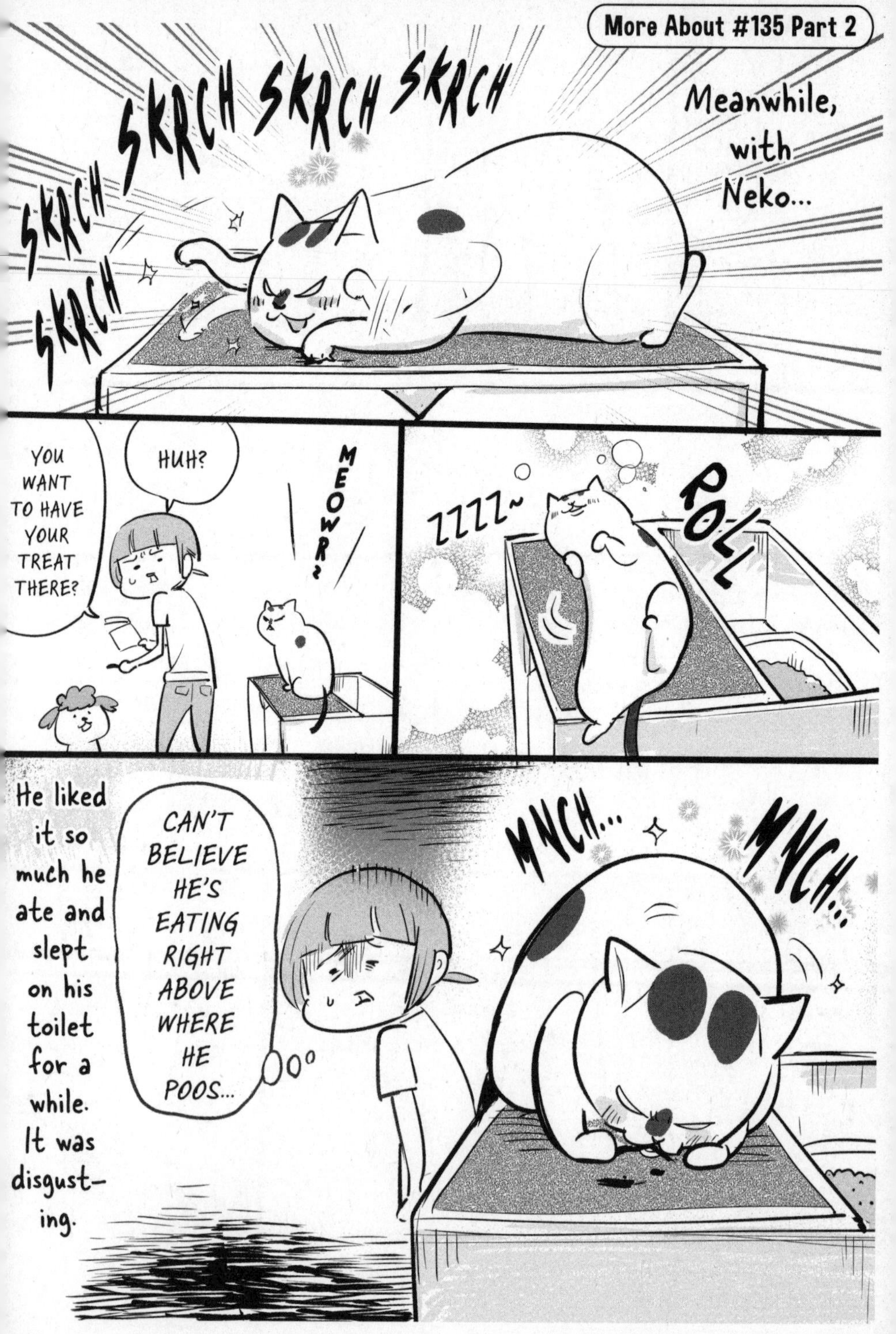
More About #135 Part 2
Meanwhile, with Neko...
SKRCH SKRCH SKRCH SKRCH SKRCH SKRCH
ROLL
ZZZZ~
MEOWR?
HUH?
YOU WANT TO HAVE YOUR TREAT THERE?
MNCH...
MNCH...
CAN'T BELIEVE HE'S EATING RIGHT ABOVE WHERE HE POOS...
He liked it so much he ate and slept on his toilet for a while. It was disgust-ing.

Neko putting pressure on me for his turn to play.

Newly-Drawn 4-Panel Strip

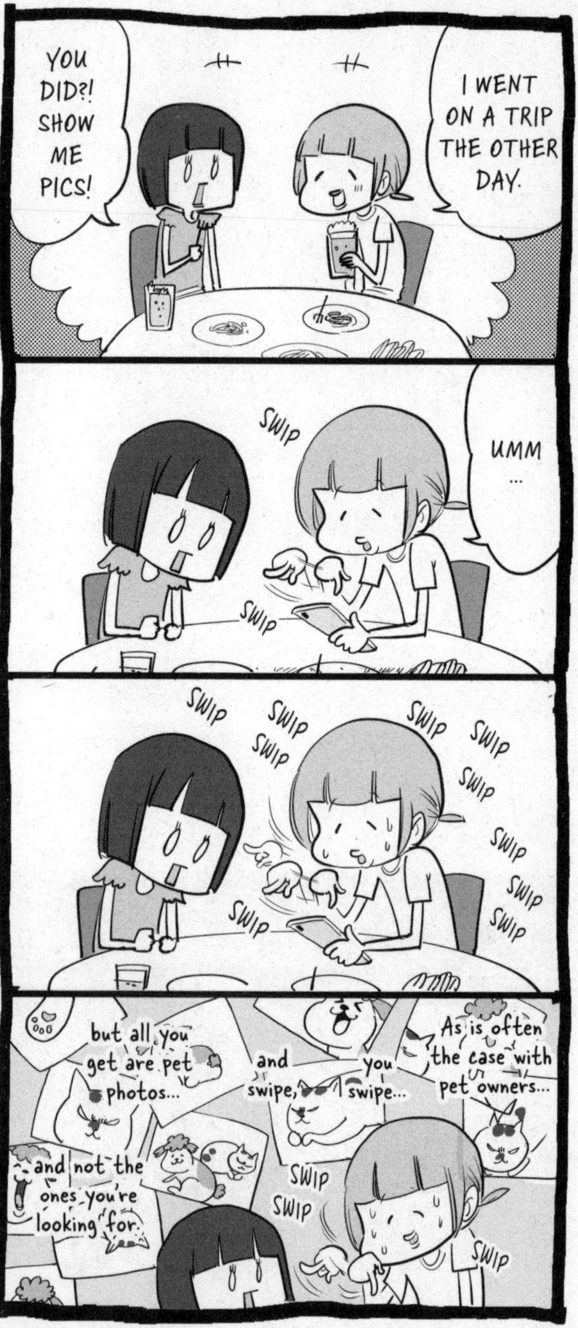
I WENT ON A TRIP THE OTHER DAY.
YOU DID?! SHOW ME PICS!
UMM ...
SWIP
SWIP
SWIP
SWIP
SWIP
SWIP
SWIP
SWIP
SWIP
SWIP
SWIP
SWIP
As is often the case with pet owners...
you swipe...
and swipe,
but all you get are pet photos...
and not the ones you're looking for.
SWIP
SWIP
SWIP

#136

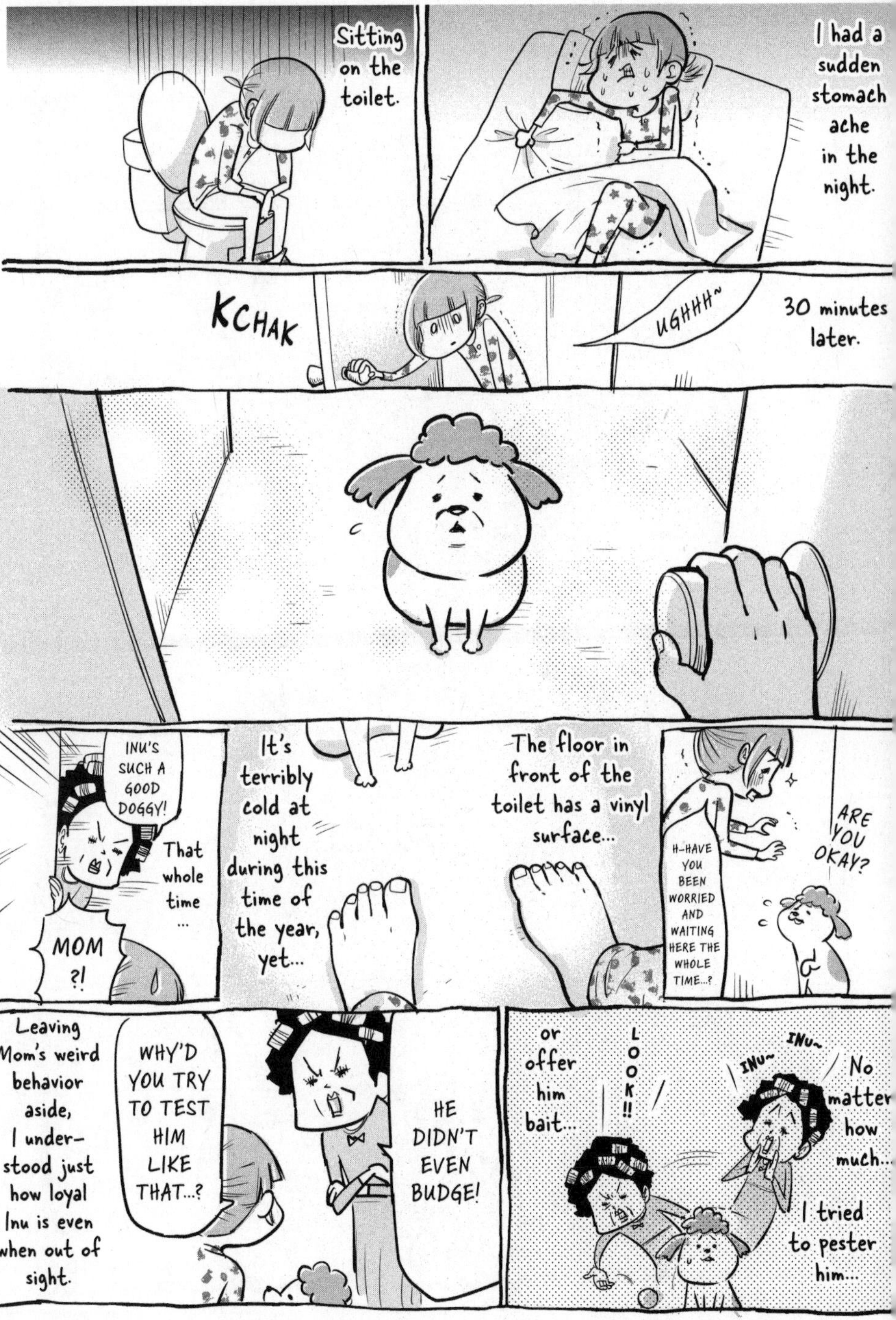
I had a sudden stomach ache in the night.
Sitting on the toilet.
30 minutes later.
UGHHH~
KCHAK
ARE YOU OKAY?
H-HAVE YOU BEEN WORRIED AND WAITING HERE THE WHOLE TIME...?
The floor in front of the toilet has a vinyl surface...
It's terribly cold at night during this time of the year, yet...
INU'S SUCH A GOOD DOGGY!
That whole time ...
MOM ?!
No matter how much...
INU~
INU~
I tried to pester him...
LOOK!!
or offer him bait...
HE DIDN'T EVEN BUDGE!
WHY'D YOU TRY TO TEST HIM LIKE THAT...?
Leaving Mom's weird behavior aside, I understood just how loyal Inu is even when out of sight.

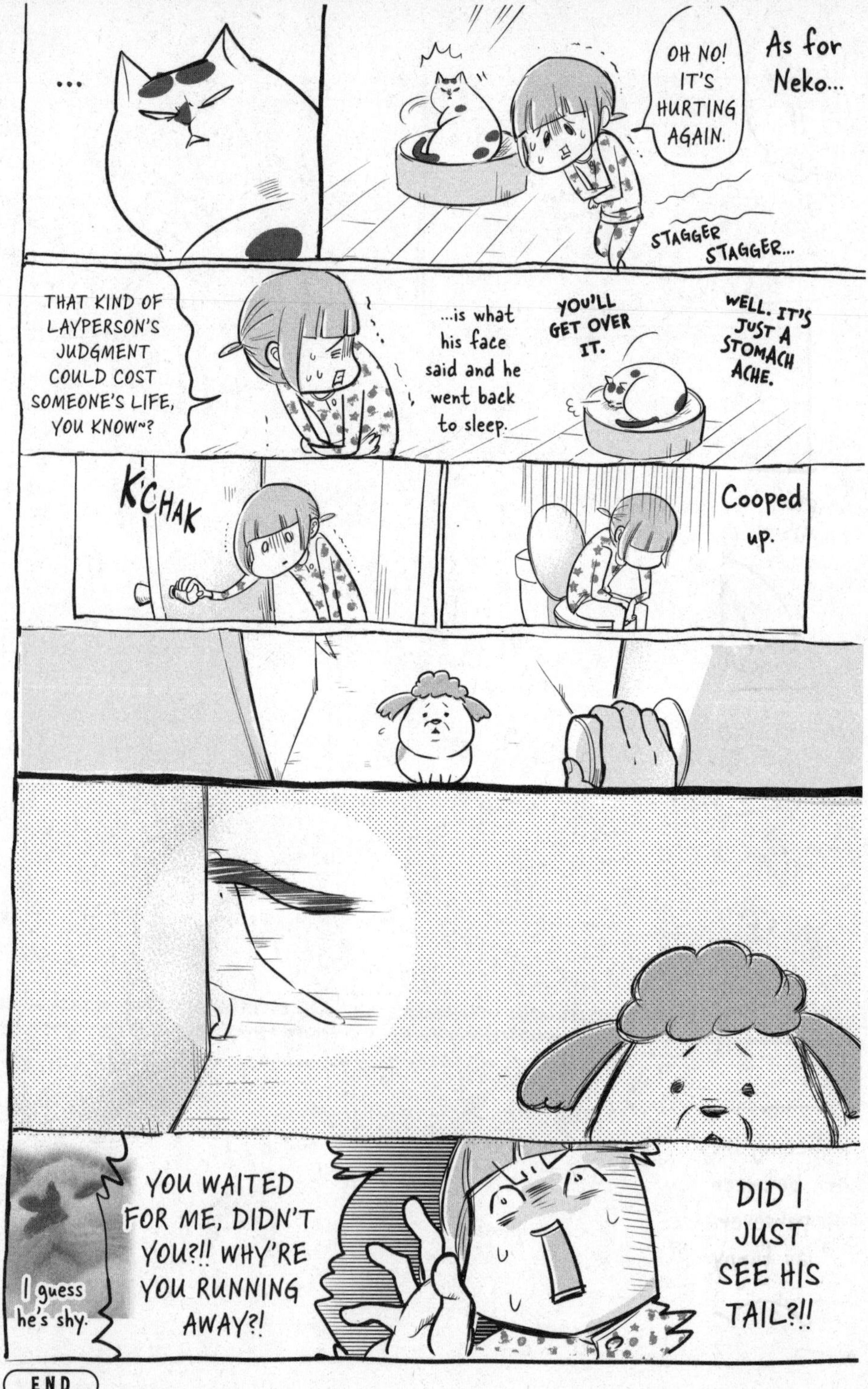
As for Neko...
OH NO! IT'S HURTING AGAIN.
STAGGER STAGGER...
...
WELL. IT'S JUST A STOMACH ACHE.
YOU'LL GET OVER IT.
...is what his face said and he went back to sleep.
THAT KIND OF LAYPERSON'S JUDGMENT COULD COST SOMEONE'S LIFE, YOU KNOW~?
Cooped up.
K'CHAK
DID I JUST SEE HIS TAIL?!!
YOU WAITED FOR ME, DIDN'T YOU?!! WHY'RE YOU RUNNING AWAY?!
I guess he's shy.

END

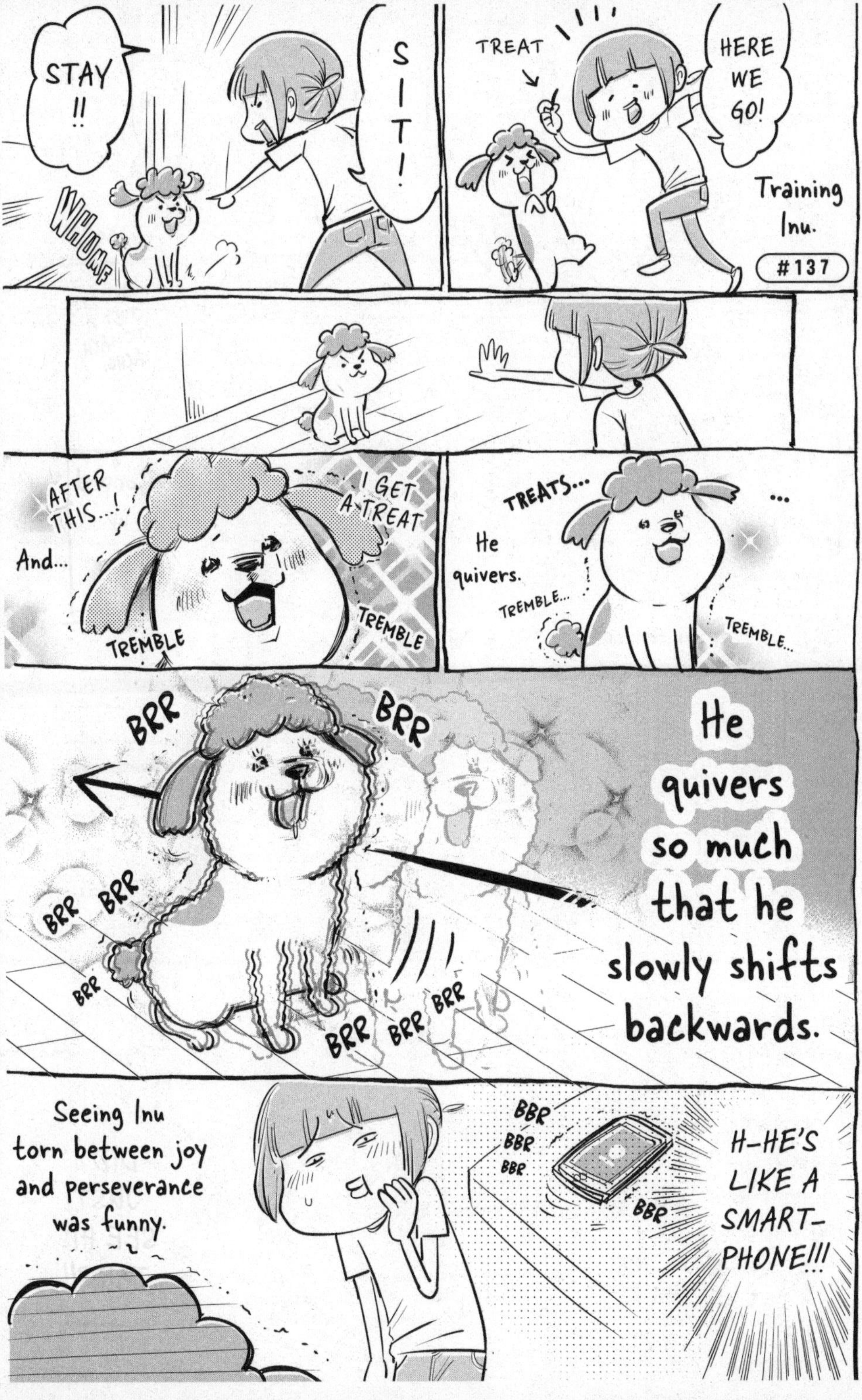
Training Inu.
#137
HERE WE GO!
TREAT
SIT!
STAY!!
WHUMF
TREATS...
...
He quivers.
TREMBLE...
TREMBLE...
I GET A TREAT
AFTER THIS...!
And...
TREMBLE
TREMBLE
He quivers so much that he slowly shifts backwards.
BRR
BRR
BRR BRR
BRR
BRR BRR BRR
H-HE'S LIKE A SMART-PHONE!!!
BBR
BBR
BBR
BBR
Seeing Inu torn between joy and perseverance was funny.

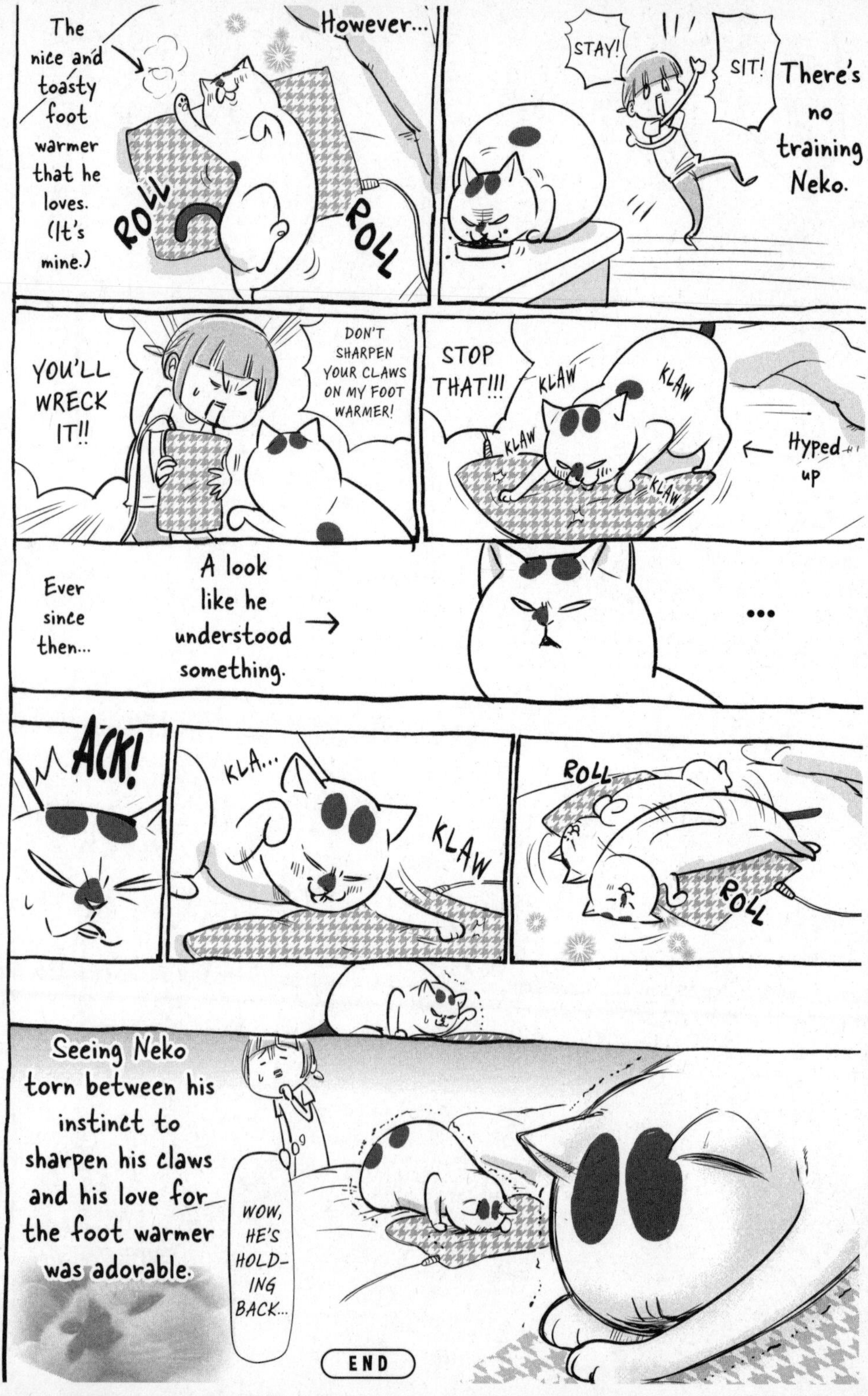
There's no training Neko.
SIT!
STAY!
However...
The nice and toasty foot warmer that he loves. (It's mine.)
ROLL
ROLL
Hyped up
KLAW
KLAW
KLAW
KLAW
STOP THAT!!!
DON'T SHARPEN YOUR CLAWS ON MY FOOT WARMER!
YOU'LL WRECK IT!!
...
A look like he understood something. →
Ever since then...
ROLL
ROLL
KLA...
KLAW
ACK!
WOW, HE'S HOLDING BACK...
Seeing Neko torn between his instinct to sharpen his claws and his love for the foot warmer was adorable.
END

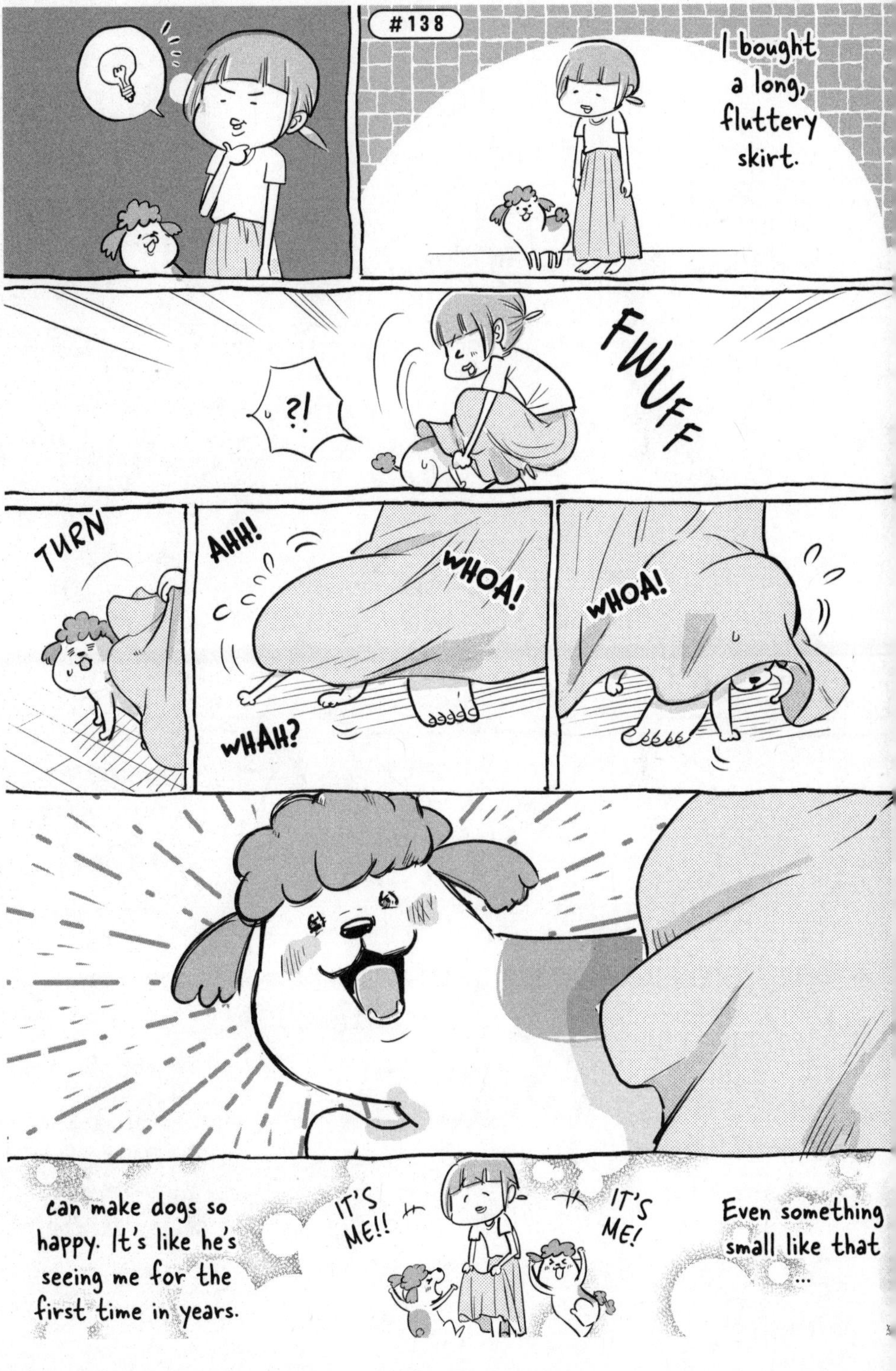
#138
I bought a long, fluttery skirt.
FWUFF
?!
WHOA!
AHH!
WHOA!
WHAH?
TURN
Even something small like that ...
IT'S ME!
IT'S ME!!
can make dogs so happy. It's like he's seeing me for the first time in years.

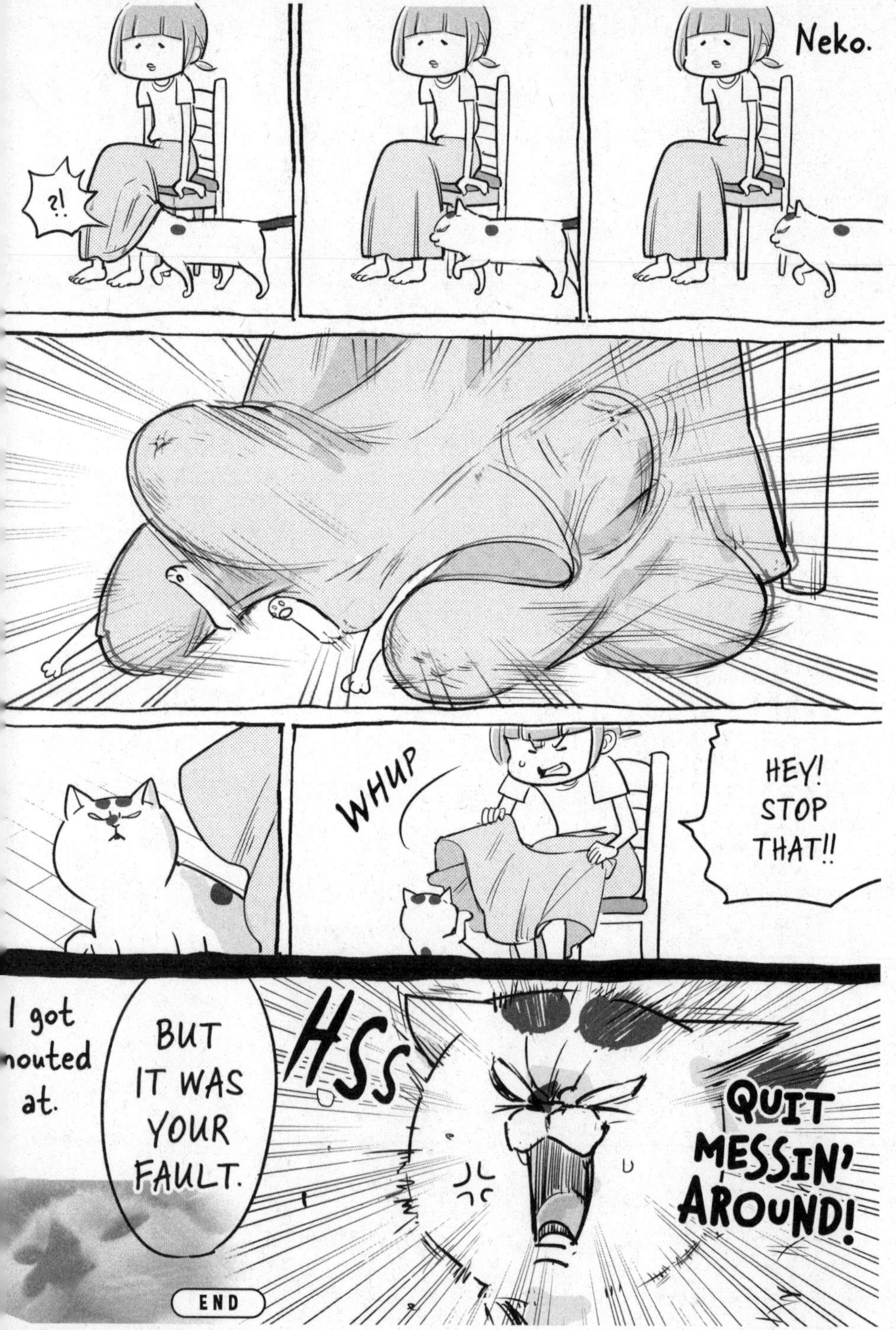
Neko.
?!
HEY! STOP THAT!!
WHUP
QUIT MESSIN' AROUND!
HSS
BUT IT WAS YOUR FAULT.
I got nouted at.
END

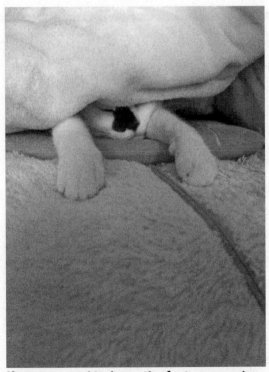

You never see him leave the foot warmer in the winter.

Newly-Drawn 4-Panel Strip

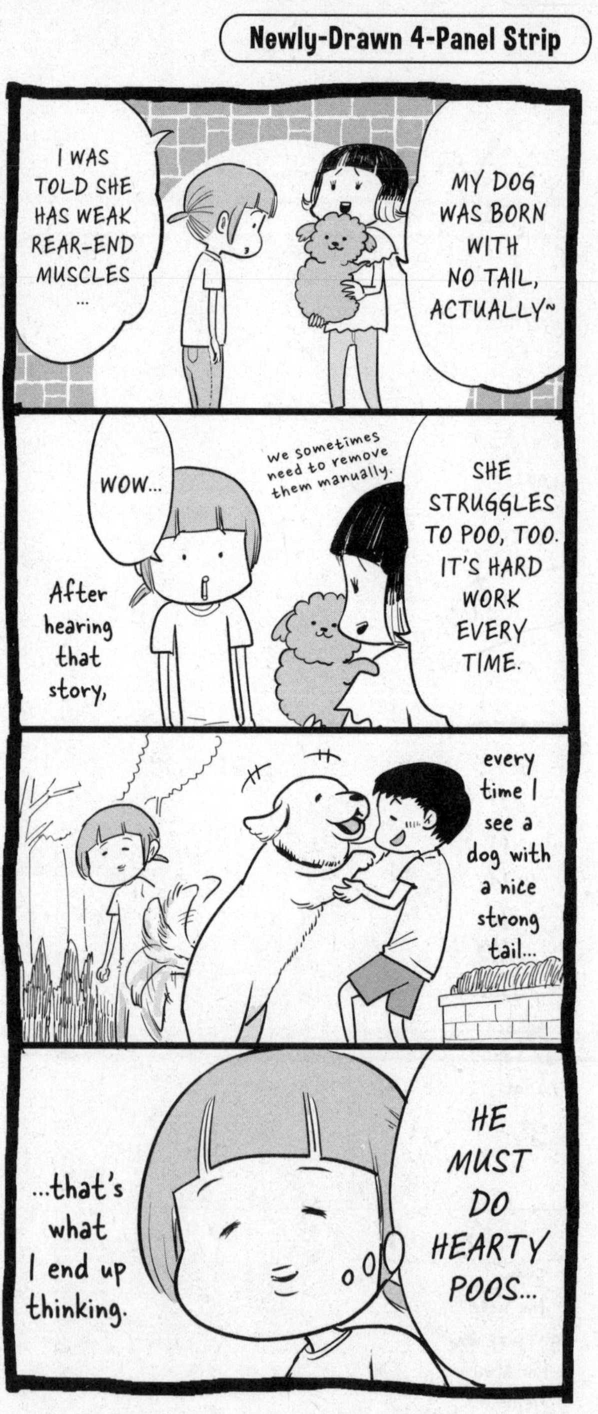
MY DOG WAS BORN WITH NO TAIL, ACTUALLY~
I WAS TOLD SHE HAS WEAK REAR-END MUSCLES ...
SHE STRUGGLES TO POO, TOO. IT'S HARD WORK EVERY TIME.
we sometimes need to remove them manually.
WOW...
After hearing that story,
every time I see a dog with a nice strong tail...
HE MUST DO HEARTY POOS...
...that's what I end up thinking.

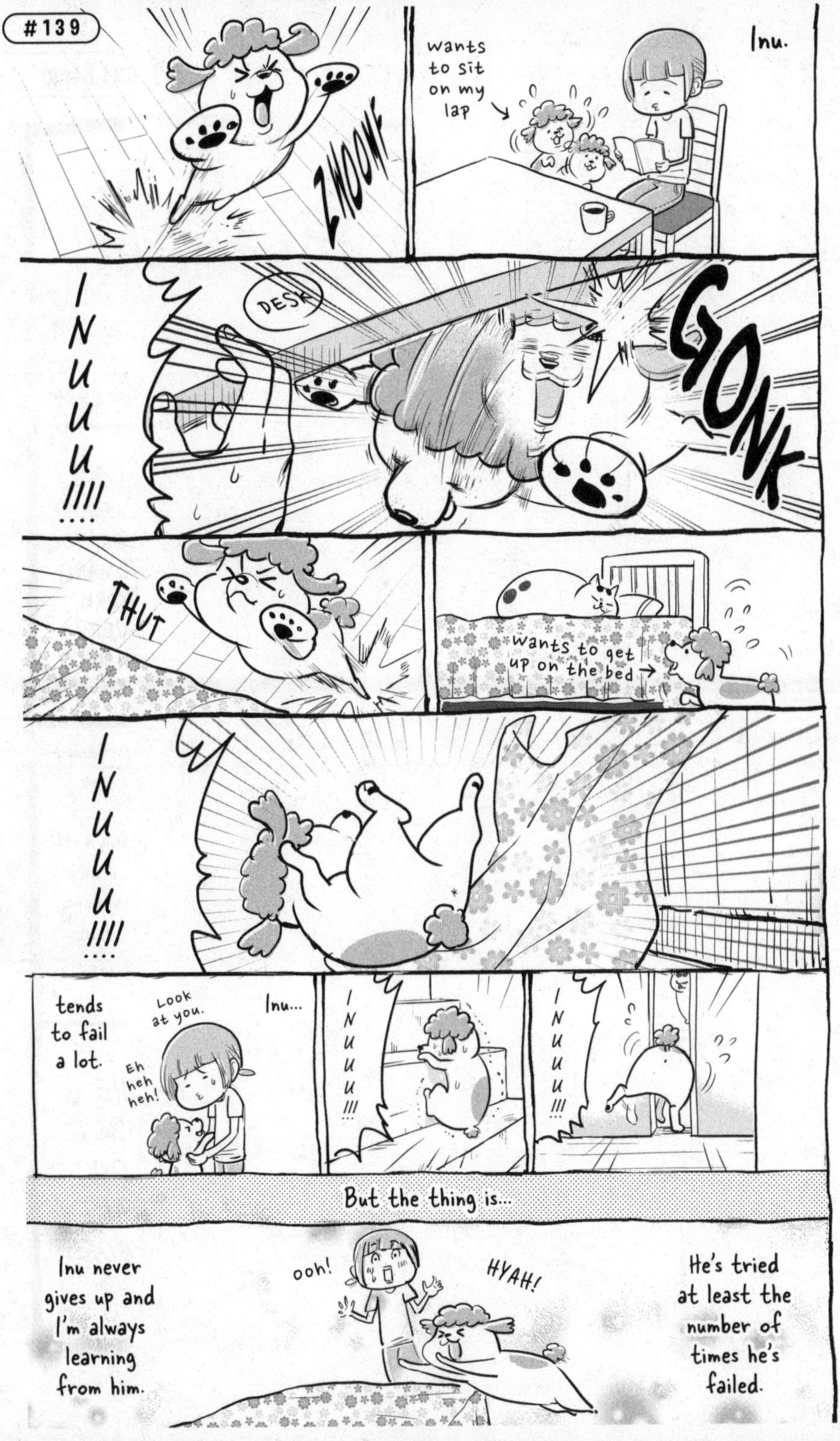
#139
Inu.
wants to sit on my lap
ZWOOMF
GONK
DESK
INUUUU!!!!....
wants to get up on the bed →
THUT
INUUUU!!!!....
INUUU!!!
INUUU!!!
Inu...
Look at you.
tends to fail a lot.
Eh heh heh!
But the thing is...
He's tried at least the number of times he's failed.
HYAH!
ooh!
Inu never gives up and I'm always learning from him.

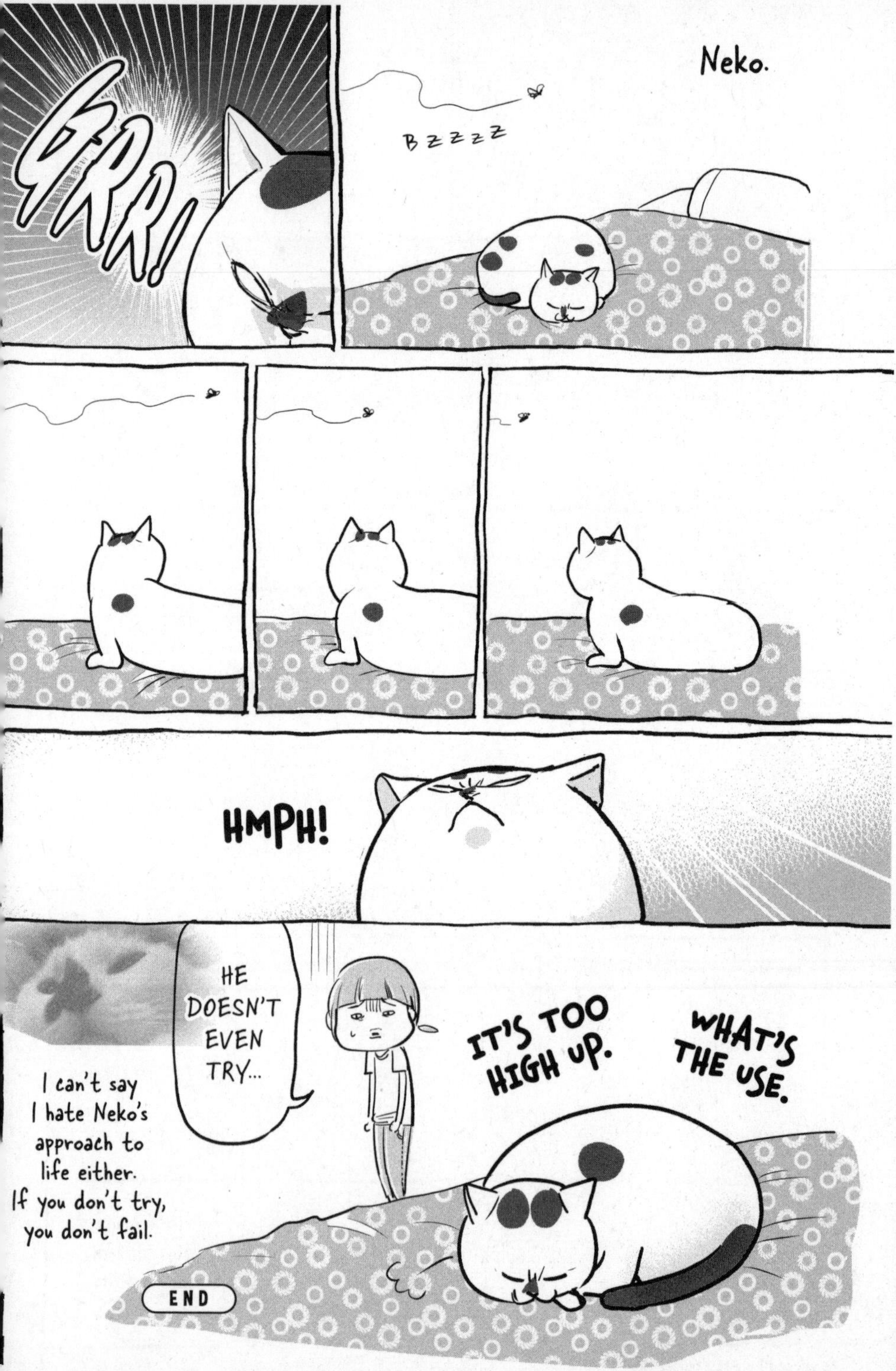

Neko.
BZZZZ
GRR!
HMPH!
WHAT'S THE USE.
IT'S TOO HIGH UP.
HE DOESN'T EVEN TRY...
I can't say I hate Neko's approach to life either. If you don't try, you don't fail.
END

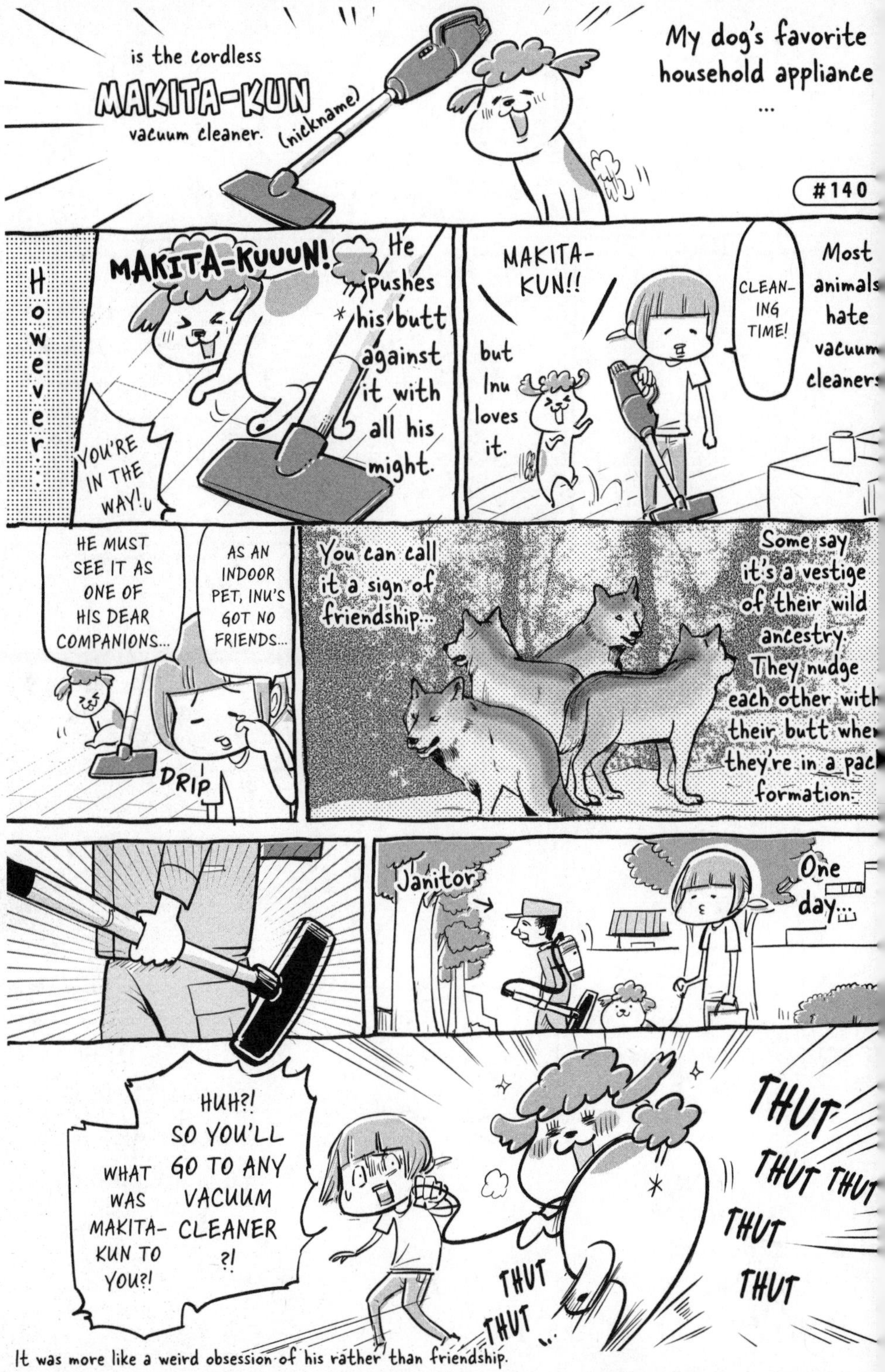
My dog's favorite household appliance ...
#140
is the cordless
MAKITA-KUN
vacuum cleaner.
(nickname)
Most animals hate vacuum cleaner
CLEANING TIME!
MAKITA-KUN!!
but Inu loves it.
He pushes his butt against it with all his might.
MAKITA-KUUUN!
YOU'RE IN THE WAY!
However...
Some say it's a vestige of their wild ancestry. They nudge each other wit their butt whe they're in a pac formation.
You can call it a sign of friendship...
AS AN INDOOR PET, INU'S GOT NO FRIENDS...
HE MUST SEE IT AS ONE OF HIS DEAR COMPANIONS...
DRIP
One day...
Janitor
THUT
THUT THU
THUT
THUT
HUH?! SO YOU'LL GO TO ANY VACUUM CLEANER ?!
WHAT WAS MAKITA-KUN TO YOU?!
THUT
THUT
It was more like a weird obsession of his rather than friendship.

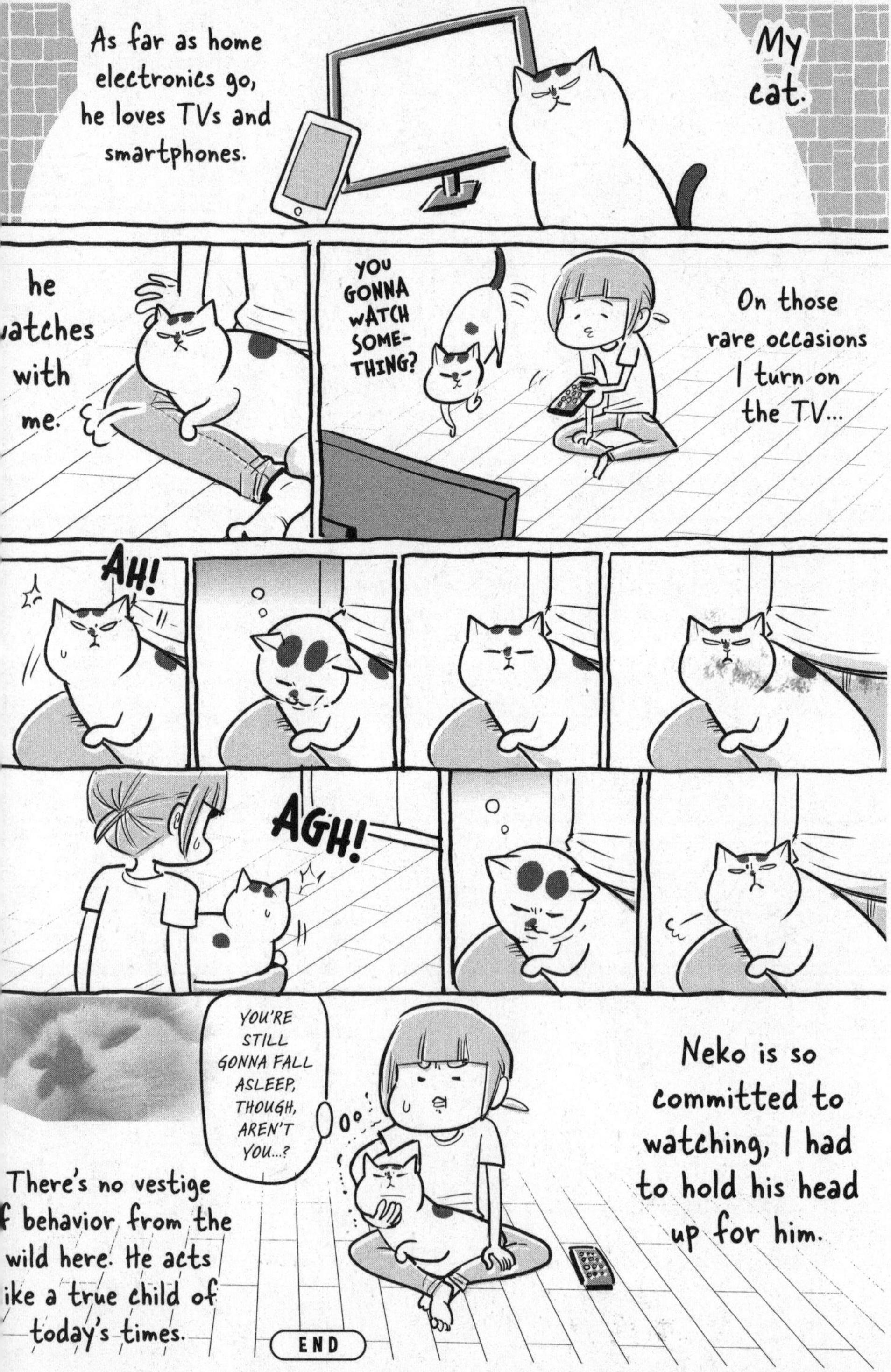
My cat.
As far as home electronics go, he loves TVs and smartphones.
On those rare occasions I turn on the TV...
YOU GONNA WATCH SOMETHING?
he atches with me.
AH!
AGH!
Neko is so committed to watching, I had to hold his head up for him.
YOU'RE STILL GONNA FALL ASLEEP, THOUGH, AREN'T YOU...?
There's no vestige f behavior from the wild here. He acts ike a true child of today's times.
END

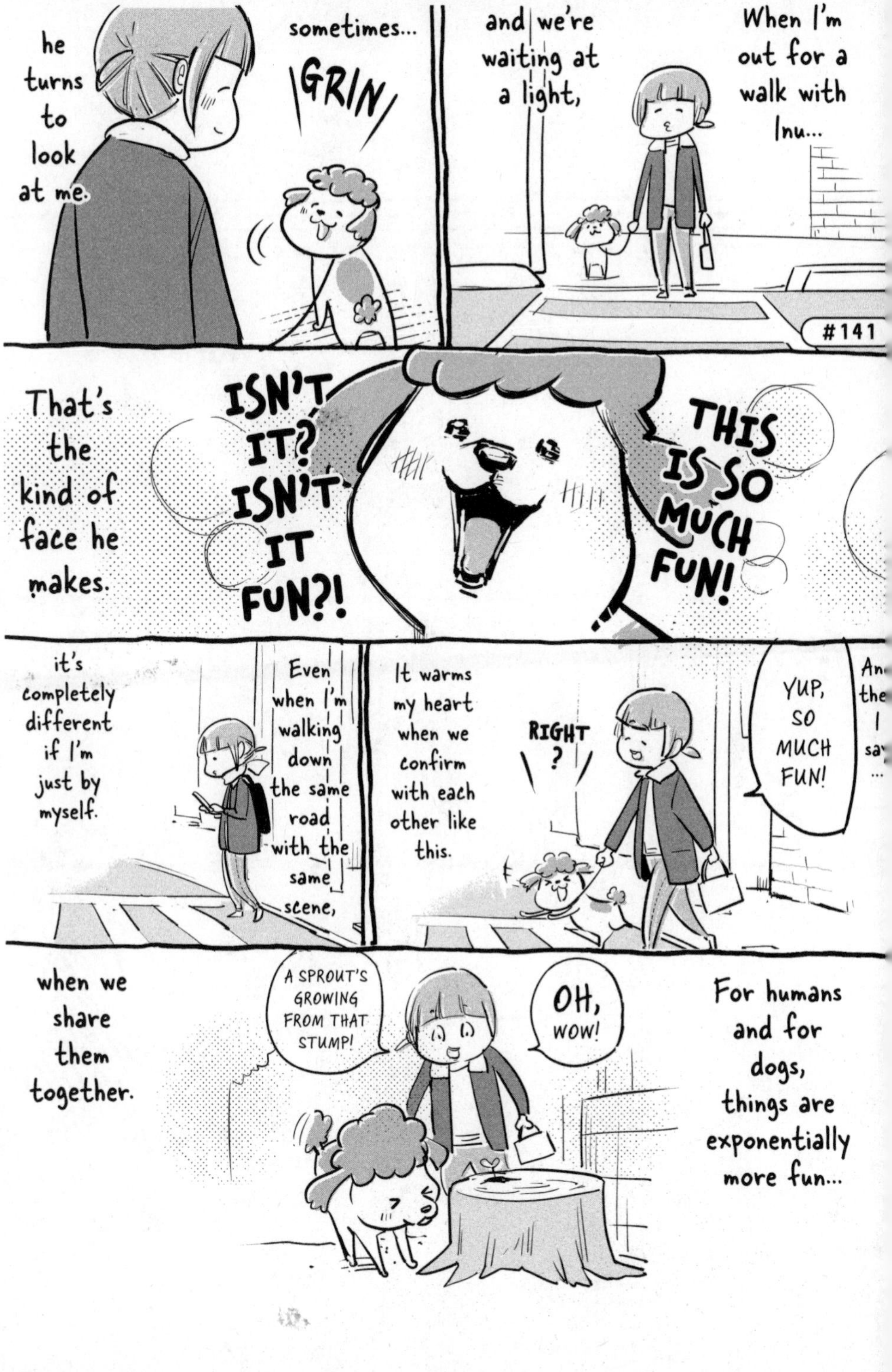
#141
When I'm out for a walk with Inu...
and we're waiting at a light,
sometimes...
GRIN
he turns to look at me.
THIS IS SO MUCH FUN!
ISN'T IT? ISN'T IT FUN?!
That's the kind of face he makes.
YUP, SO MUCH FUN!
RIGHT?
It warms my heart when we confirm with each other like this.
Even when I'm walking down the same road with the same scene,
it's completely different if I'm just by myself.
For humans and for dogs, things are exponentially more fun...
OH, WOW!
A SPROUT'S GROWING FROM THAT STUMP!
when we share them together.

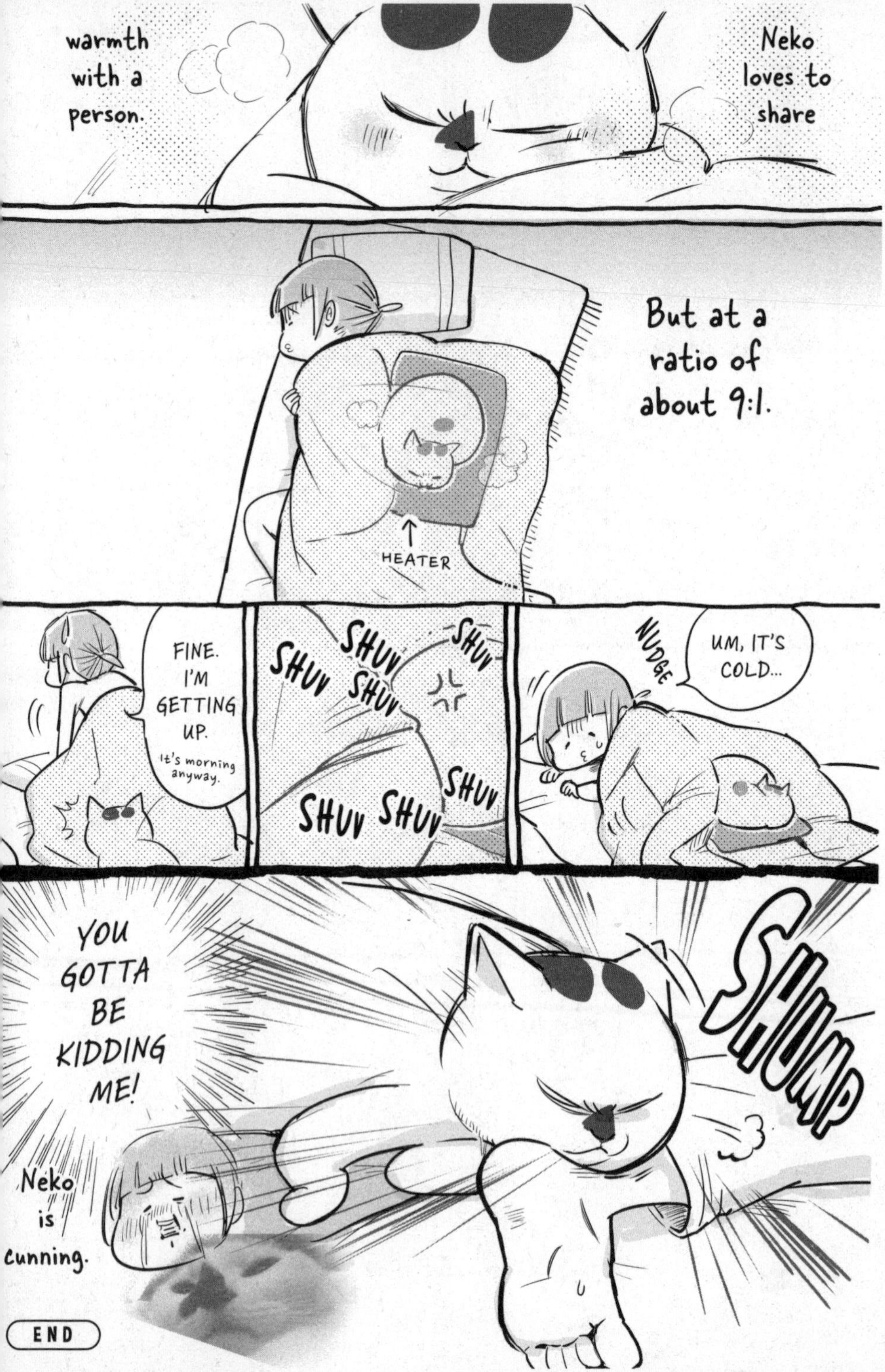
Neko loves to share
warmth with a person.
But at a ratio of about 9:1.
HEATER
NUDGE
UM, IT'S COLD...
SHUV
SHUV
SHUV
SHUV
SHUV
SHUV
SHUV
FINE. I'M GETTING UP.
It's morning anyway.
SHUMP
YOU GOTTA BE KIDDING ME!
Neko is cunning.
END

Newly-Drawn 4-Panel Strip

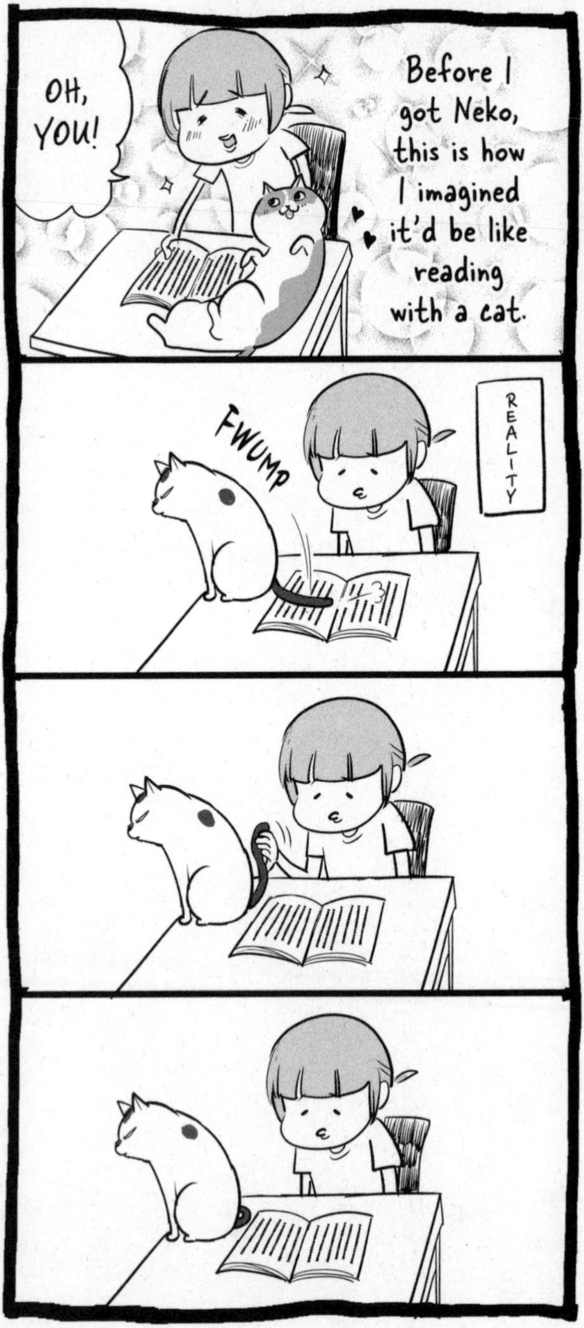
Before I got Neko, this is how I imagined it'd be like reading with a cat.
OH, YOU!
REALITY
FWUMP

Bonus

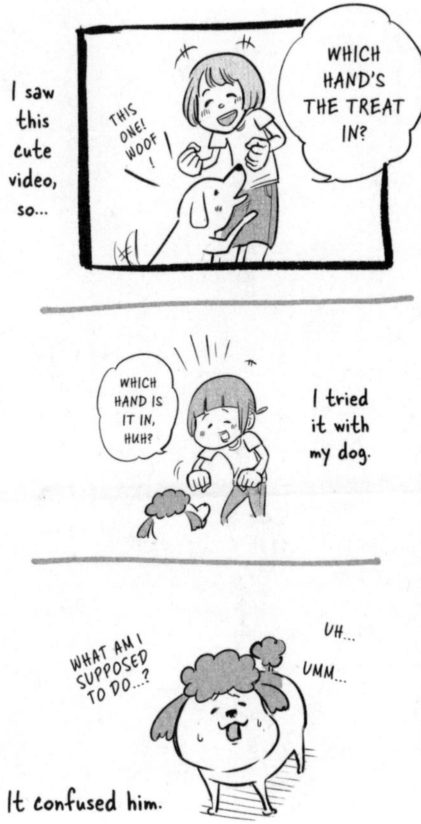
WHICH HAND'S THE TREAT IN?
THIS ONE! WOOF!
I saw this cute video, so...
I tried it with my dog.
WHICH HAND IS IT IN, HUH?
UH...
UMM...
WHAT AM I SUPPOSED TO DO...?
It confused him.

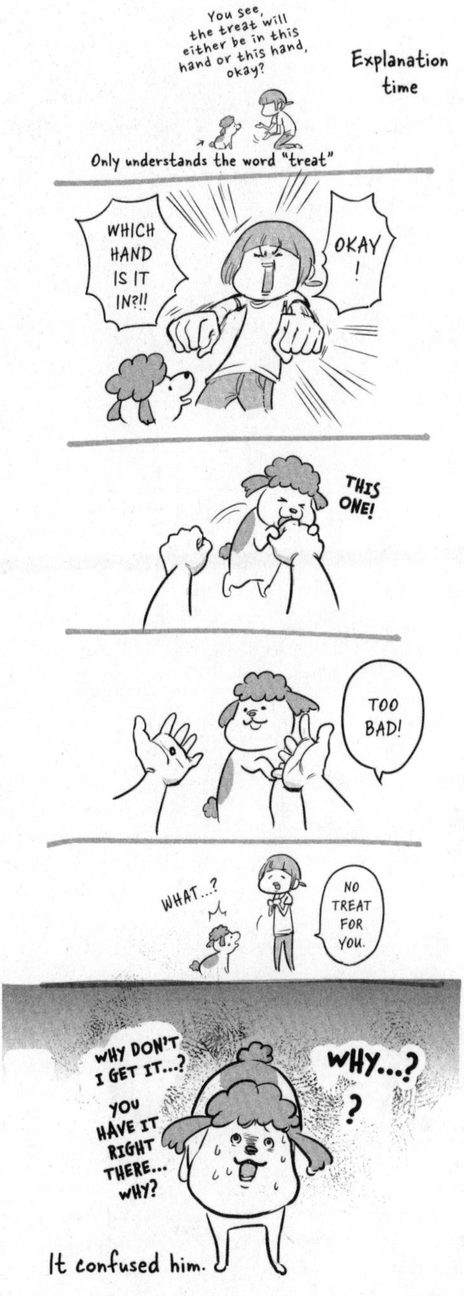
Explanation time
You see, the treat will either be in this hand or this hand, okay?
Only understands the word "treat"
OKAY!
WHICH HAND IS IT IN?!!
THIS ONE!
TOO BAD!
NO TREAT FOR YOU.
WHAT...?
WHY...?
?
WHY DON'T I GET IT...?
YOU HAVE IT RIGHT THERE... WHY?
It confused him.

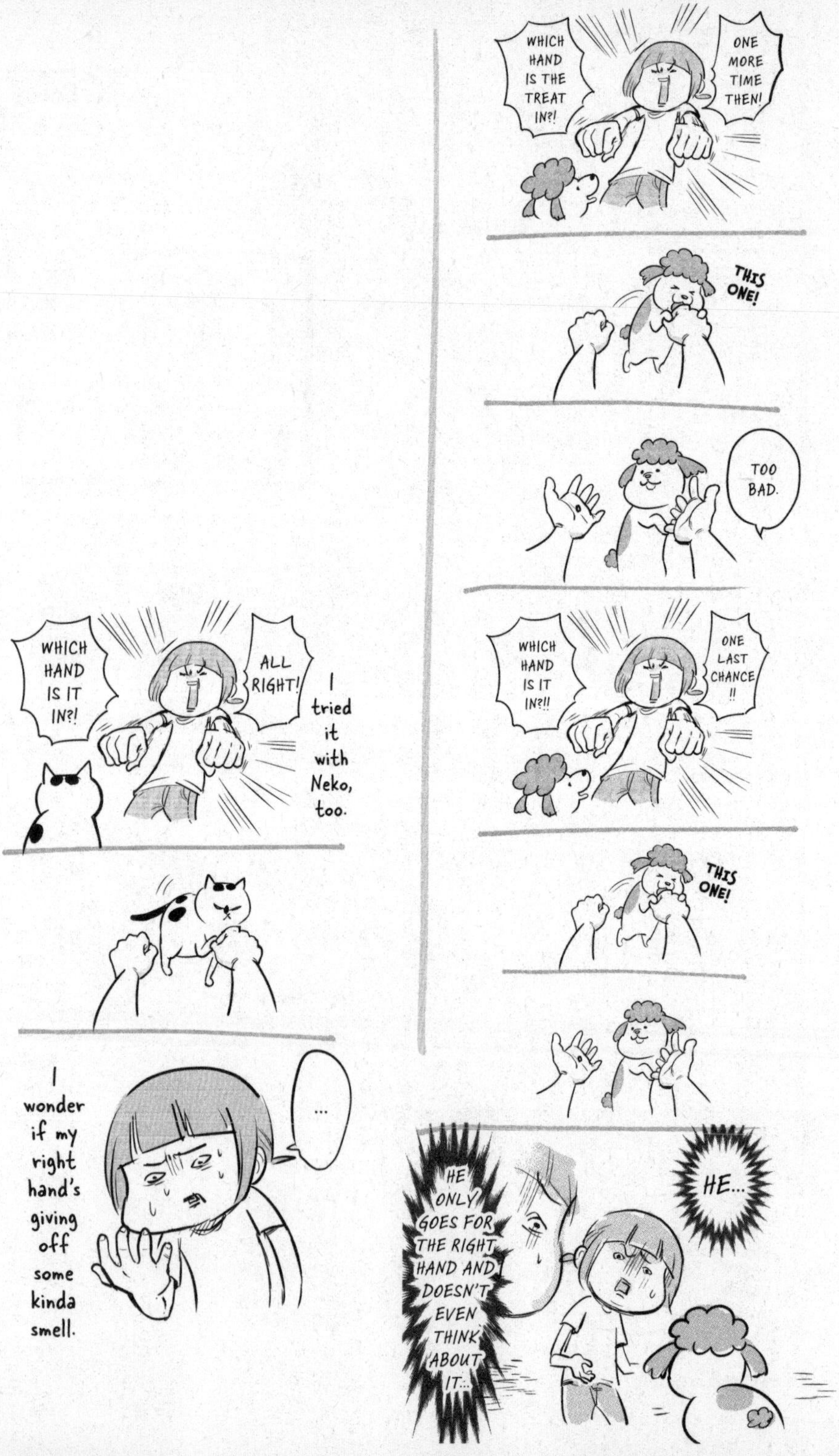
ONE MORE TIME THEN!
WHICH HAND IS THE TREAT IN?!
THIS ONE!
TOO BAD.
ONE LAST CHANCE!!
WHICH HAND IS IT IN?!!
THIS ONE!
HE...
HE ONLY GOES FOR THE RIGHT HAND AND DOESN'T EVEN THINK ABOUT IT...
I tried it with Neko, too.
ALL RIGHT!
WHICH HAND IS IT IN?!
...
I wonder if my right hand's giving off some kinda smell.

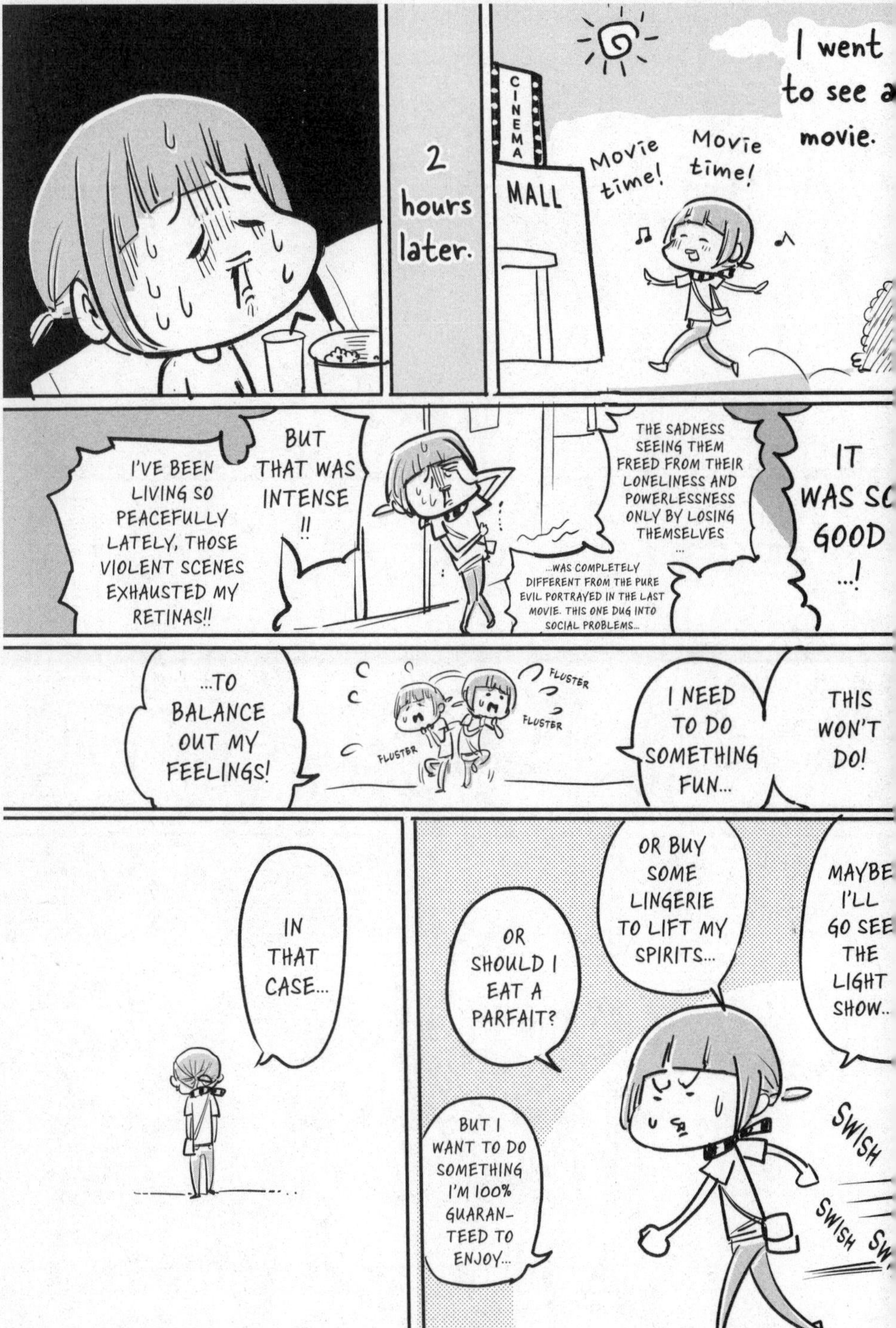
I went to see a movie.
Movie time!
Movie time!
CINEMA
MALL
2 hours later.
IT WAS S GOOD ...!
THE SADNESS SEEING THEM FREED FROM THEIR LONELINESS AND POWERLESSNESS ONLY BY LOSING THEMSELVES ...
...WAS COMPLETELY DIFFERENT FROM THE PURE EVIL PORTRAYED IN THE LAST MOVIE. THIS ONE DUG INTO SOCIAL PROBLEMS...
BUT THAT WAS INTENSE !!
I'VE BEEN LIVING SO PEACEFULLY LATELY, THOSE VIOLENT SCENES EXHAUSTED MY RETINAS!!
THIS WON'T DO!
I NEED TO DO SOMETHING FUN...
FLUSTER
FLUSTER
FLUSTER
...TO BALANCE OUT MY FEELINGS!
MAYBE I'LL GO SEE THE LIGHT SHOW..
OR BUY SOME LINGERIE TO LIFT MY SPIRITS...
OR SHOULD I EAT A PARFAIT?
SWISH
SWISH
BUT I WANT TO DO SOMETHING I'M 100% GUARANTEED TO ENJOY...
IN THAT CASE...

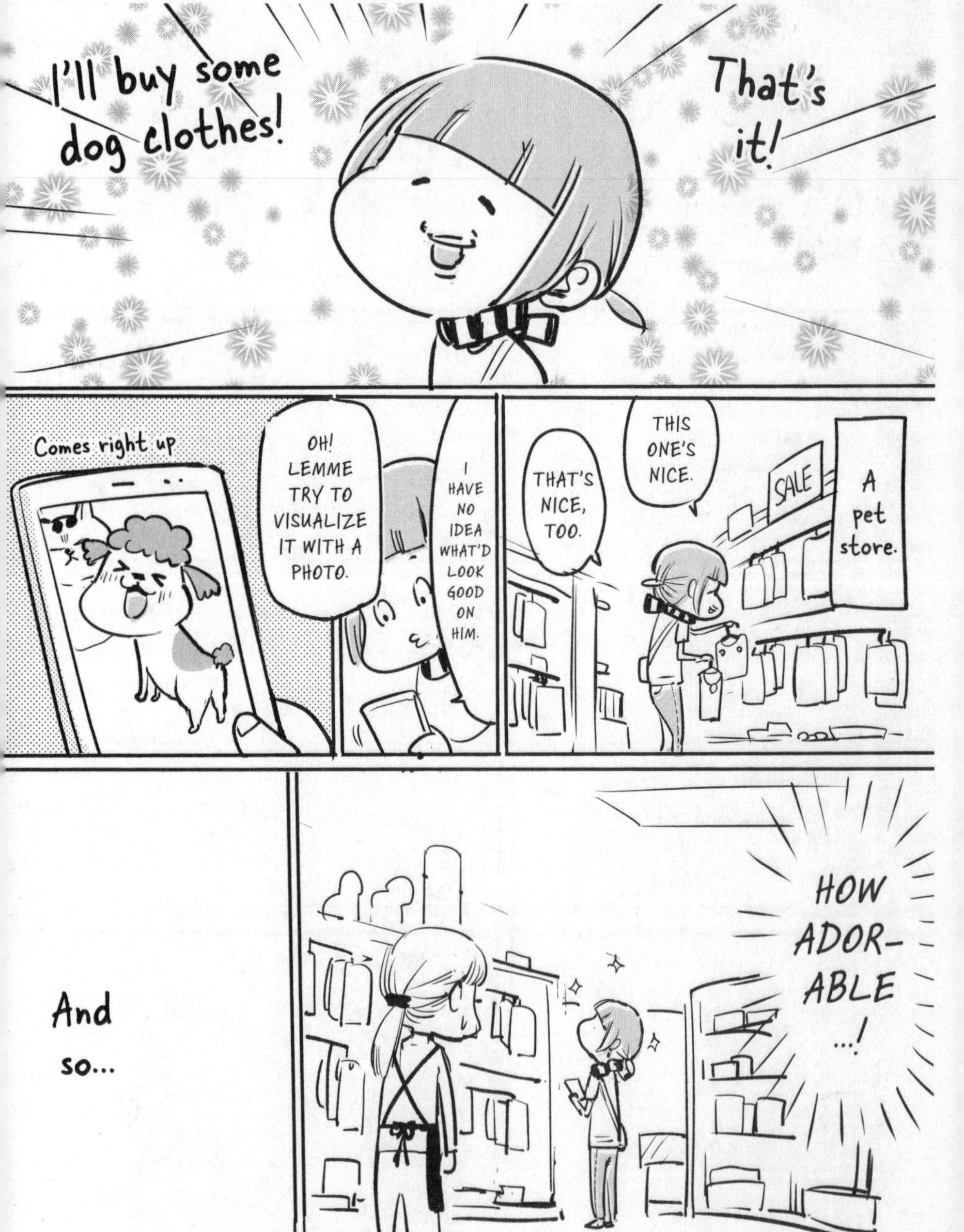
That's it!
I'll buy some dog clothes!
A pet store.
SALE
THIS ONE'S NICE.
THAT'S NICE, TOO.
I HAVE NO IDEA WHAT'D LOOK GOOD ON HIM.
OH! LEMME TRY TO VISUALIZE IT WITH A PHOTO.
Comes right up
HOW ADORABLE ...!
And so...

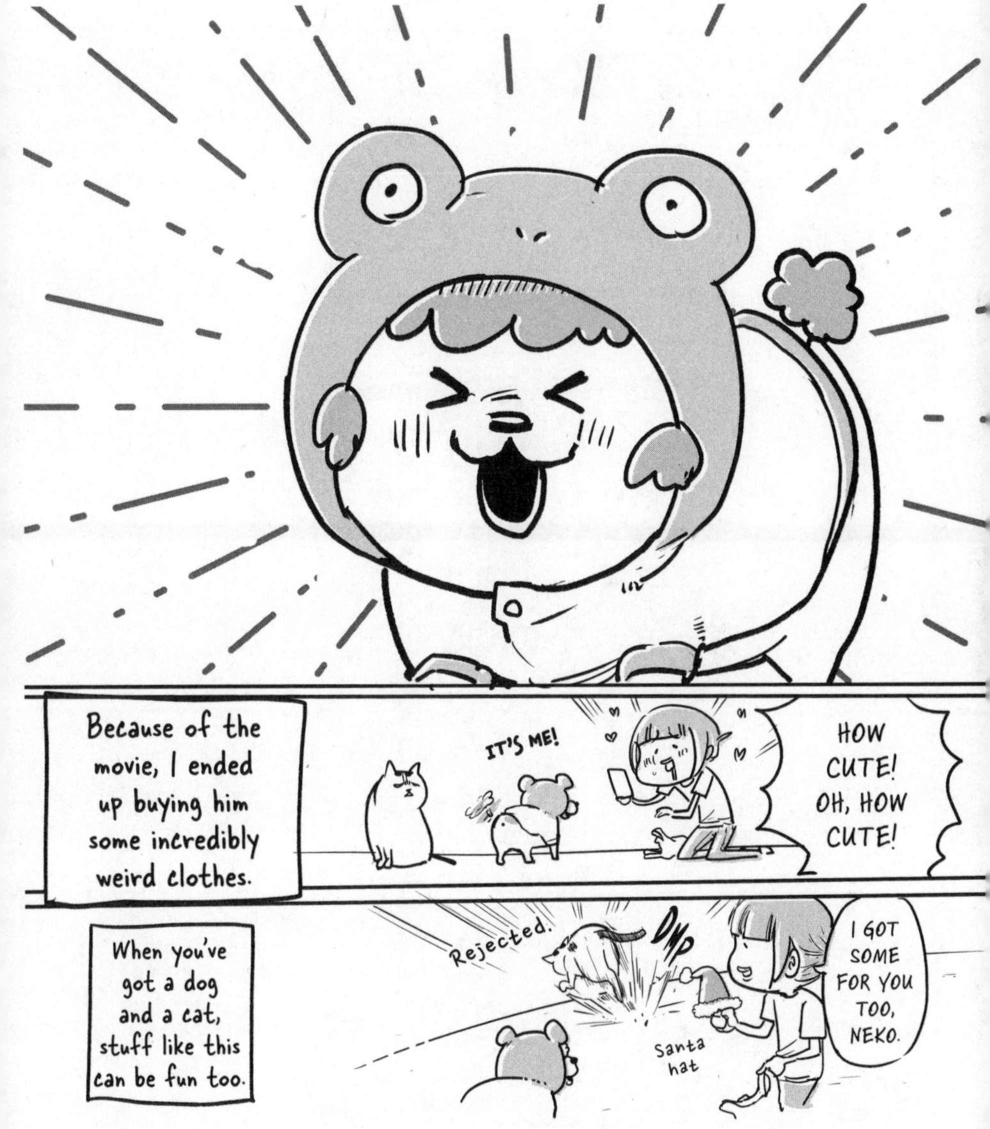
HOW CUTE! OH, HOW CUTE!
IT'S ME!
Because of the movie, I ended up buying him some incredibly weird clothes.
I GOT SOME FOR YOU TOO, NEKO.
DWP
Rejected.
Santa hat
When you've got a dog and a cat, stuff like this can be fun too.

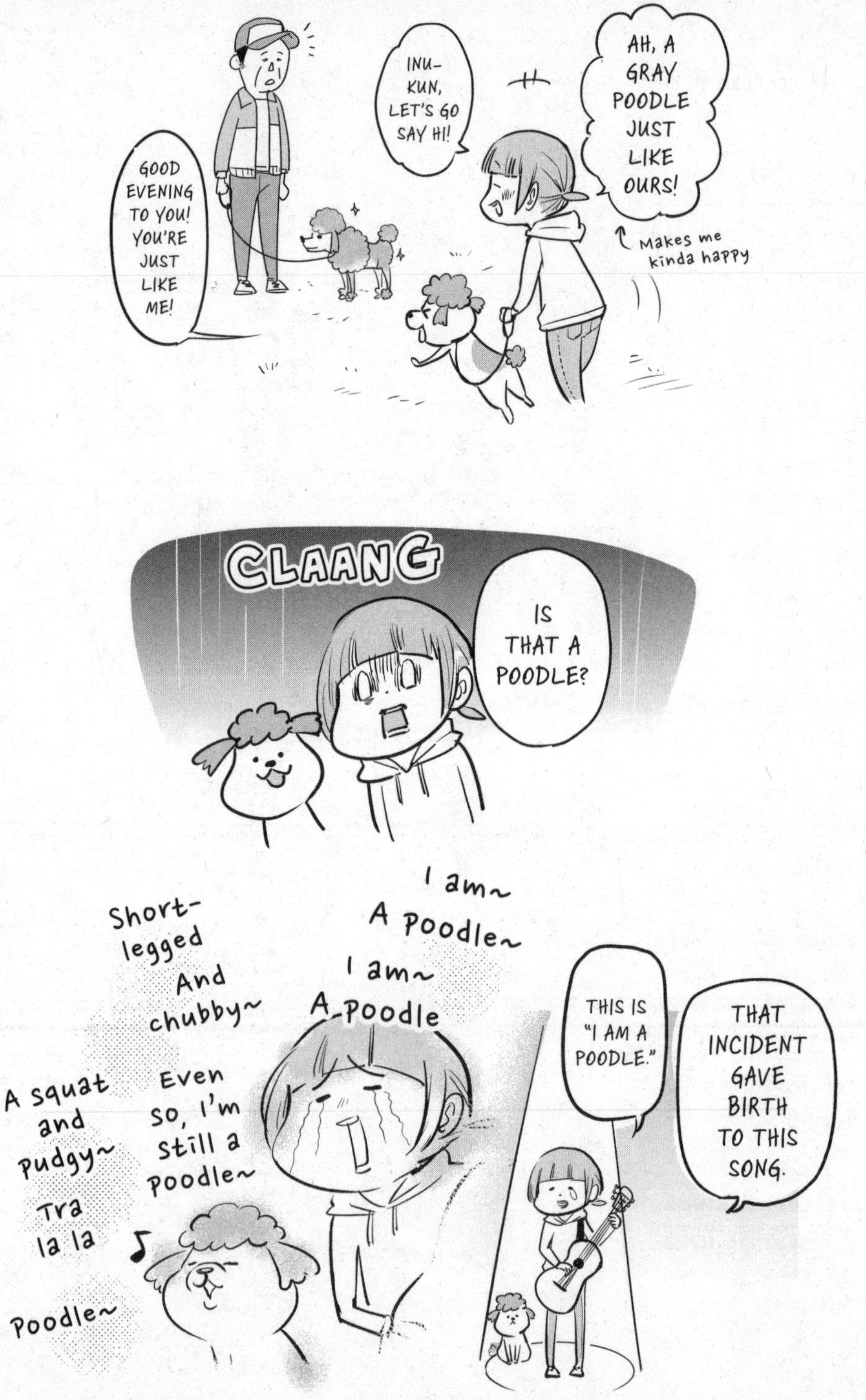
AH, A GRAY POODLE JUST LIKE OURS!
Makes me kinda happy
INU-KUN, LET'S GO SAY HI!
GOOD EVENING TO YOU! YOU'RE JUST LIKE ME!
CLAANG
IS THAT A POODLE?
THAT INCIDENT GAVE BIRTH TO THIS SONG.
THIS IS "I AM A POODLE."
I am~ A poodle~
I am~ A poodle
Short-legged And chubby~
Even so, I'm still a poodle~
A squat and pudgy~
Tra la la
Poodle~

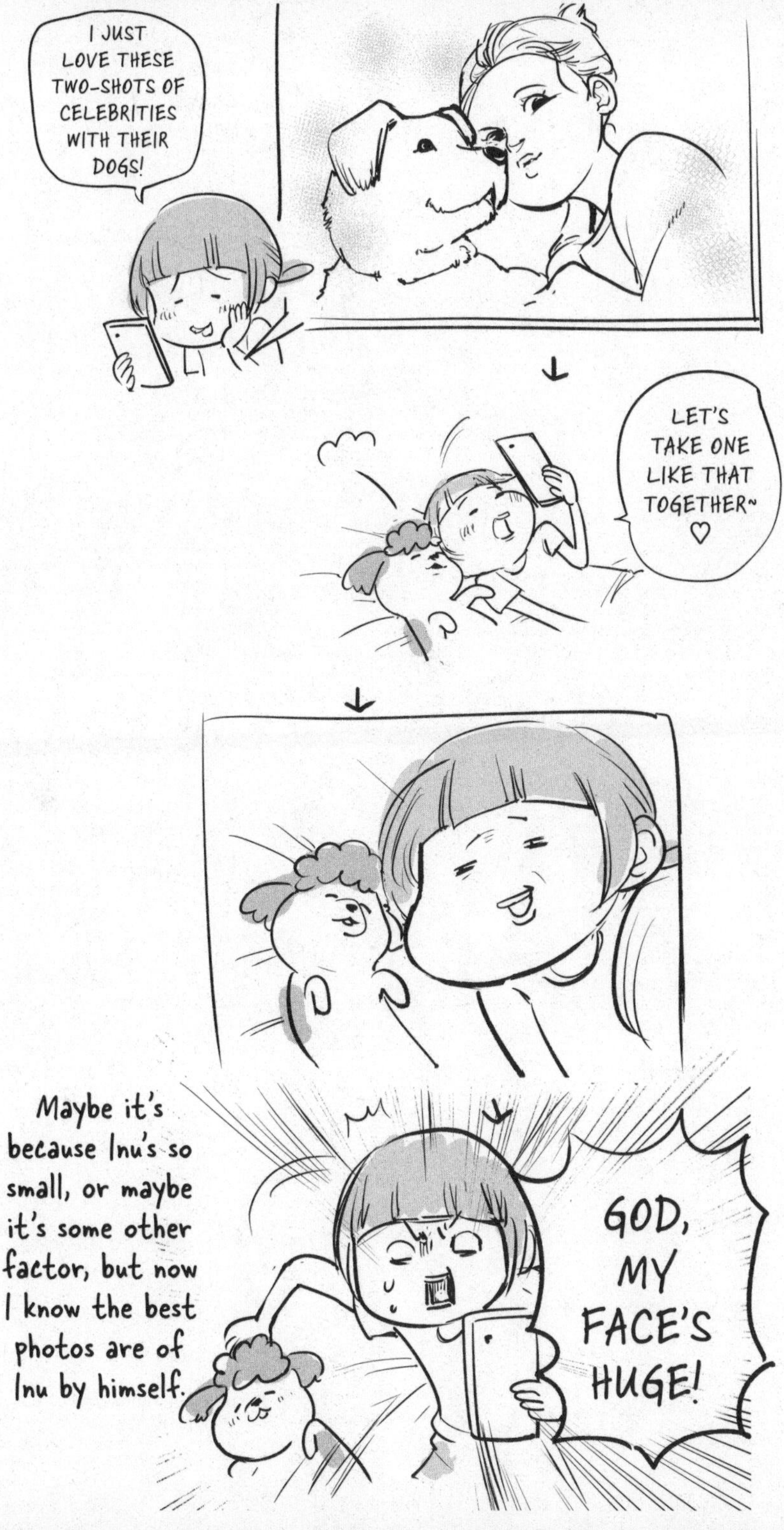
I JUST LOVE THESE TWO-SHOTS OF CELEBRITIES WITH THEIR DOGS!
LET'S TAKE ONE LIKE THAT TOGETHER~ ♡
GOD, MY FACE'S HUGE!
Maybe it's because Inu's so small, or maybe it's some other factor, but now I know the best photos are of Inu by himself.

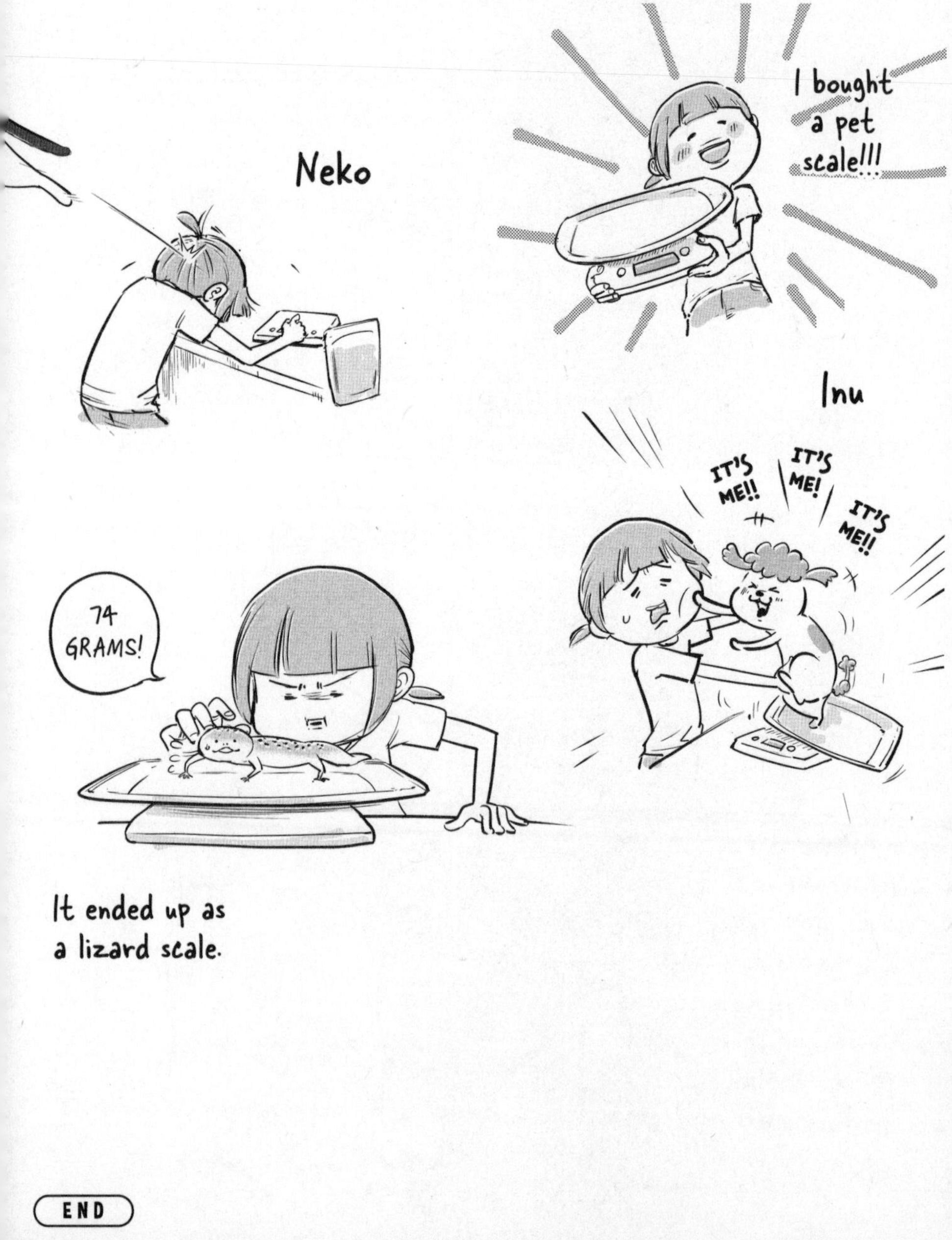

I bought a pet scale!!!
Neko
Inu
IT'S ME!!
IT'S ME!
IT'S ME!!
74 GRAMS!
It ended up as a lizard scale.
END

I feel like he smiles a lot on springtime walks.

Newly-Drawn 4-Panel Strip

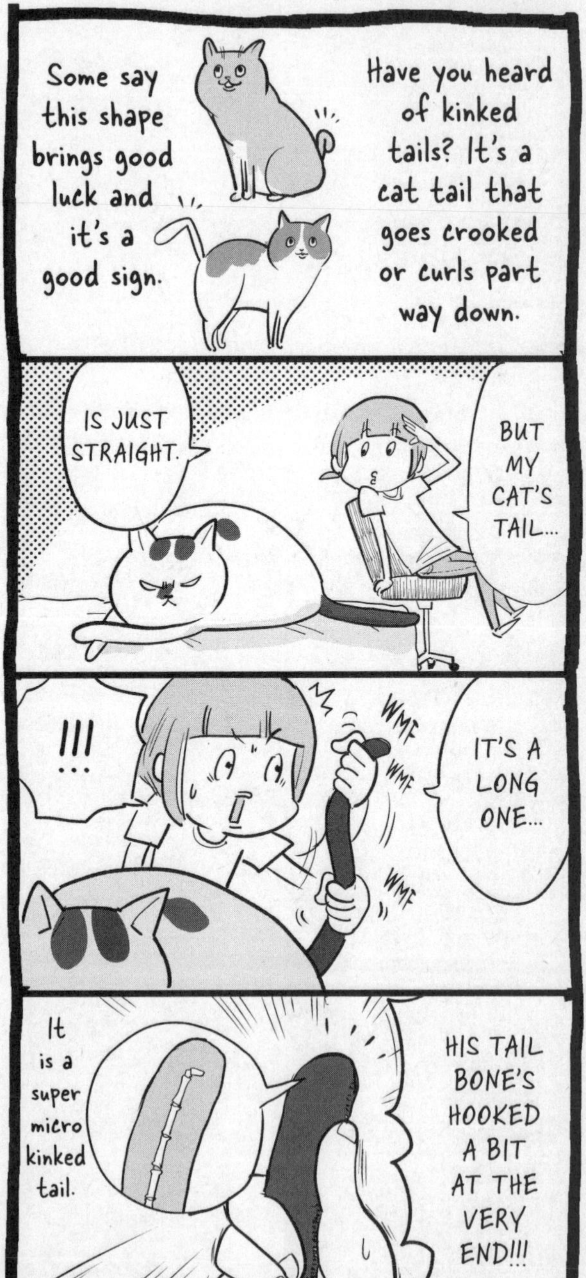
Have you heard of kinked tails? It's a cat tail that goes crooked or curls part way down.
Some say this shape brings good luck and it's a good sign.
BUT MY CAT'S TAIL...
IS JUST STRAIGHT.
IT'S A LONG ONE...
WMF
WMF
WMF
!!!
...
HIS TAIL BONE'S HOOKED A BIT AT THE VERY END!!!
It is a super micro kinked tail.

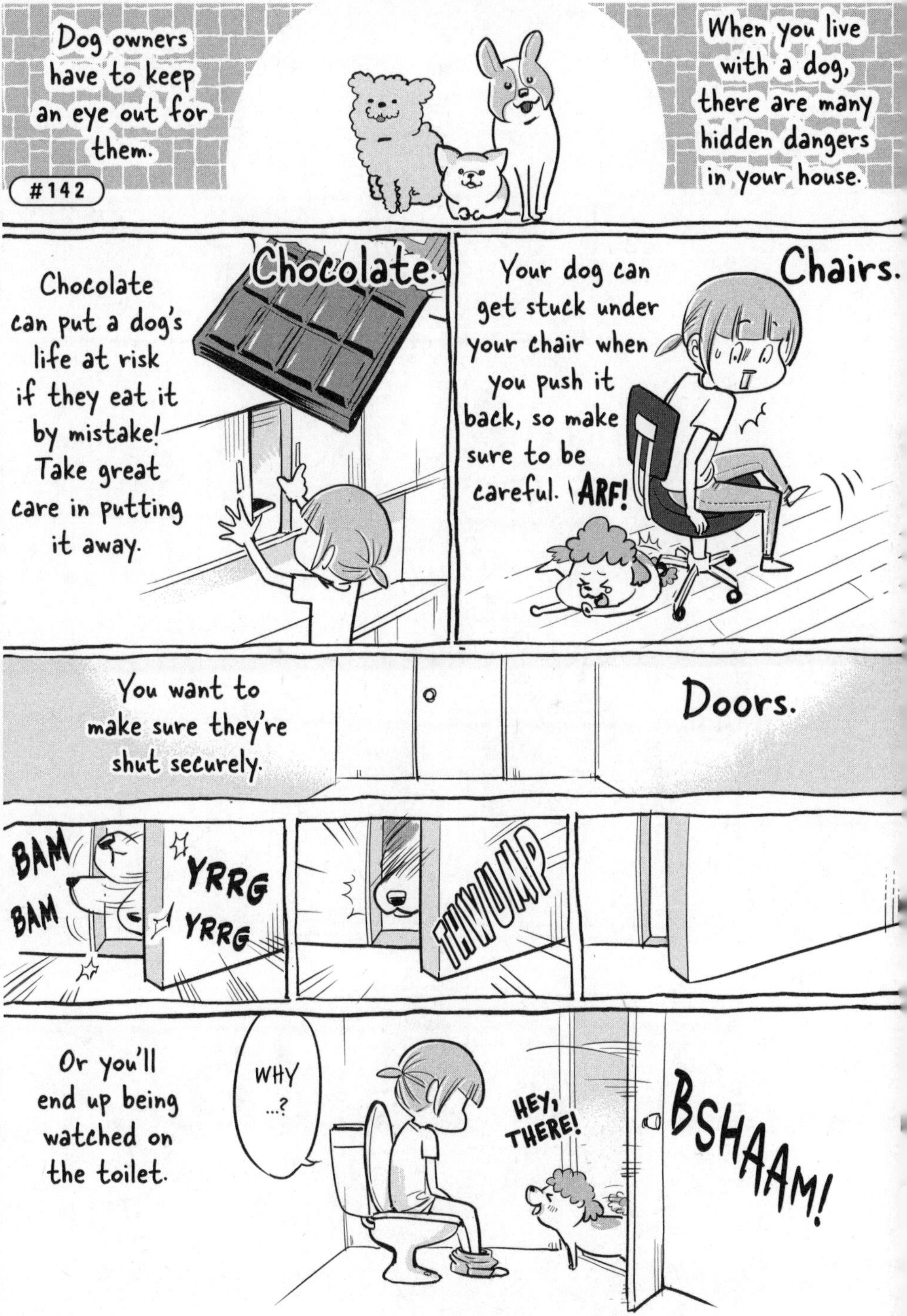
When you live with a dog, there are many hidden dangers in your house.
Dog owners have to keep an eye out for them.
#142
Chairs.
Your dog can get stuck under your chair when you push it back, so make sure to be careful.
ARF!
Chocolate.
Chocolate can put a dog's life at risk if they eat it by mistake! Take great care in putting it away.
Doors.
You want to make sure they're shut securely.
THWUMP
YRRG
YRRG
BAM
BAM
BSHAAM!
HEY, THERE!
WHY ...?
Or you'll end up being watched on the toilet.

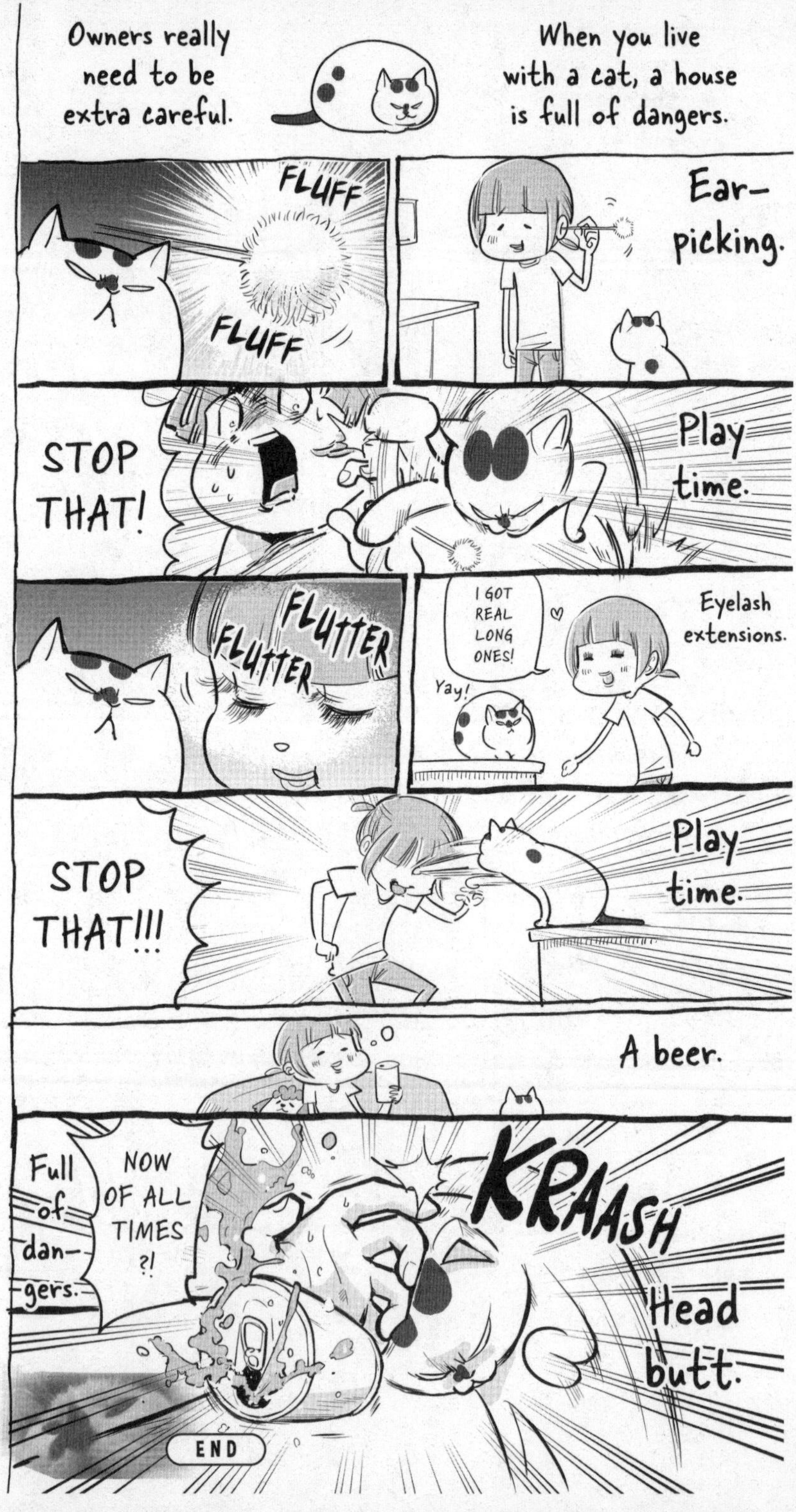
When you live with a cat, a house is full of dangers.
Owners really need to be extra careful.
Ear-picking.
FLUFF
FLUFF
Play time.
STOP THAT!
Eyelash extensions.
I GOT REAL LONG ONES!
Yay!
FLUTTER
FLUTTER
Play time.
STOP THAT!!!
A beer.
KRAASH
Head butt.
NOW OF ALL TIMES?!
Full of dan-gers.
END

#143

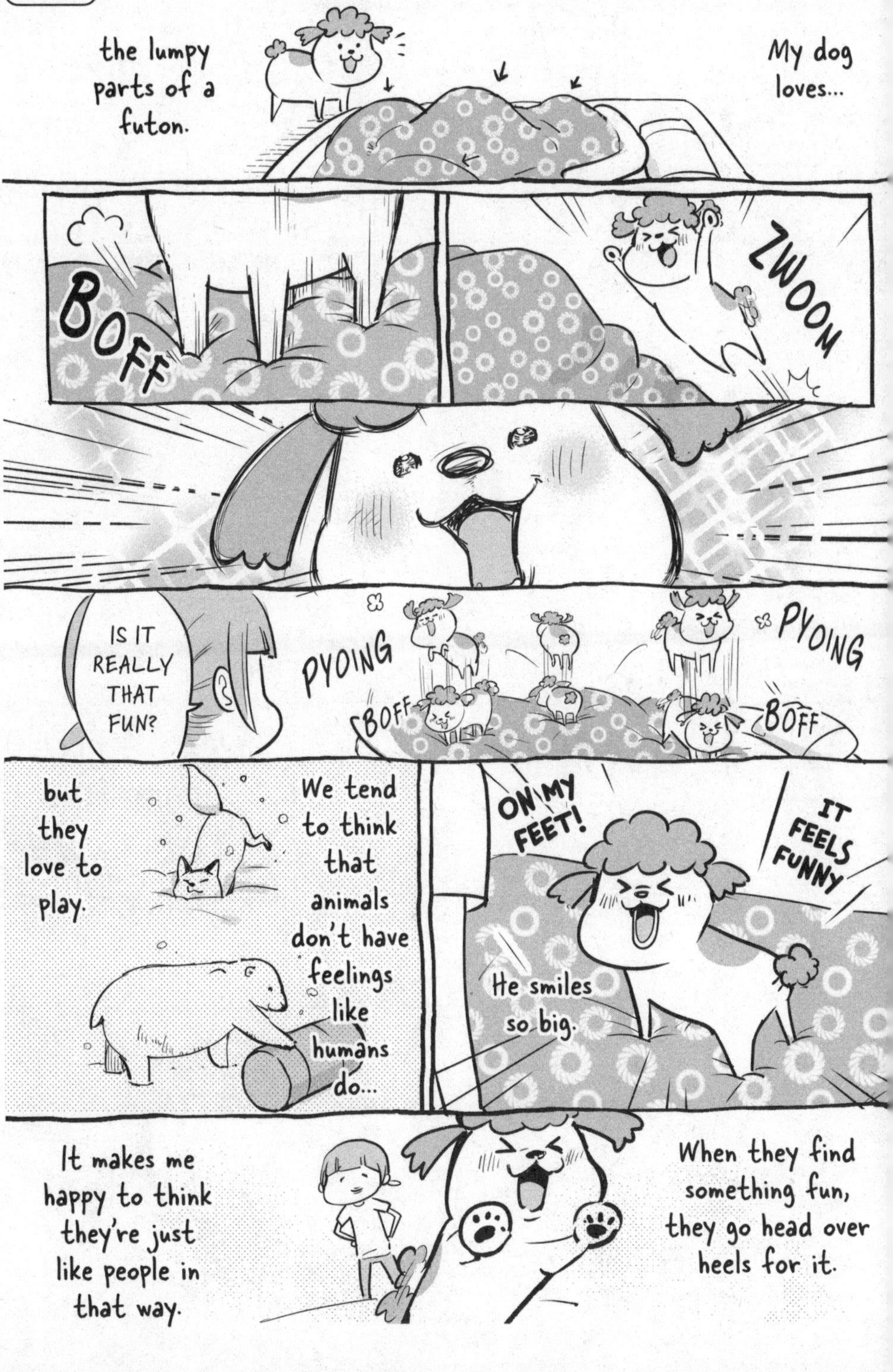
My dog loves...
the lumpy parts of a futon.
ZWOOM
BOFF
PYOING
BOFF
PYOING
BOFF
IS IT REALLY THAT FUN?
IT FEELS FUNNY
ON MY FEET!
He smiles so big.
We tend to think that animals don't have feelings like humans do...
but they love to play.
When they find something fun, they go head over heels for it.
It makes me happy to think they're just like people in that way.

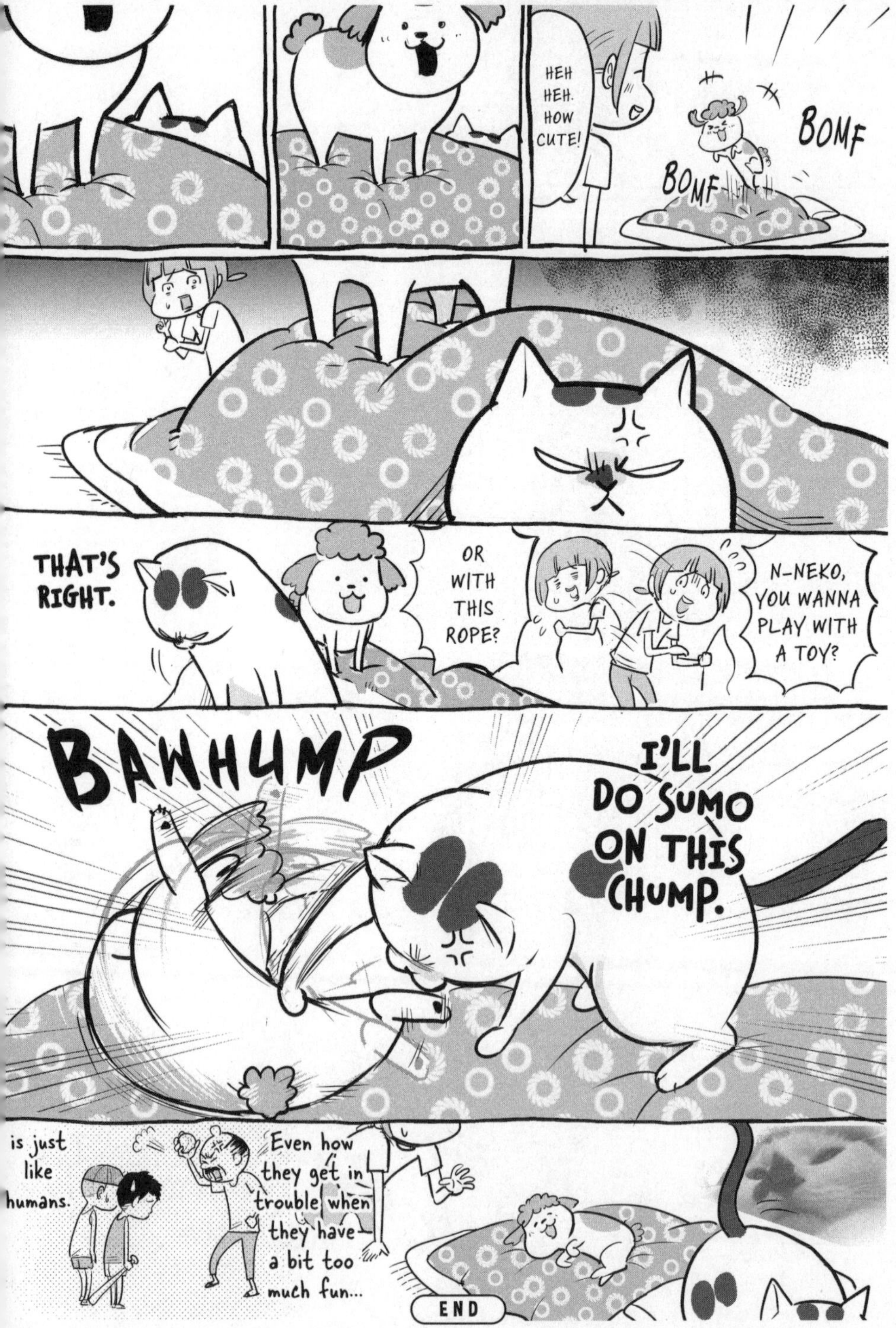
BOMF
BOMF
HEH HEH. HOW CUTE!
N-NEKO, YOU WANNA PLAY WITH A TOY?
OR WITH THIS ROPE?
THAT'S RIGHT.
I'LL DO SUMO ON THIS CHUMP.
BAWHUMP
Even how they get in trouble when they have a bit too much fun...
is just like humans.
END

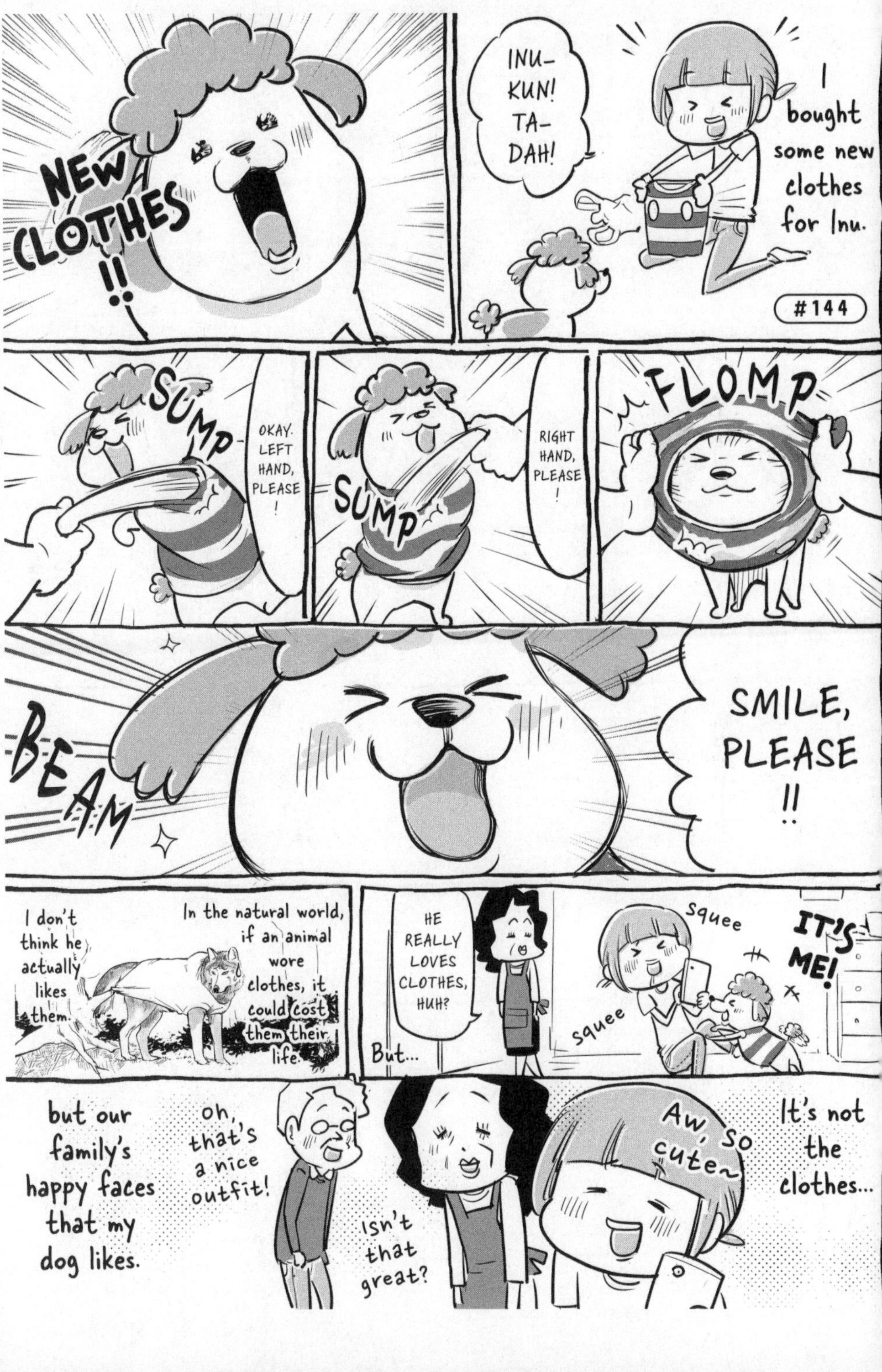
INU-KUN! TA-DAH!
I bought some new clothes for Inu.
#144
NEW CLOTHES!!
FLOMP
RIGHT HAND, PLEASE!
SUMP
OKAY. LEFT HAND, PLEASE!
SUMP
SMILE, PLEASE!!
BEAM
squee
IT'S ME!
squee
HE REALLY LOVES CLOTHES, HUH?
But...
In the natural world, if an animal wore clothes, it could cost them their life.
I don't think he actually likes them.
It's not the clothes...
Aw, so cute~
Isn't that great?
oh, that's a nice outfit!
but our family's happy faces that my dog likes.

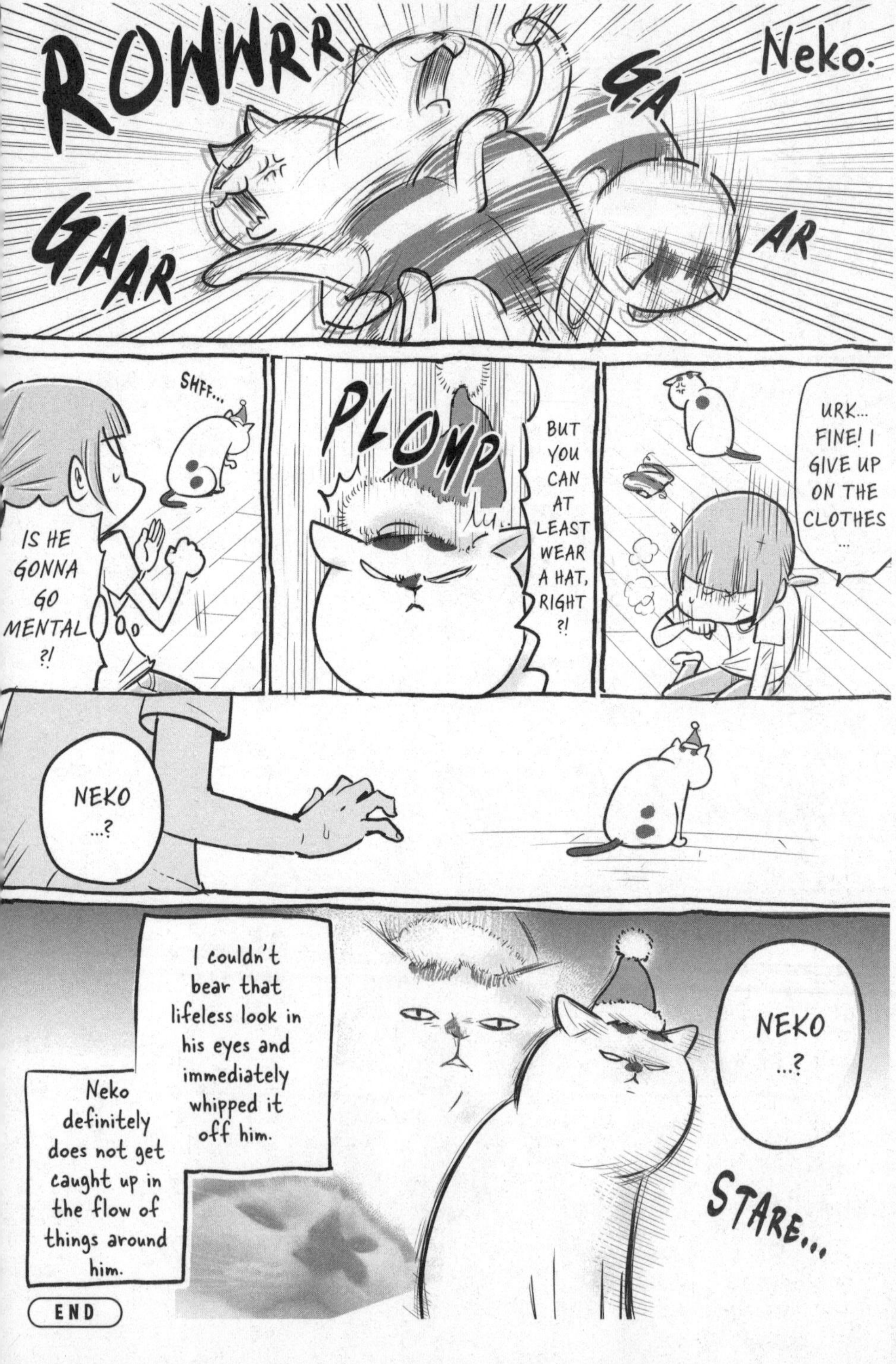
Neko.
GA
ROWWRR
AR
GAAR
URK... FINE! I GIVE UP ON THE CLOTHES ...
BUT YOU CAN AT LEAST WEAR A HAT, RIGHT ?!
PLOMP
SHFF...
IS HE GONNA GO MENTAL ?!
NEKO ...?
NEKO ...?
STARE...
I couldn't bear that lifeless look in his eyes and immediately whipped it off him.
Neko definitely does not get caught up in the flow of things around him.
END

It's the lighting... He only looks scary because of the lighting...

Newly-Drawn 4-Panel Strip

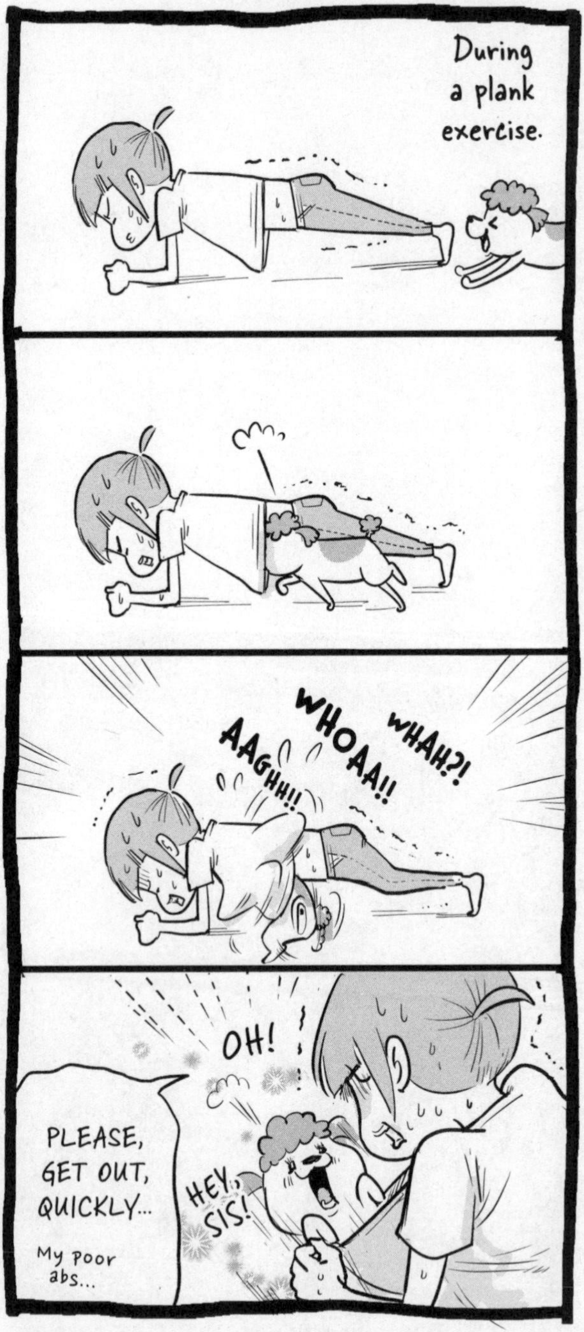
During a plank exercise.
WHAH?!
WHOAA!!
AAGHH!!
OH!
HEY, SIS!
PLEASE, GET OUT, QUICKLY...
My poor abs...

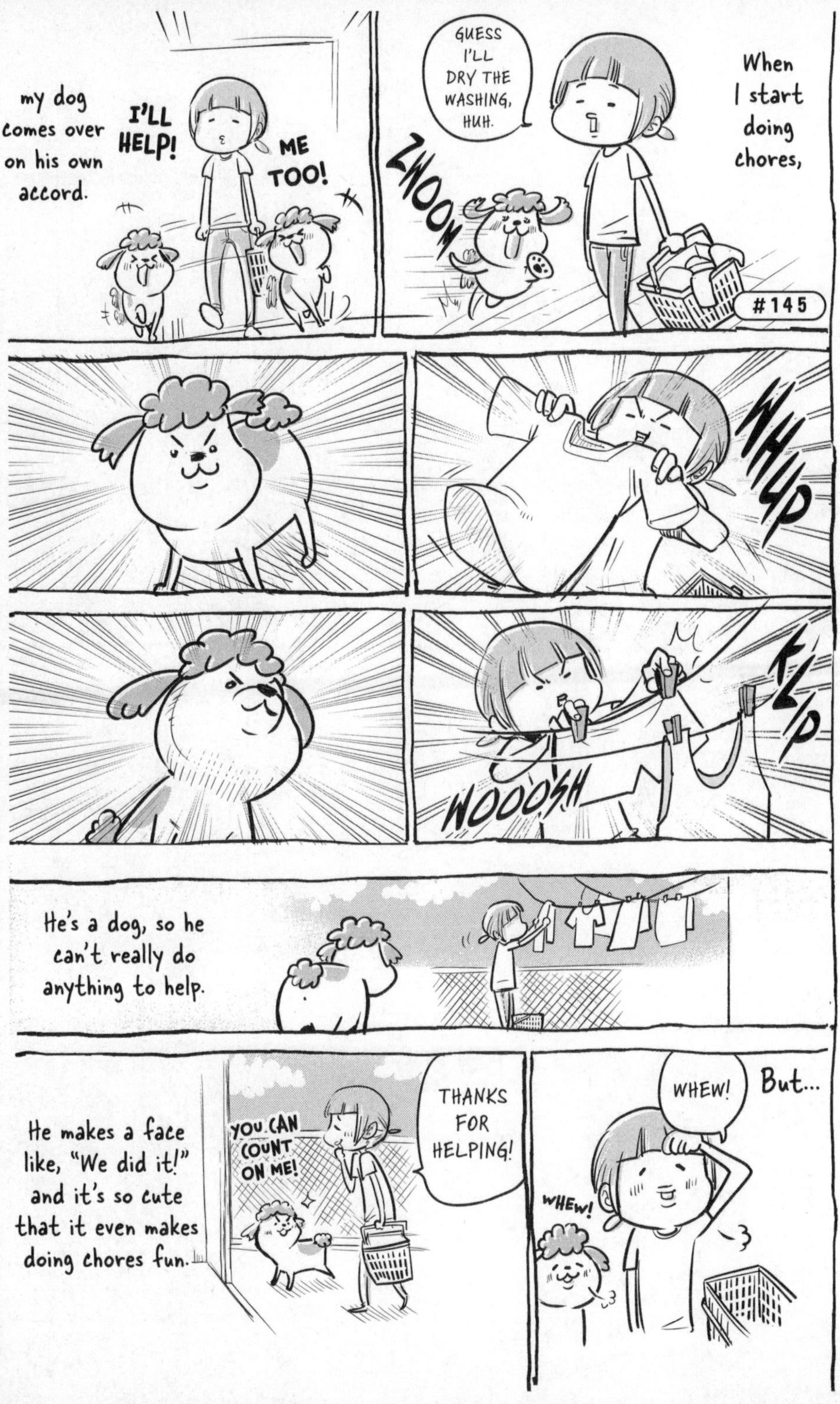

When I start doing chores,
#145
GUESS I'LL DRY THE WASHING, HUH.
ZWOOM
my dog comes over on his own accord.
I'LL HELP!
ME TOO!
WHUP
KLIP
WOOOSH
He's a dog, so he can't really do anything to help.
But...
WHEW!
WHEW!
THANKS FOR HELPING!
YOU CAN COUNT ON ME!
He makes a face like, "We did it!" and it's so cute that it even makes doing chores fun.

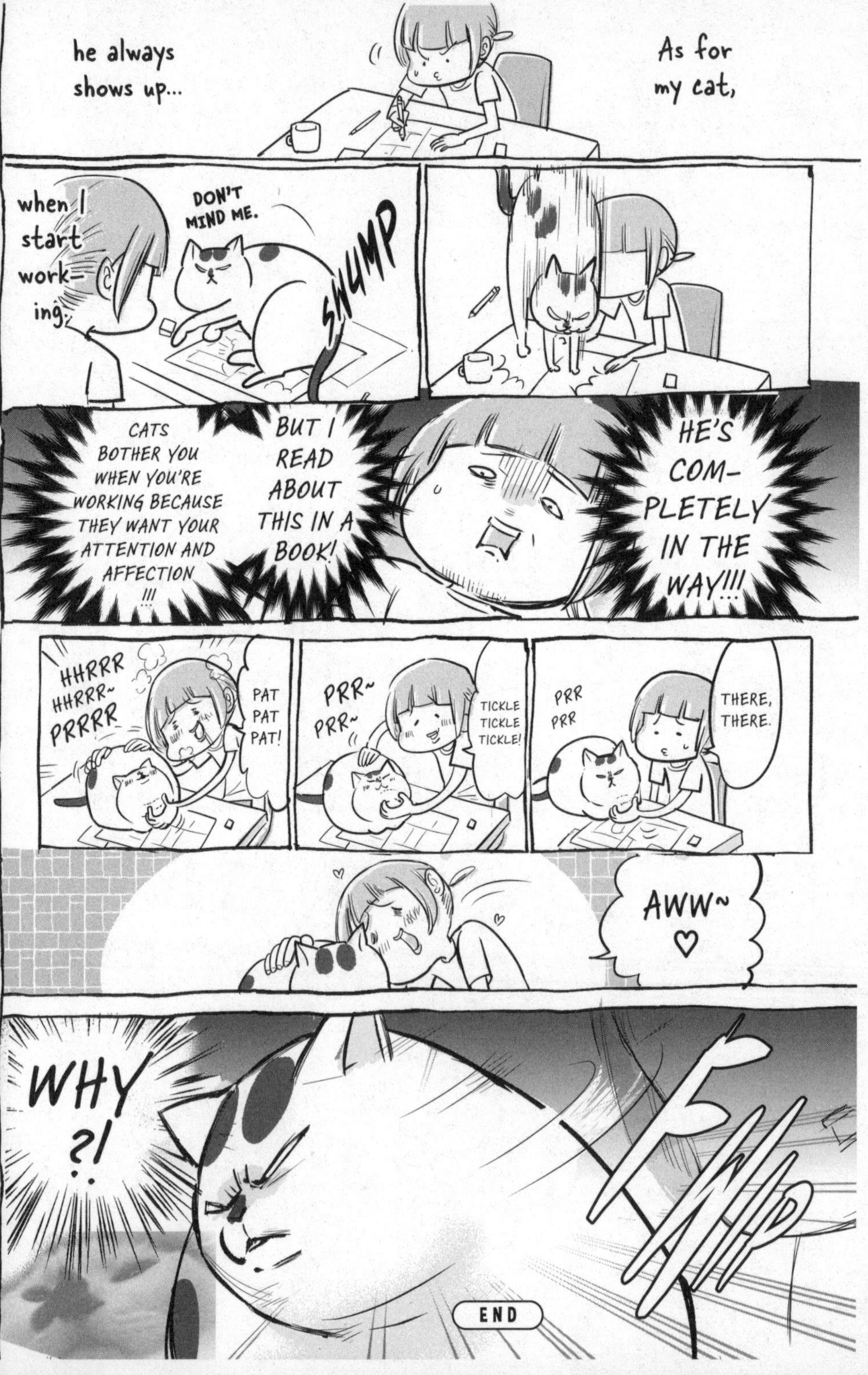
As for my cat,
he always shows up...
when I start work-ing,
DON'T MIND ME.
SHUMP
HE'S COM-PLETELY IN THE WAY!!!
BUT I READ ABOUT THIS IN A BOOK!
CATS BOTHER YOU WHEN YOU'RE WORKING BECAUSE THEY WANT YOUR ATTENTION AND AFFECTION!!!
THERE, THERE.
PRR PRR
TICKLE TICKLE TICKLE!
PRR~ PRR~
PAT PAT PAT!
HHRRR HHRRR~ PRRRR
AWW~ ♡
WHY?!
END

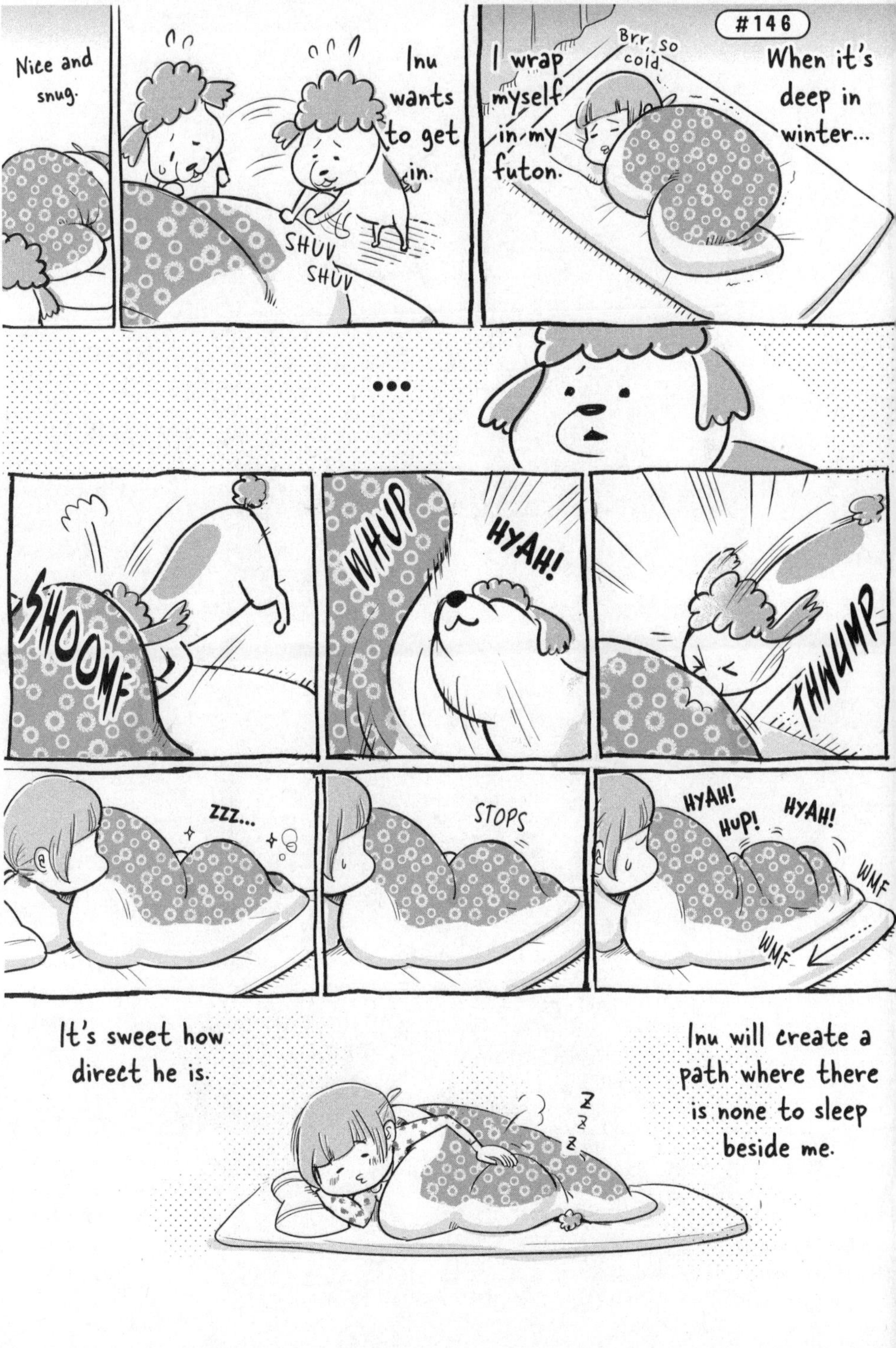
#146
When it's deep in winter...
Brr, so cold.
I wrap myself in my futon.
Inu wants to get in.
SHUV
SHUV
Nice and snug.
...
THWUMP
HYAH!
WHUP
SHOOMF
HYAH!
HUP!
HYAH!
WMF
WMF
STOPS
ZZZ...
Inu will create a path where there is none to sleep beside me.
Z
Z
Z
It's sweet how direct he is.

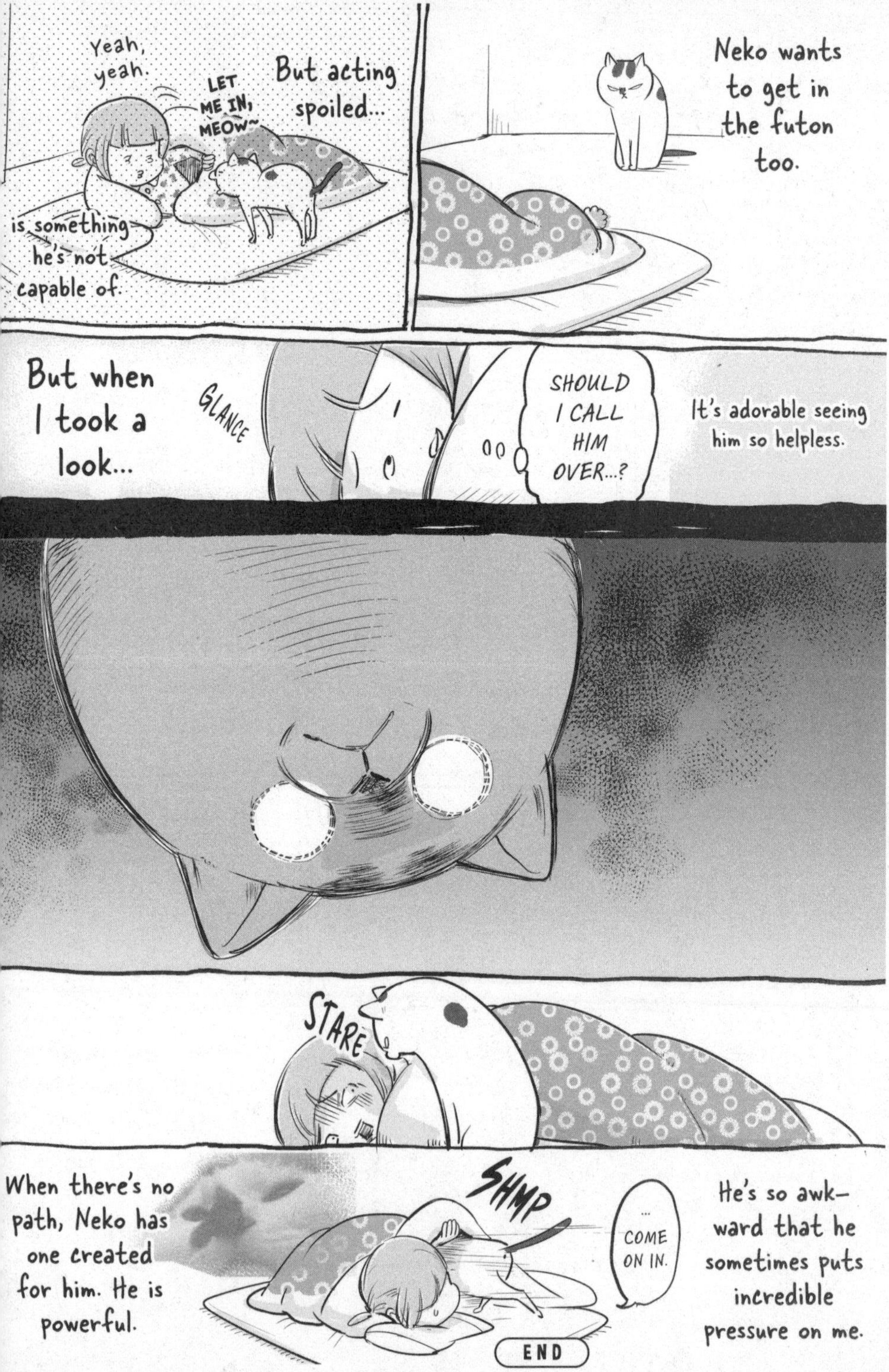
Neko wants to get in the futon too.
But acting spoiled...
LET ME IN, MEOW~
Yeah, yeah.
is something he's not capable of.
It's adorable seeing him so helpless.
SHOULD I CALL HIM OVER...?
GLANCE
But when I took a look...
STARE
He's so awk-ward that he sometimes puts incredible pressure on me.
... COME ON IN.
SHMP
When there's no path, Neko has one created for him. He is powerful.
END

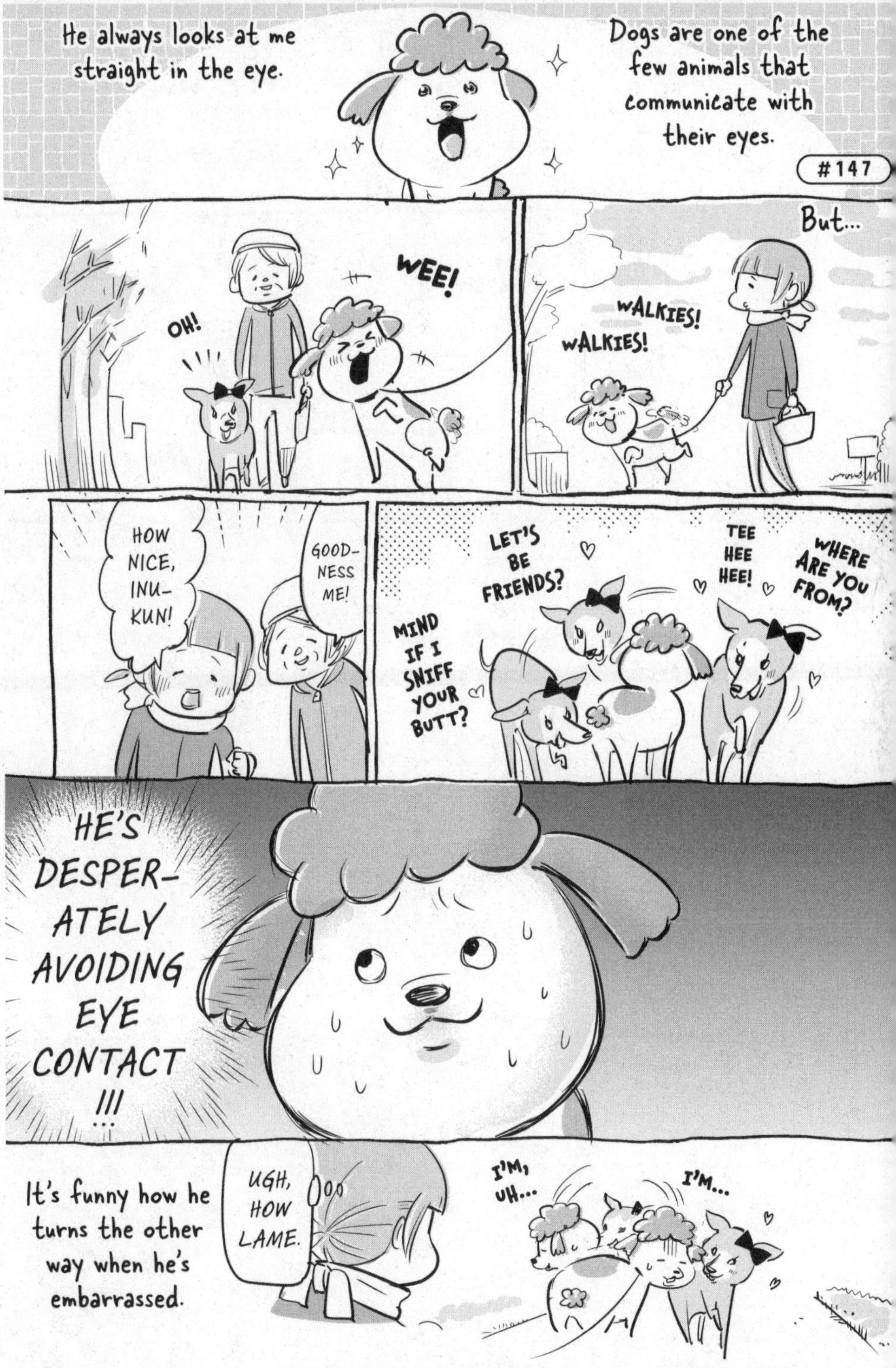

#147
Dogs are one of the few animals that communicate with their eyes.
He always looks at me straight in the eye.
But...
WALKIES!
WALKIES!
WEE!
OH!
WHERE ARE YOU FROM?
TEE HEE HEE!
LET'S BE FRIENDS?
MIND IF I SNIFF YOUR BUTT?
GOOD-NESS ME!
HOW NICE, INU-KUN!
HE'S DESPER-ATELY AVOIDING EYE CONTACT !!! ...
I'M...
I'M, UH...
UGH, HOW LAME.
It's funny how he turns the other way when he's embarrassed.

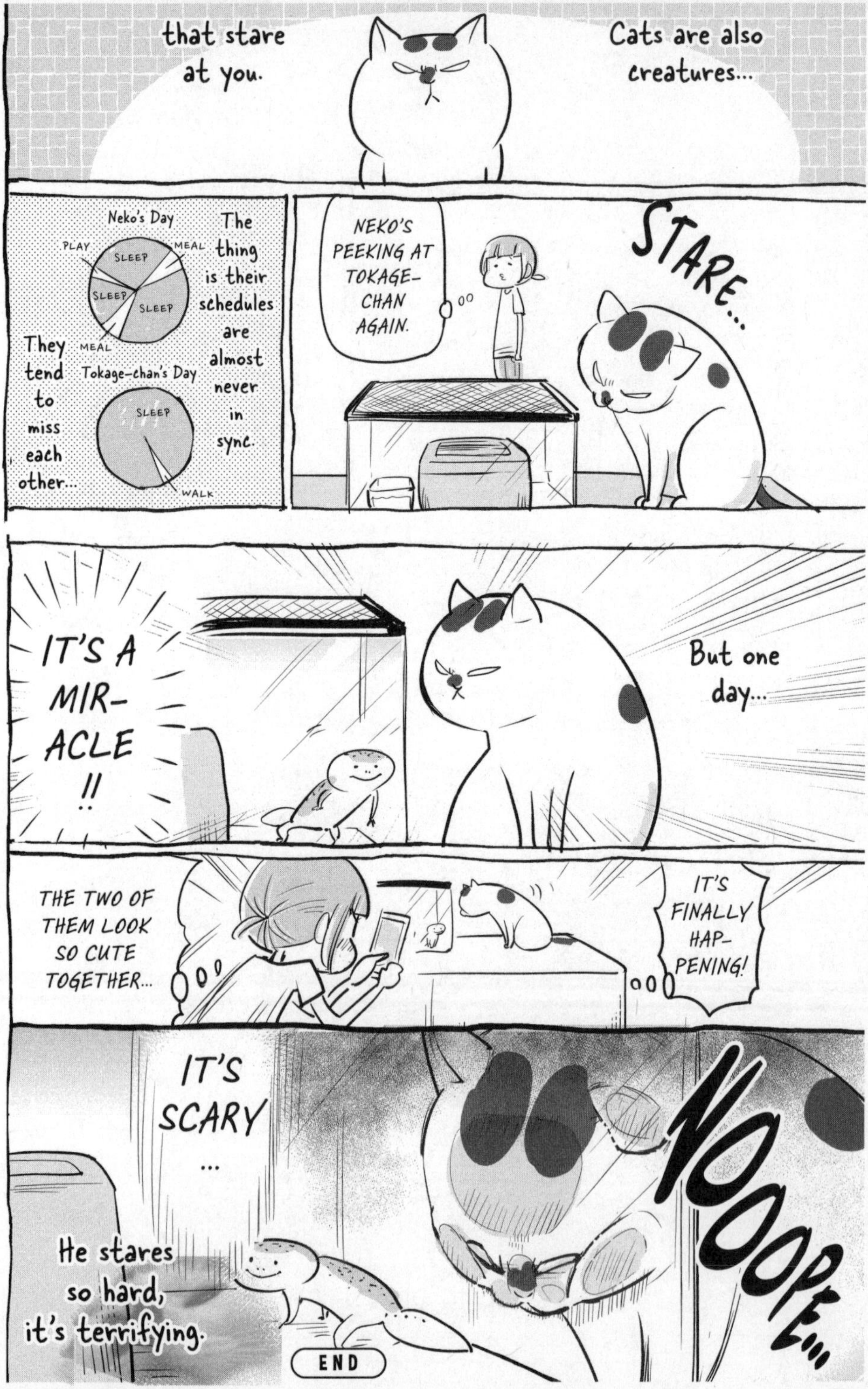
Cats are also creatures...
that stare at you.
STARE...
NEKO'S PEEKING AT TOKAGE-CHAN AGAIN.
The thing is their schedules are almost never in sync.
Neko's Day
PLAY
SLEEP
MEAL
SLEEP
SLEEP
MEAL
Tokage-chan's Day
SLEEP
WALK
They tend to miss each other...
But one day...
IT'S A MIRACLE!!
IT'S FINALLY HAPPENING!
THE TWO OF THEM LOOK SO CUTE TOGETHER...
NOOOPE...
IT'S SCARY...
He stares so hard, it's terrifying.
END

Nailed it.

Newly-Drawn 4-Panel Strip

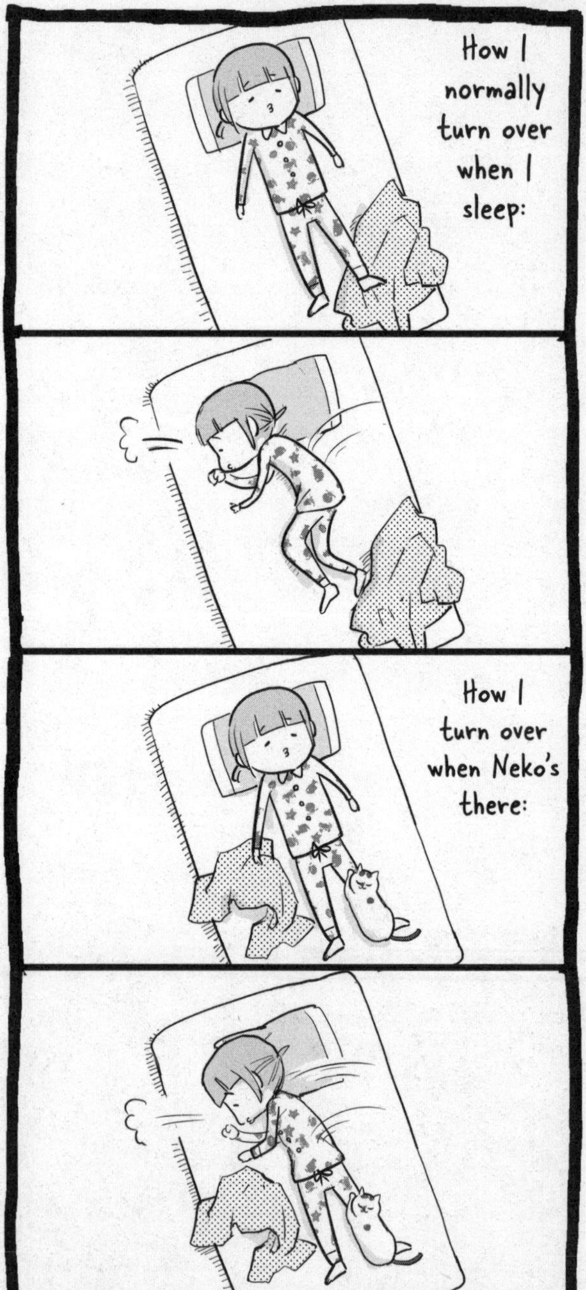
How I normally turn over when I sleep:
How I turn over when Neko's there:

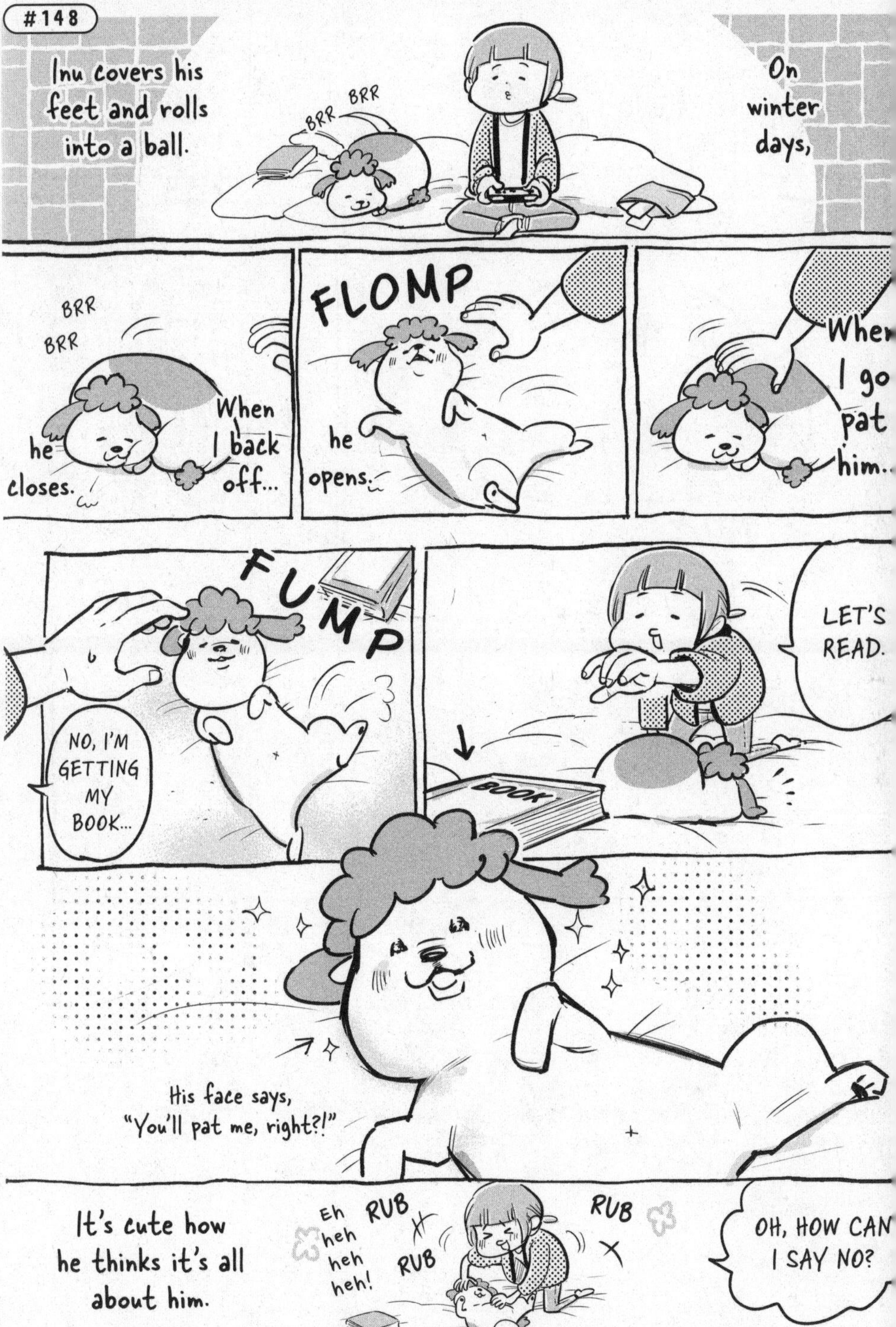
#148
On winter days,
BRR BRR
Inu covers his feet and rolls into a ball.
When I go pat him...
FLOMP
he opens.
BRR
BRR
When I back off...
he closes.
LET'S READ.
BOOK
FUMP
NO, I'M GETTING MY BOOK...
His face says, "You'll pat me, right?!"
OH, HOW CAN I SAY NO?
RUB
RUB
RUB
Eh heh heh heh!
It's cute how he thinks it's all about him.

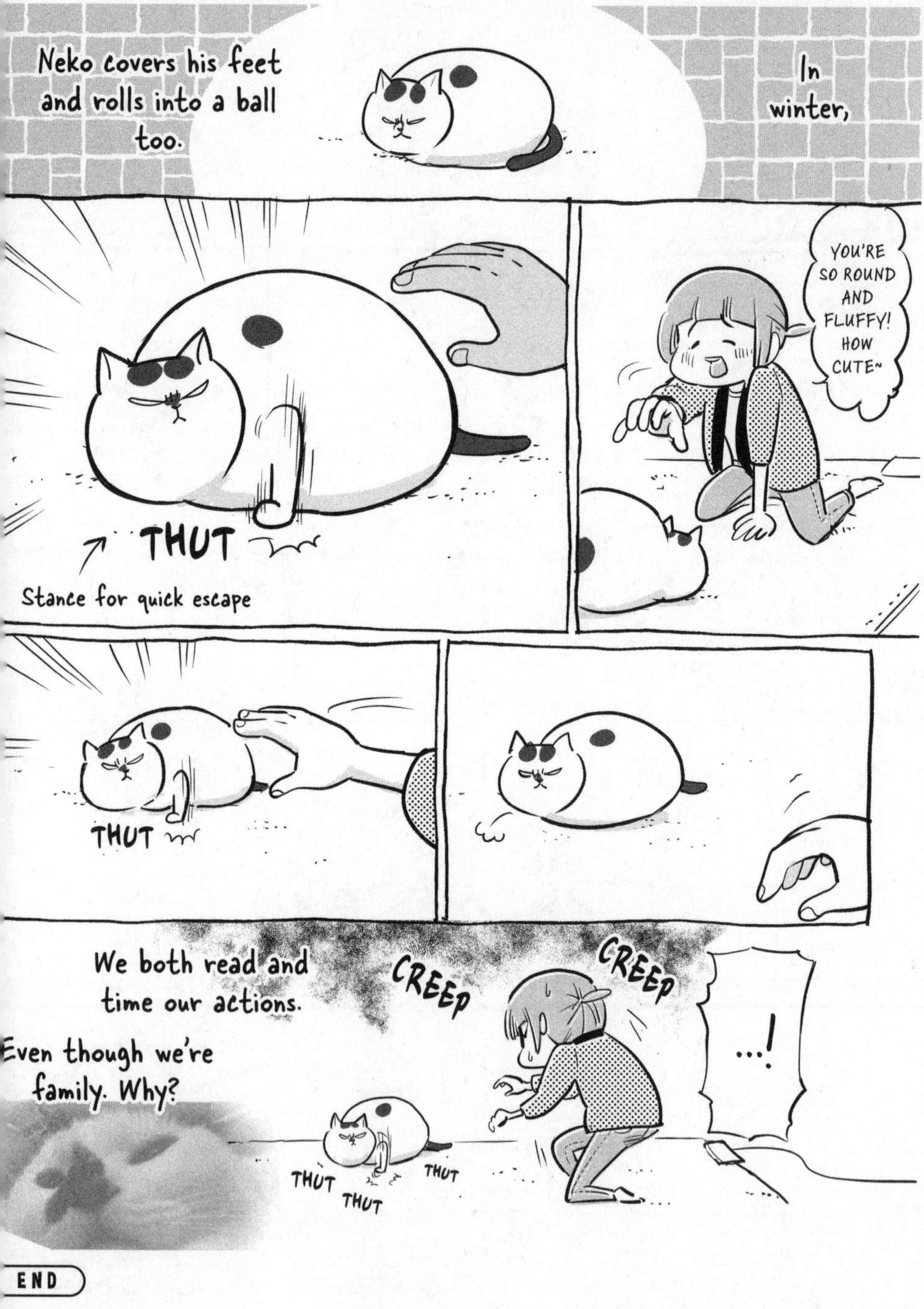
In winter,
Neko covers his feet and rolls into a ball too.
YOU'RE SO ROUND AND FLUFFY! HOW CUTE~
THUT
Stance for quick escape
THUT
...!
CREEP
CREEP
We both read and time our actions.
Even though we're family. Why?
THUT
THUT
THUT
END

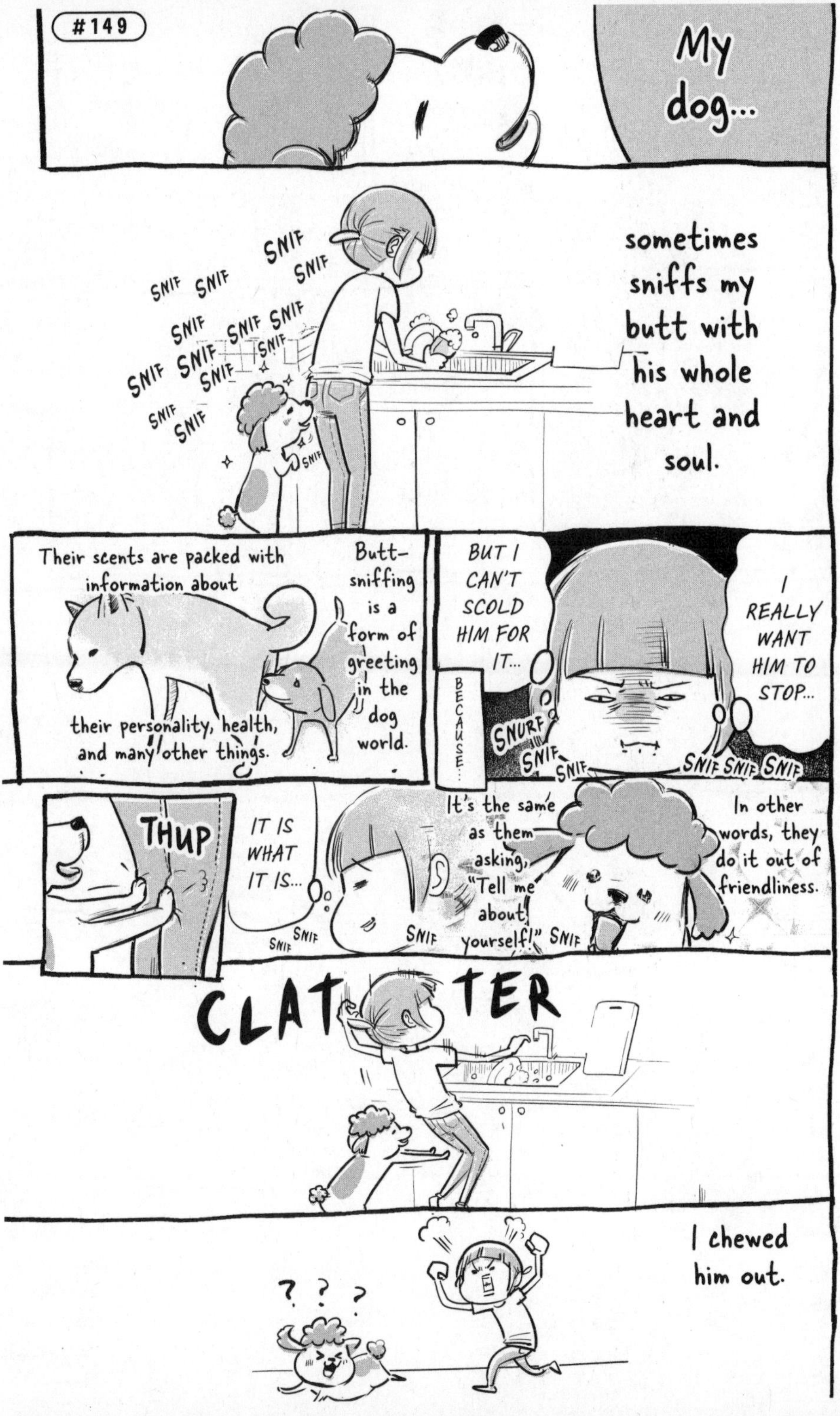
#149
My dog...
sometimes sniffs my butt with his whole heart and soul.
SNIF SNIF SNIF SNIF SNIF SNIF SNIF SNIF SNIF SNIF SNIF SNIF SNIF SNIF SNIF
I REALLY WANT HIM TO STOP...
BUT I CAN'T SCOLD HIM FOR IT...
BECAUSE...
SNURF SNIF SNIF SNIF SNIF SNIF
Butt-sniffing is a form of greeting in the dog world.
Their scents are packed with information about their personality, health, and many other things.
In other words, they do it out of friendliness.
It's the same as them asking, "Tell me about yourself!"
SNIF SNIF
IT IS WHAT IT IS...
SNIF SNIF
THUP
CLATTER
I chewed him out.
? ? ?

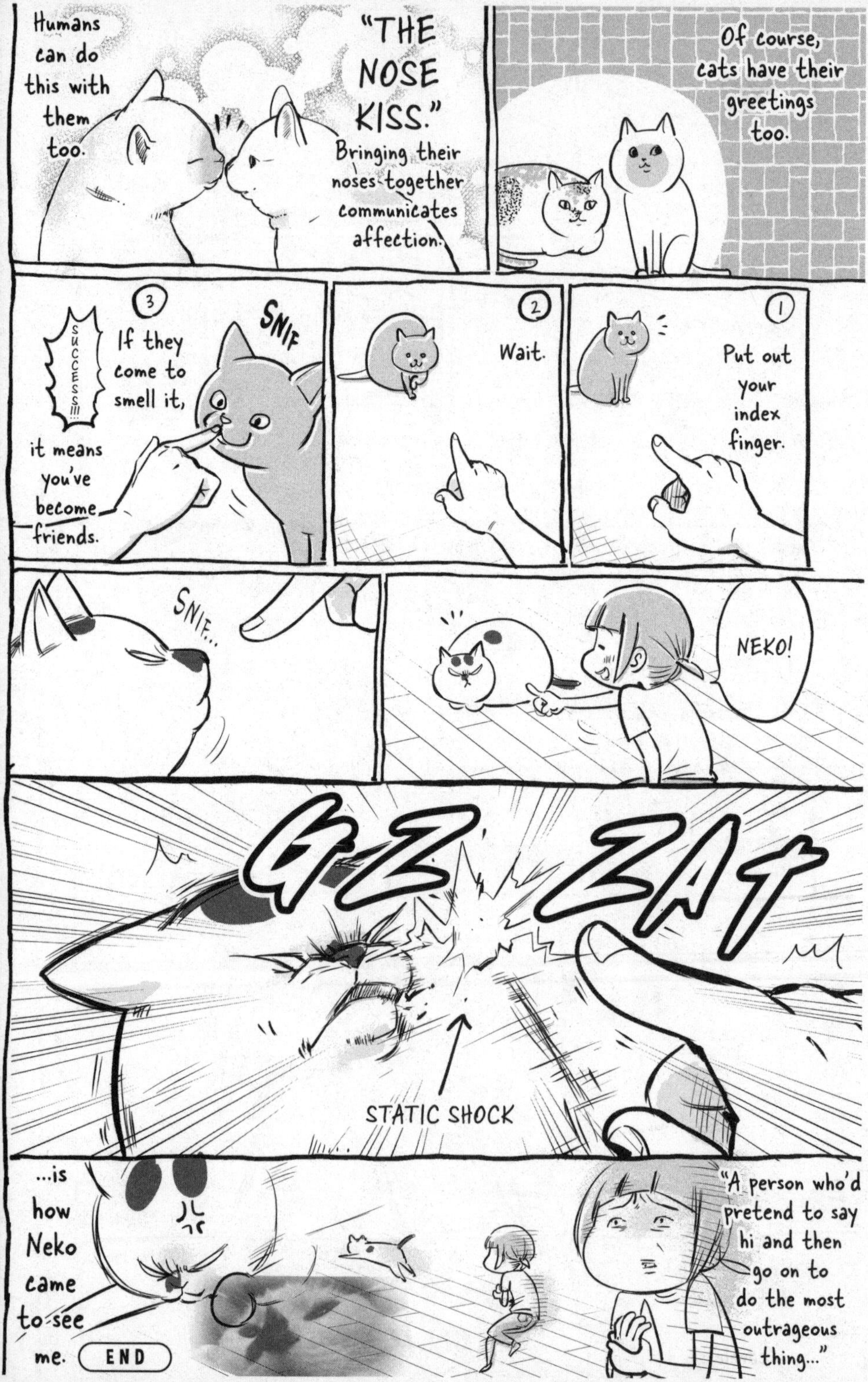
Of course, cats have their greetings too.
"THE NOSE KISS."
Bringing their noses together communicates affection.
Humans can do this with them too.
1
Put out your index finger.
2
Wait.
3
SNIF
If they come to smell it,
SUCCESS!!!
it means you've become friends.
NEKO!
SNIF...
GZ ZAT
STATIC SHOCK
"A person who'd pretend to say hi and then go on to do the most outrageous thing..."
...is how Neko came to see me.
END

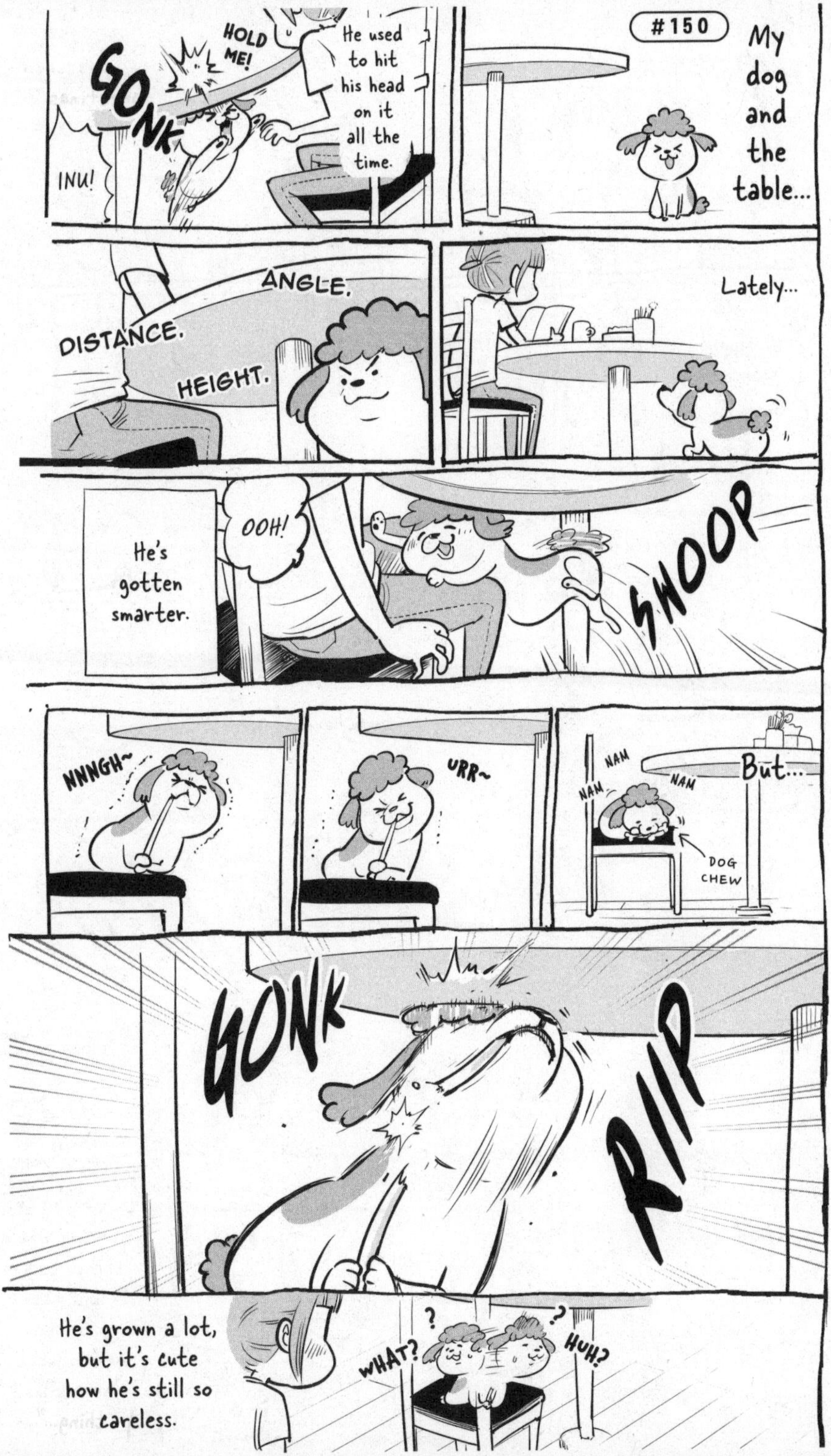
#150
My dog and the table...
He used to hit his head on it all the time.
HOLD ME!
GONK
INU!
Lately...
ANGLE.
DISTANCE.
HEIGHT.
SHOOP
OOH!
He's gotten smarter.
But...
NAM
NAM
NAM
DOG CHEW
URR~
NNNGH~
RIIP
GONK
HUH?
WHAT?
He's grown a lot, but it's cute how he's still so careless.

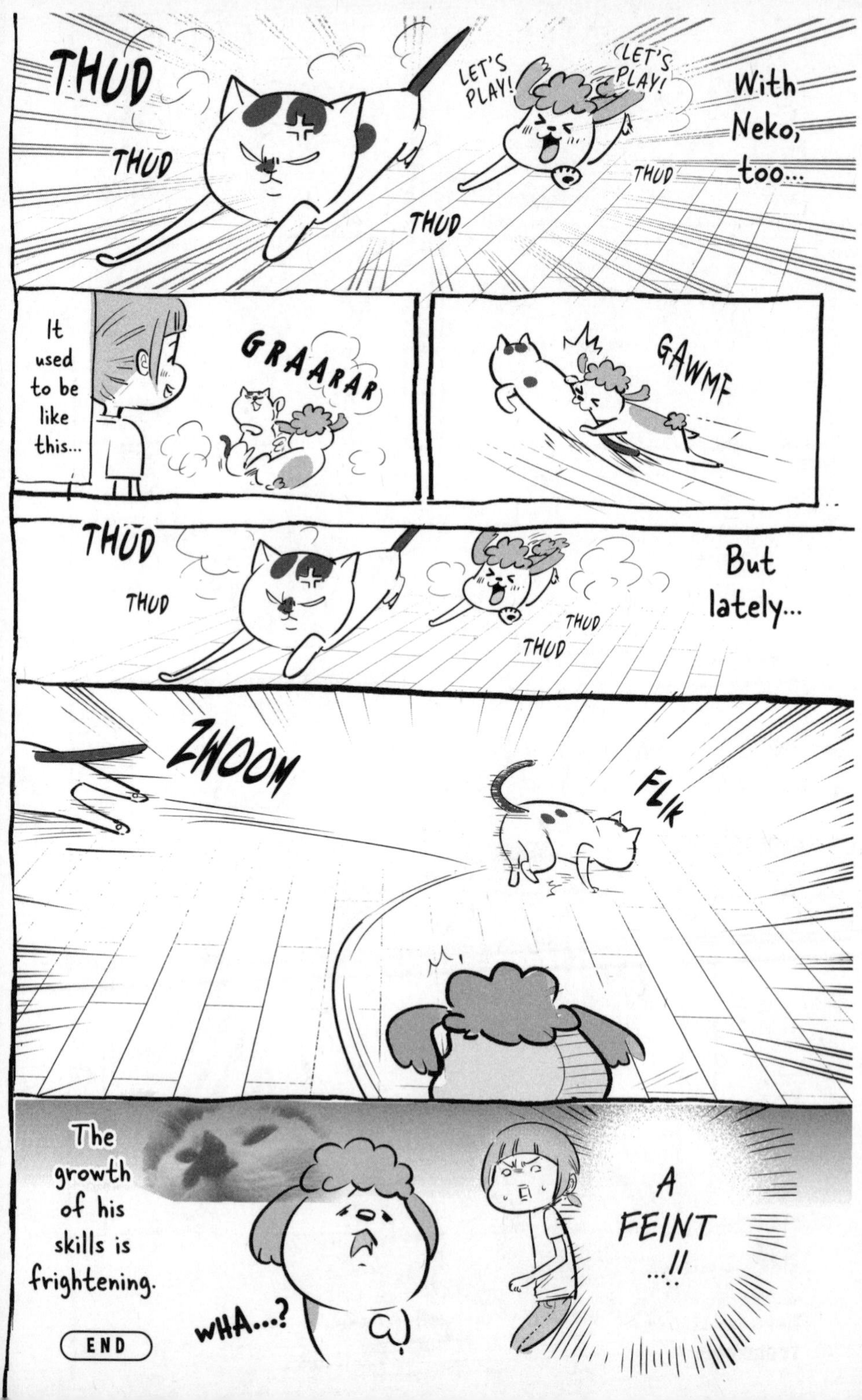

With Neko, too...
LET'S PLAY!
LET'S PLAY!
THUD
THUD
THUD
THUD
GAWMF
GRAARAR
It used to be like this...
But lately...
THUD
THUD
THUD
THUD
FLIK
ZWOOM
A FEINT ...!!
WHA...?
The growth of his skills is frightening.
END

Neko getting a bit too warm and cooling just his front half.

Newly-Drawn 4-Panel Strip

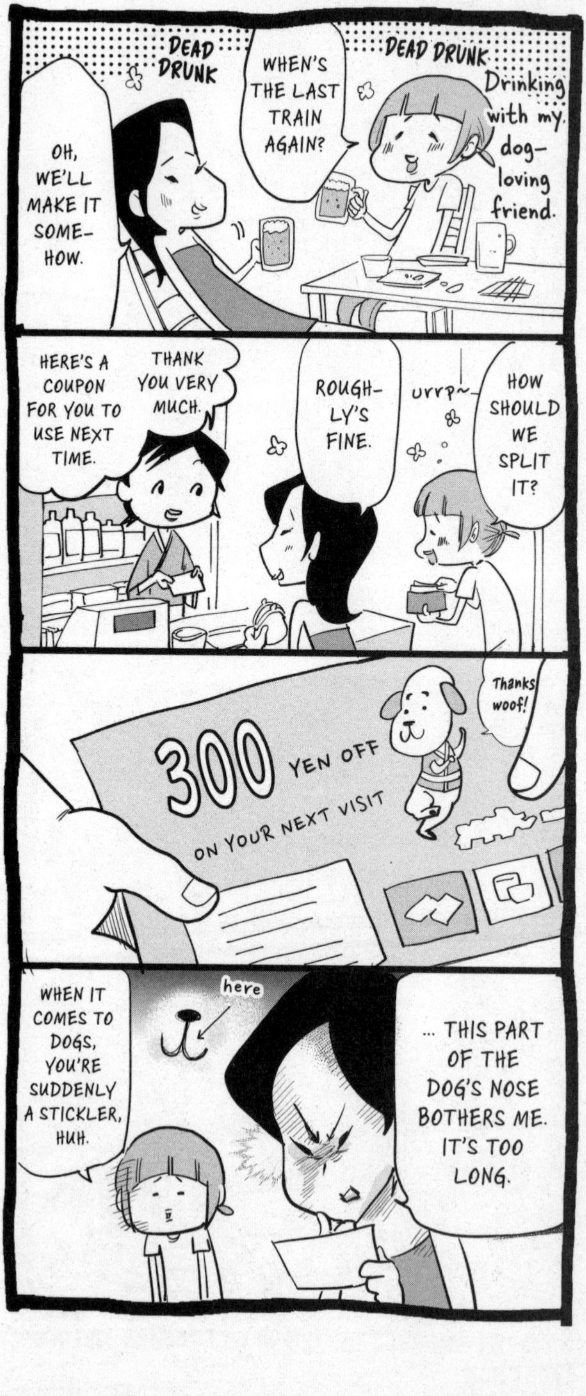
Drinking with my dog-loving friend.
DEAD DRUNK
WHEN'S THE LAST TRAIN AGAIN?
DEAD DRUNK
OH, WE'LL MAKE IT SOMEHOW.
HOW SHOULD WE SPLIT IT?
urrp~
ROUGHLY'S FINE.
THANK YOU VERY MUCH.
HERE'S A COUPON FOR YOU TO USE NEXT TIME.
Thanks woof!
300 YEN OFF
ON YOUR NEXT VISIT
... THIS PART OF THE DOG'S NOSE BOTHERS ME. IT'S TOO LONG.
here
WHEN IT COMES TO DOGS, YOU'RE SUDDENLY A STICKLER, HUH.

Bonus

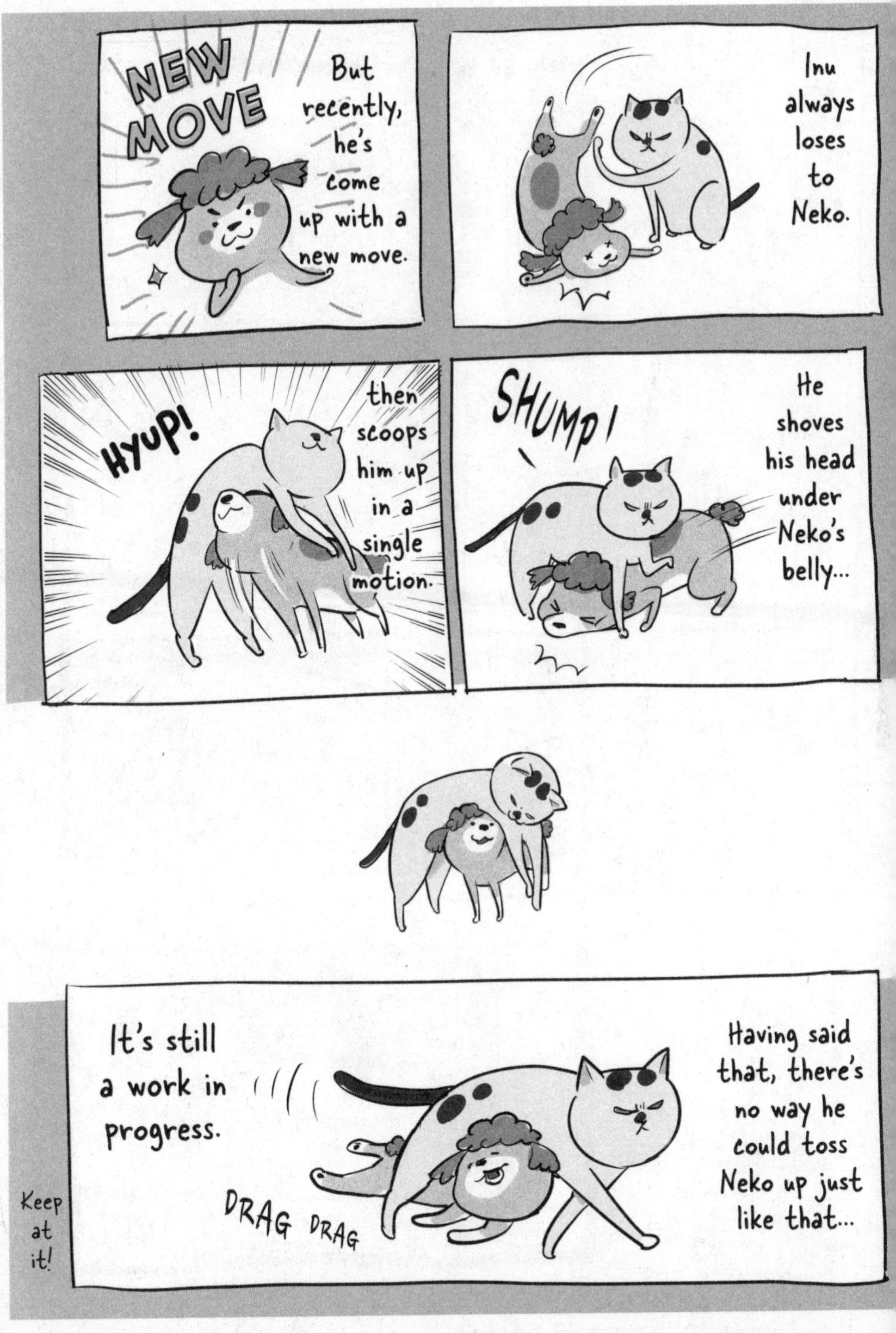
Inu always loses to Neko.
But recently, he's come up with a new move.
NEW MOVE
He shoves his head under Neko's belly...
SHUMP!
then scoops him up in a single motion.
HYUP!
Having said that, there's no way he could toss Neko up just like that...
It's still a work in progress.
DRAG DRAG
Keep at it!

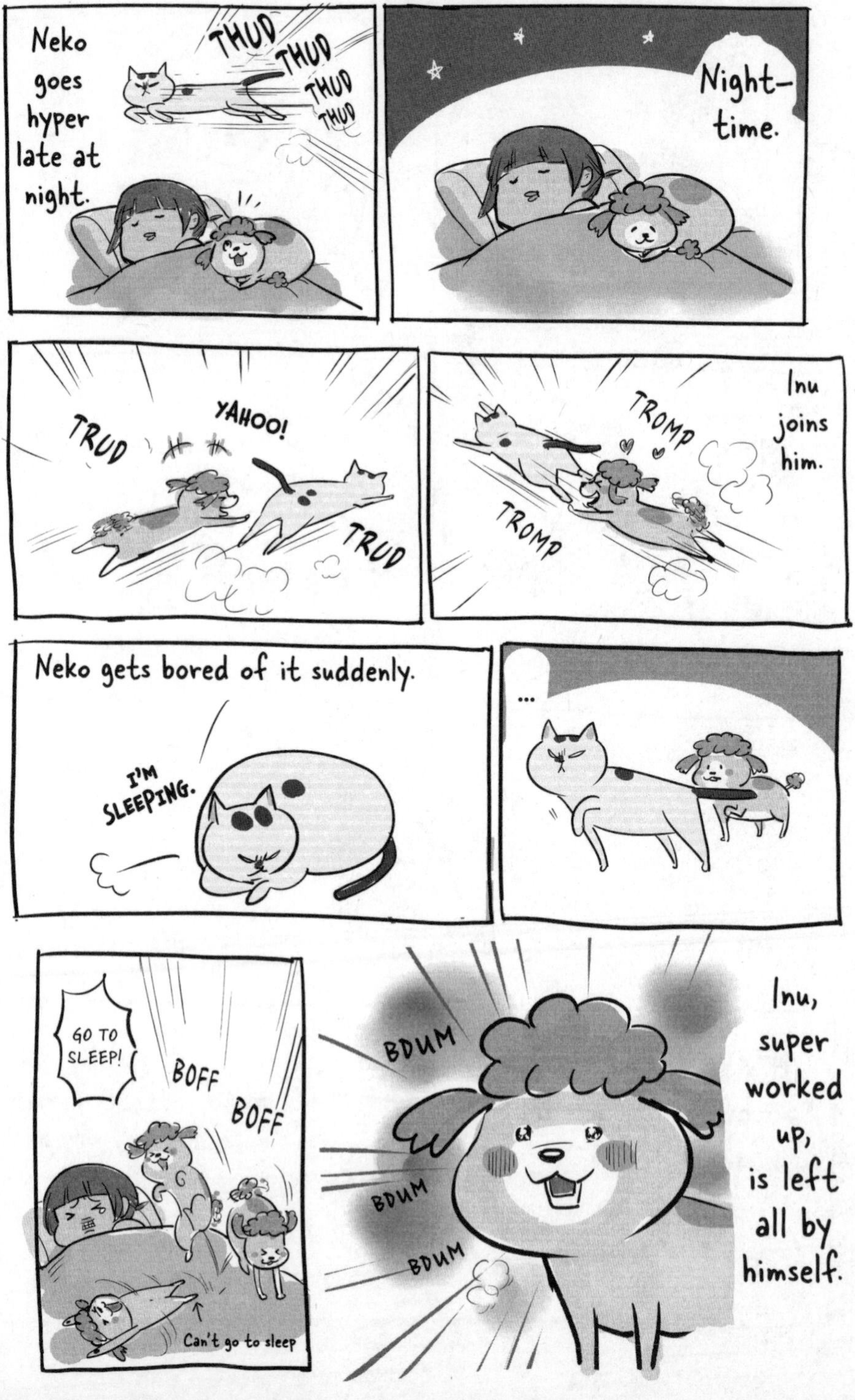
Night-time.
Neko goes hyper late at night.
THUD
THUD
THUD
THUD
Inu joins him.
TROMP
TROMP
YAHOO!
TRUD
TRUD
...
Neko gets bored of it suddenly.
I'M SLEEPING.
Inu, super worked up, is left all by himself.
BDUM
BDUM
BDUM
GO TO SLEEP!
BOFF
BOFF
Can't go to sleep

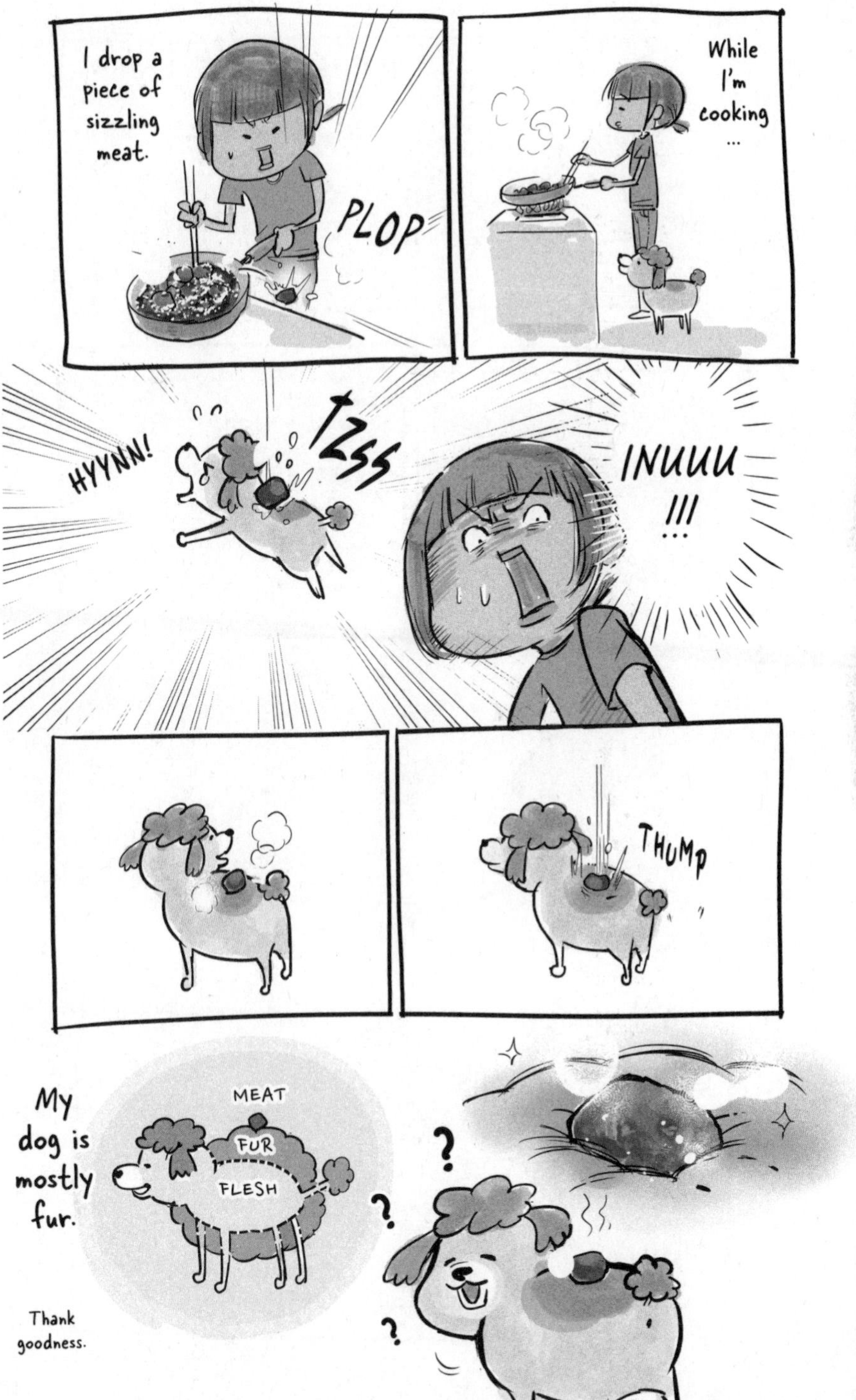
While I'm cooking ...
I drop a piece of sizzling meat.
PLOP
INUUU !!!
TZSS
HYYNN!
THUMP
? ? ?
My dog is mostly fur.
MEAT
FUR
FLESH
Thank goodness.

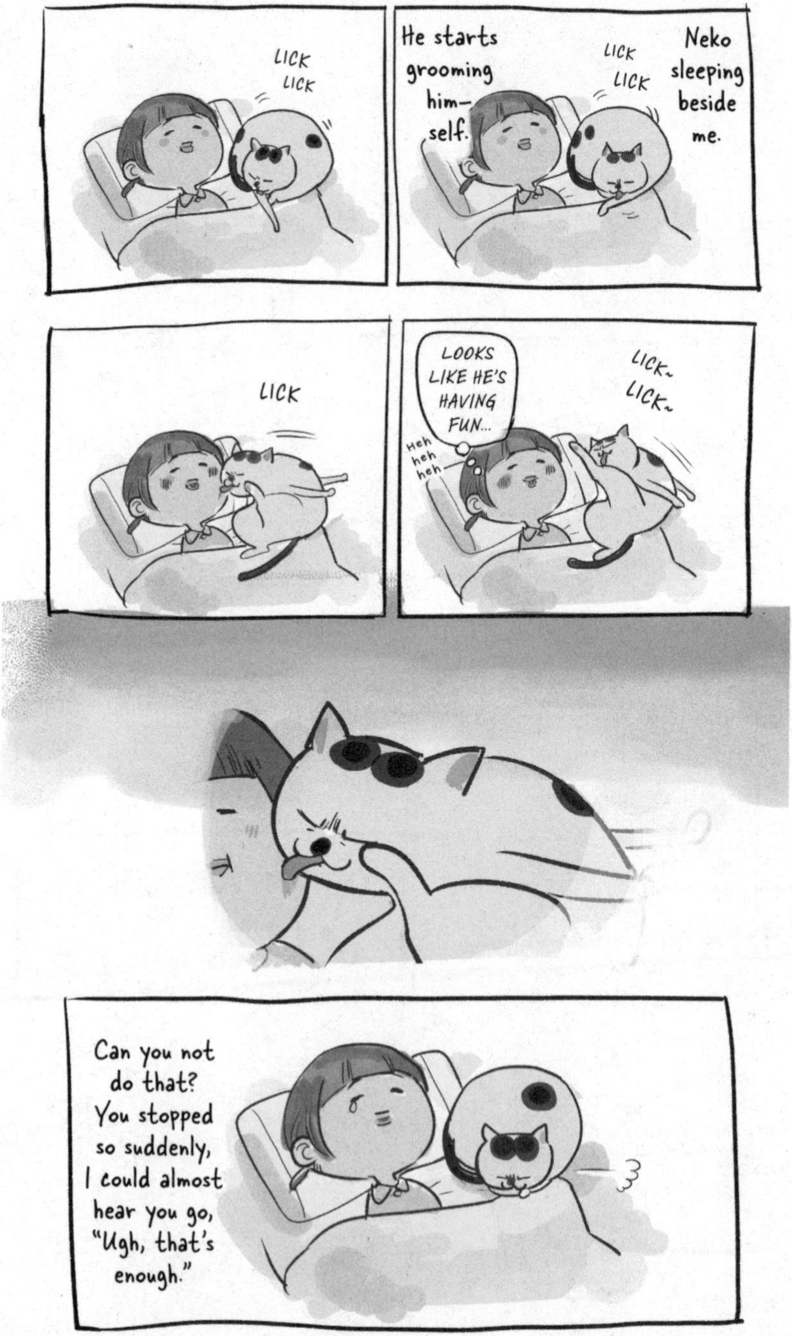
Neko sleeping beside me.
LICK LICK
He starts grooming him-self.
LICK LICK
LICK~ LICK~
LOOKS LIKE HE'S HAVING FUN...
Heh heh heh
LICK
Can you not do that? You stopped so suddenly, I could almost hear you go, "Ugh, that's enough."

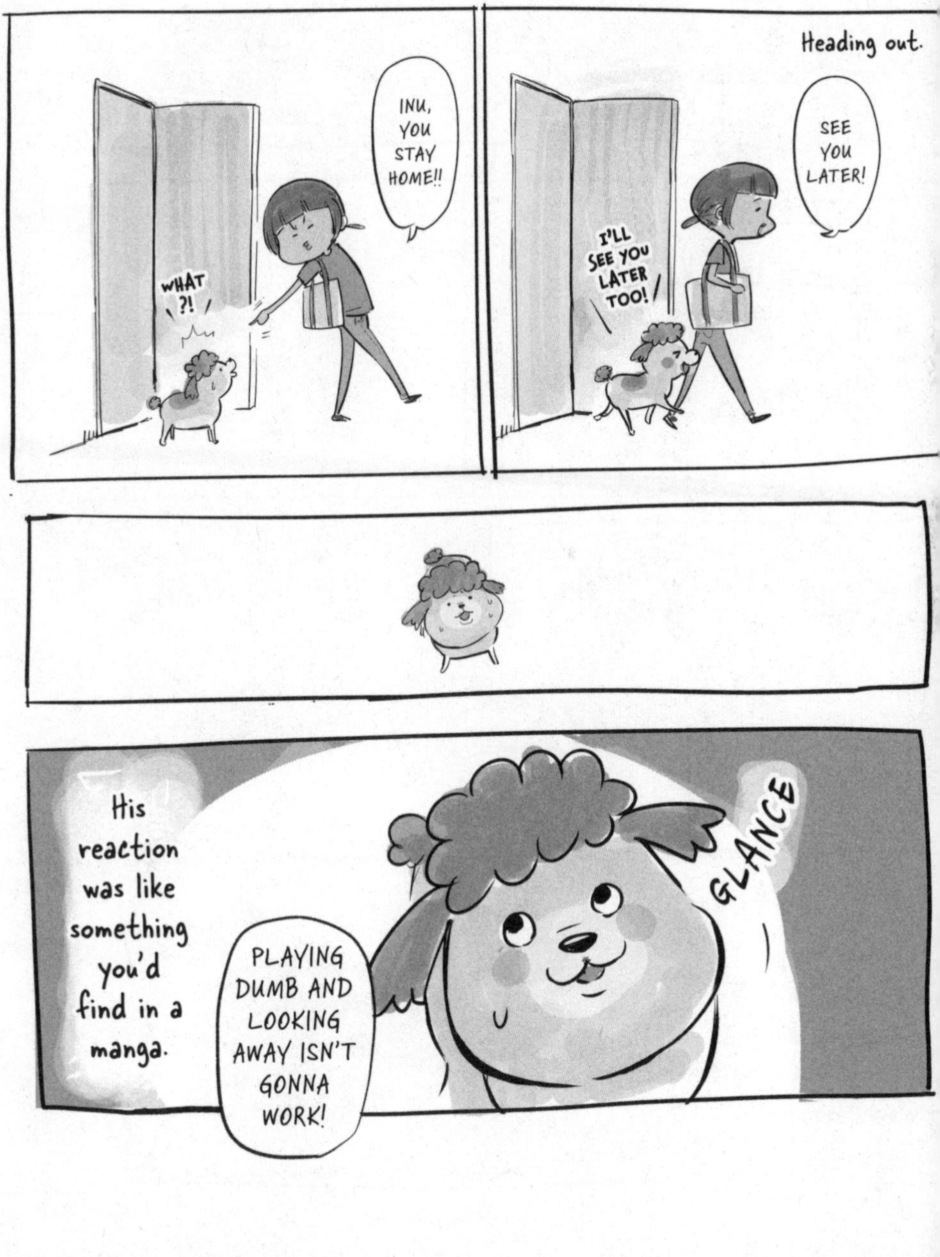
Heading out.
SEE YOU LATER!
I'LL SEE YOU LATER TOO!
INU, YOU STAY HOME!!
WHAT ?!
GLANCE
His reaction was like something you'd find in a manga.
PLAYING DUMB AND LOOKING AWAY ISN'T GONNA WORK!

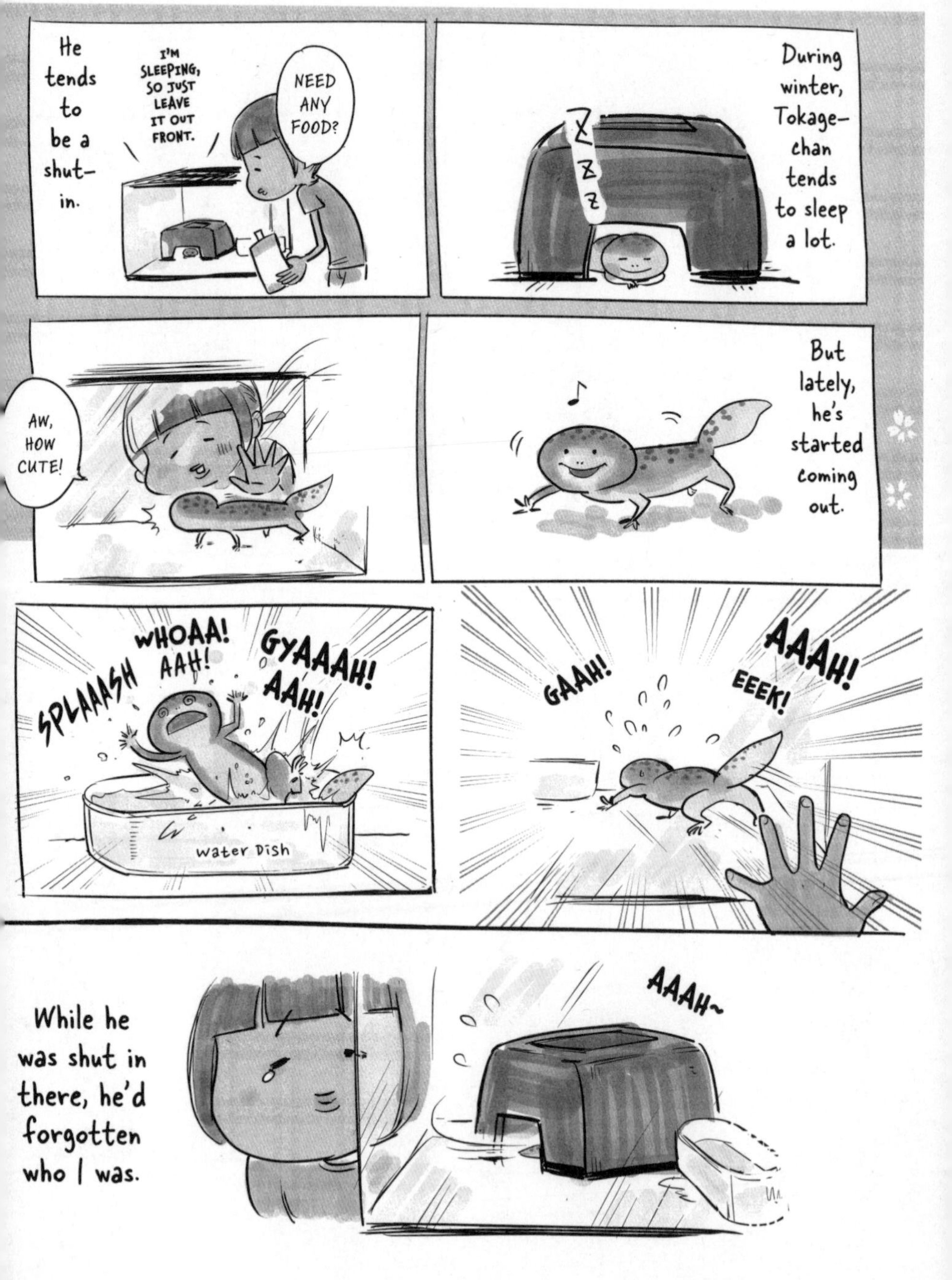

ZZZ
During winter, Tokage-chan tends to sleep a lot.
NEED ANY FOOD?
I'M SLEEPING, SO JUST LEAVE IT OUT FRONT.
He tends to be a shut-in.
But lately, he's started coming out.
AW, HOW CUTE!
AAAH!
EEEK!
GAAH!
GYAAAH! AAH!
WHOAA! AAH!
SPLAAASH
water Dish
AAAH~
While he was shut in there, he'd forgotten who I was.

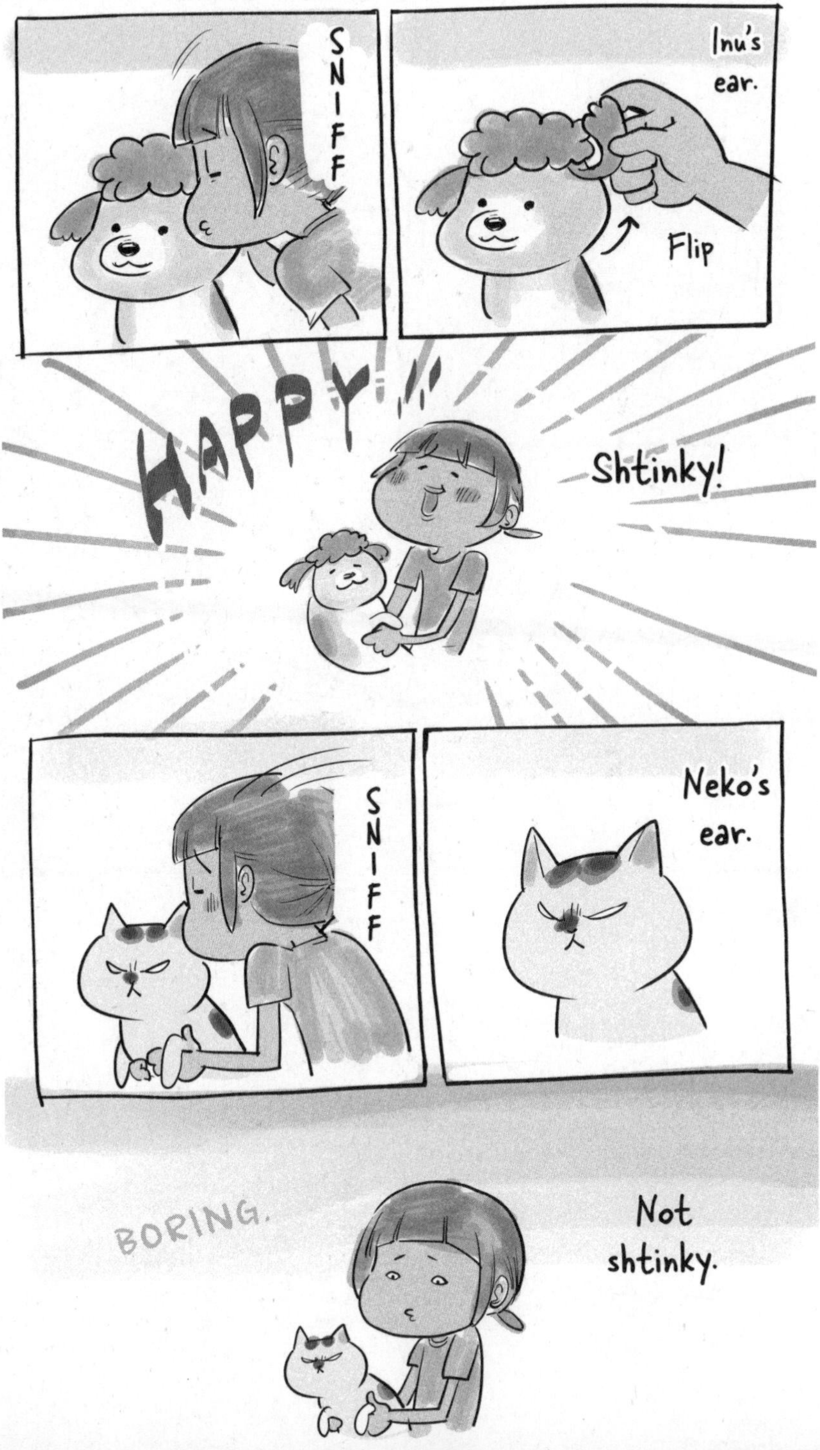
Inu's ear.
Flip
SNIFF
Shtinky!
HAPPY!!
Neko's ear.
SNIFF
Not shtinky.
BORING.

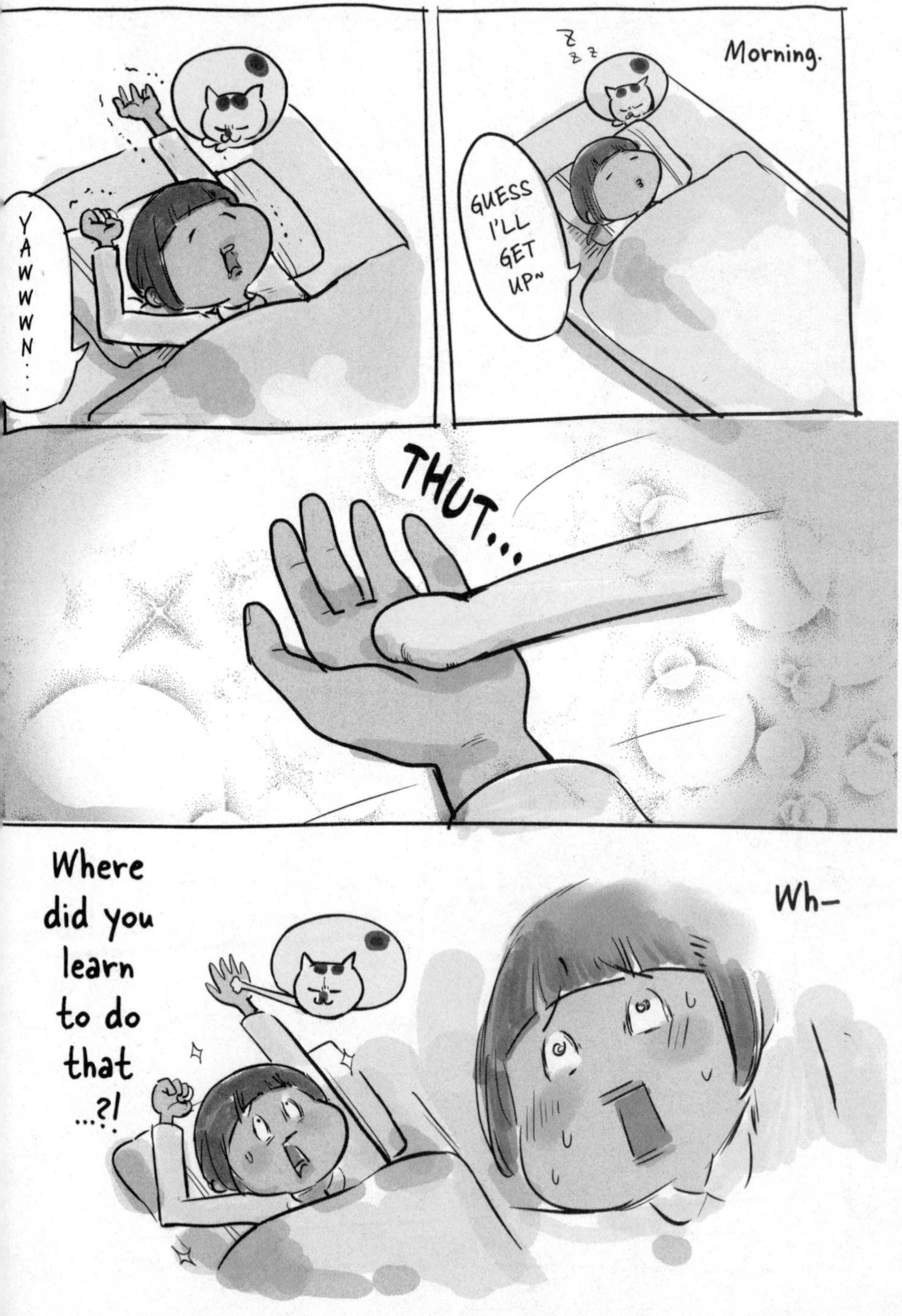
Morning.
Z z z
GUESS I'LL GET UP~
YAWWWN...
THUT...
Wh-
Where did you learn to do that ...?!

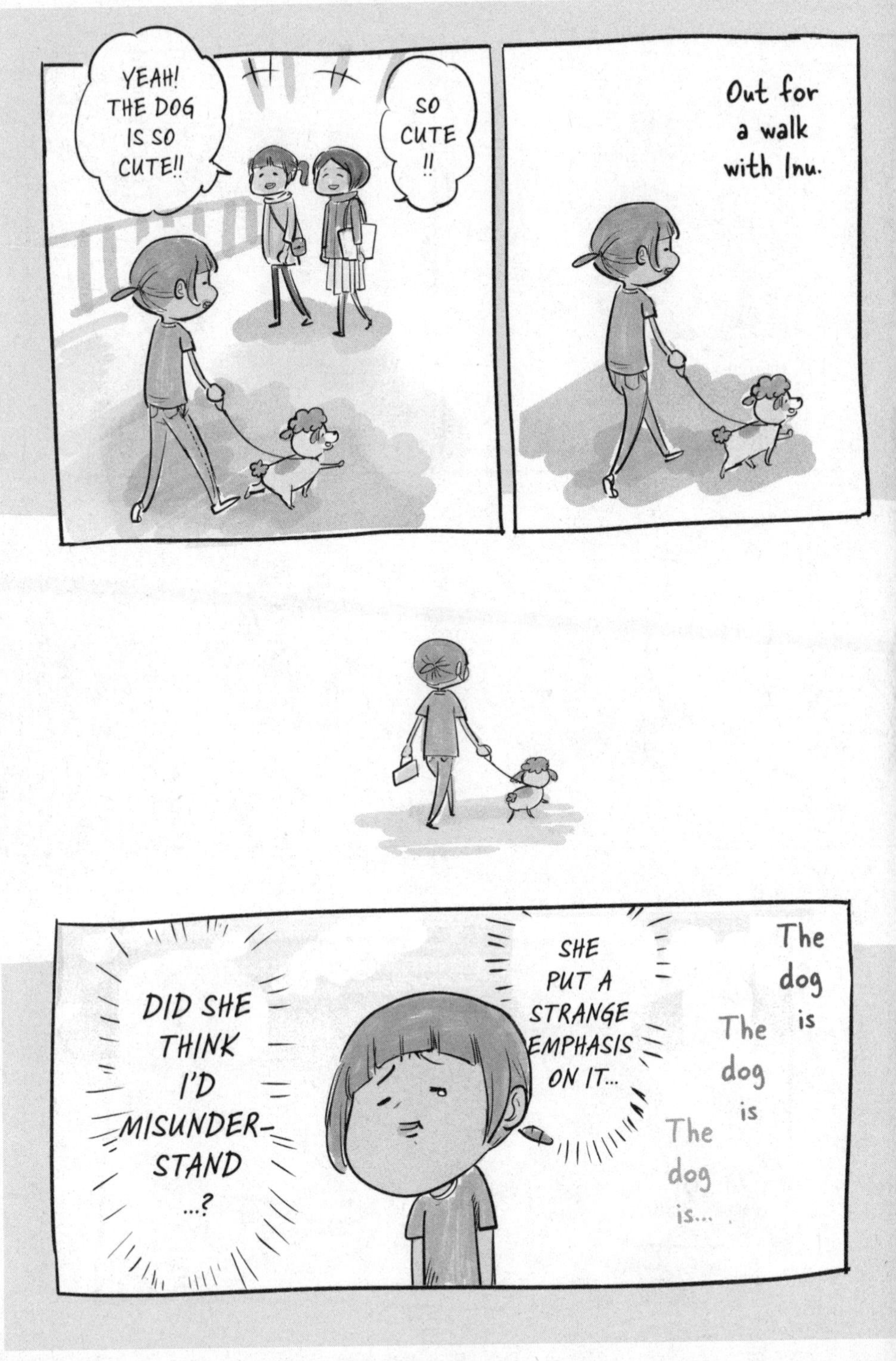
Out for a walk with Inu.
SO CUTE!!
YEAH! THE DOG IS SO CUTE!!
The dog is
The dog is
The dog is...
SHE PUT A STRANGE EMPHASIS ON IT...
DID SHE THINK I'D MISUNDERSTAND...?

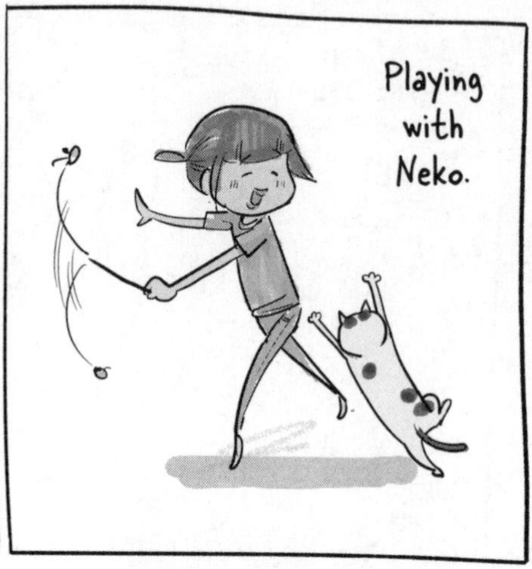
Playing
with
Neko.

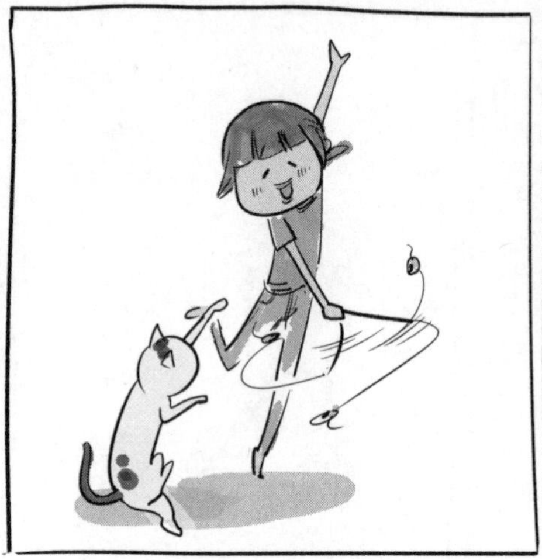

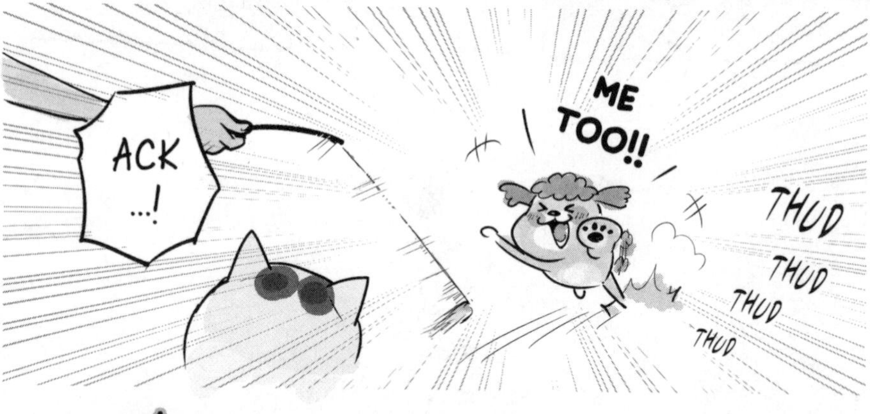
ME TOO!!
THUD
THUD
THUD
THUD
ACK
...!

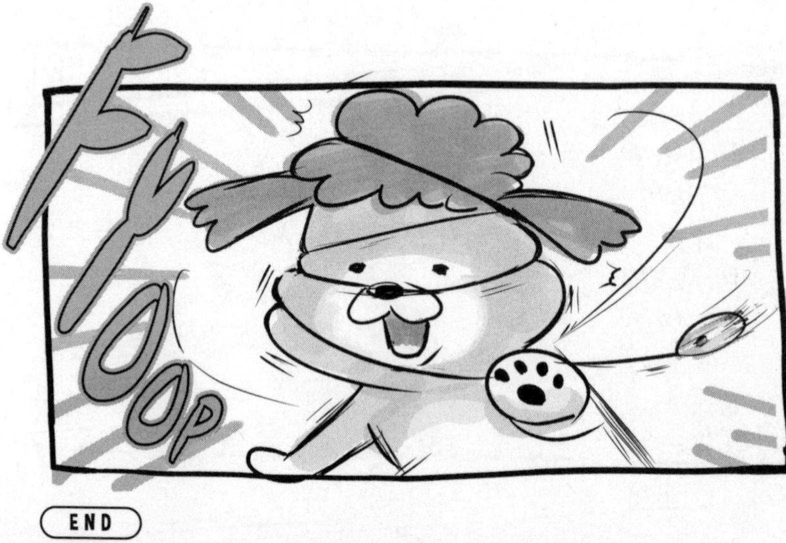

END

Give that back.

#151

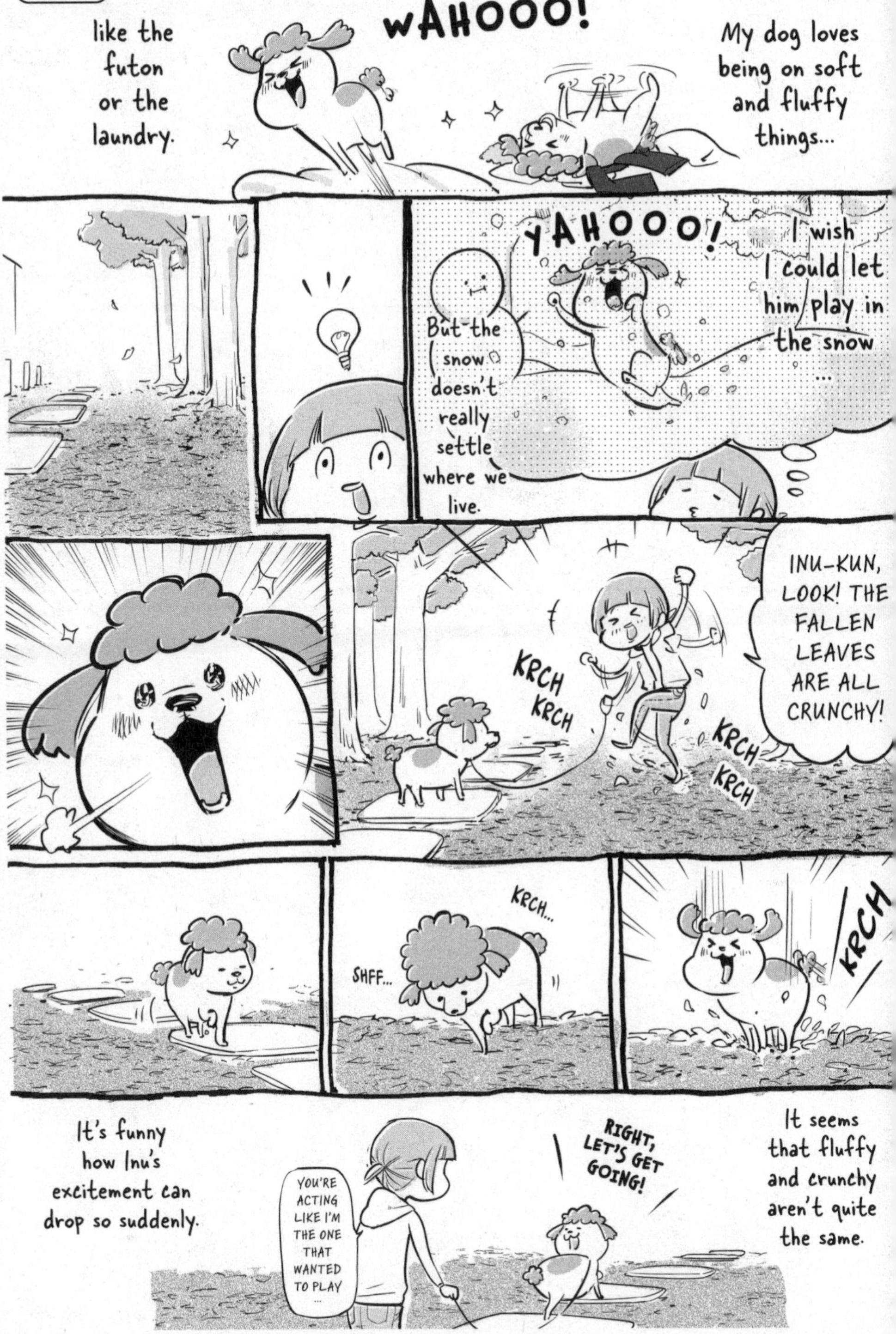
My dog loves being on soft and fluffy things...
WAHOOO!
like the futon or the laundry.
I wish I could let him play in the snow ...
YAHOOO!
But the snow doesn't really settle where we live.
INU-KUN, LOOK! THE FALLEN LEAVES ARE ALL CRUNCHY!
KRCH KRCH
KRCH KRCH
KRCH
KRCH...
SHFF...
It seems that fluffy and crunchy aren't quite the same.
RIGHT, LET'S GET GOING!
YOU'RE ACTING LIKE I'M THE ONE THAT WANTED TO PLAY ...
It's funny how Inu's excitement can drop so suddenly.

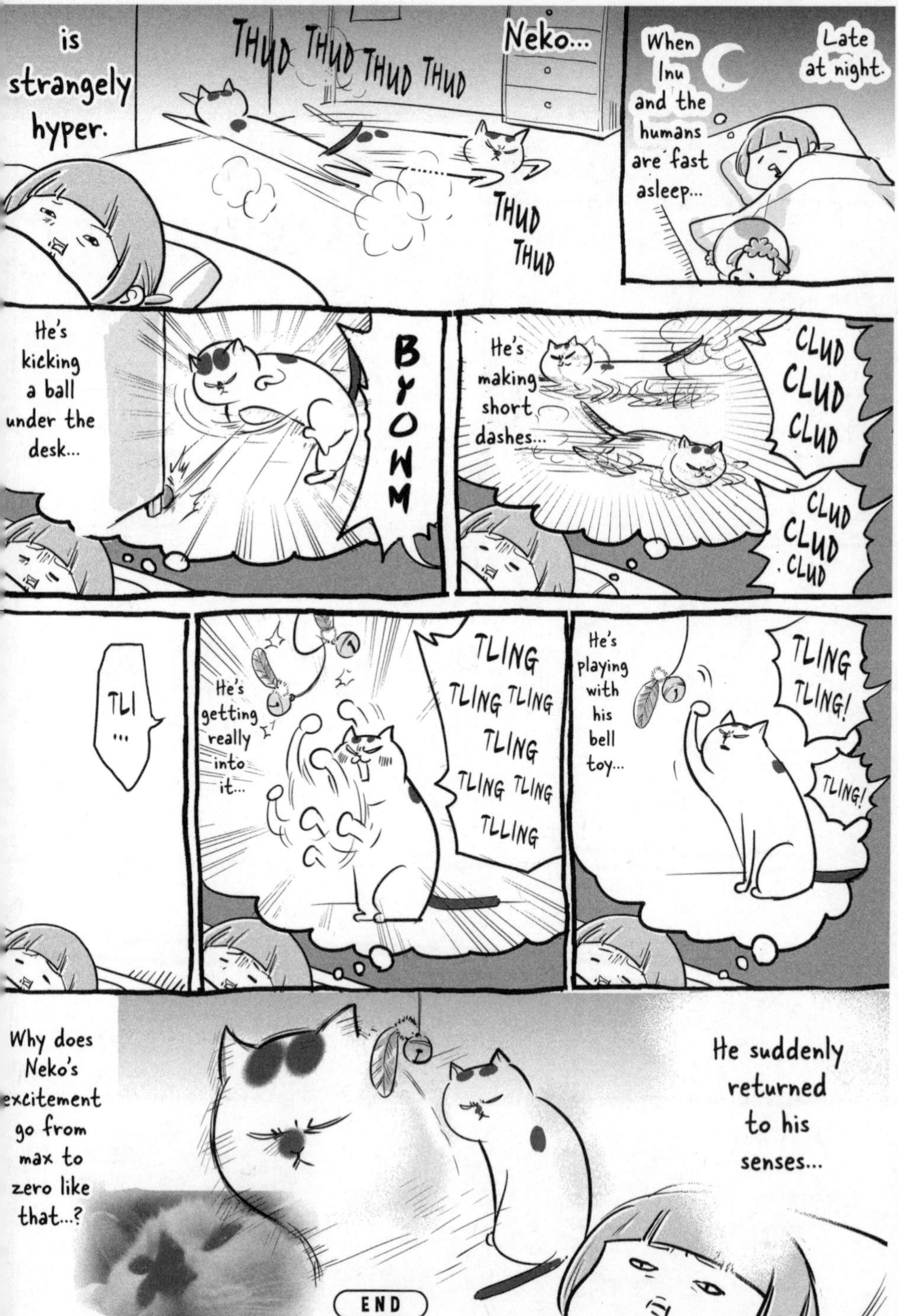
Late at night.
When Inu and the humans are fast asleep...
Neko...
THUD THUD THUD THUD
THUD THUD
is strangely hyper.
He's making short dashes...
CLUD CLUD CLUD
CLUD CLUD CLUD
He's kicking a ball under the desk...
BYOWM
He's playing with his bell toy...
TLING TLING!
TLING!
He's getting really into it...
TLING TLING TLING TLING TLING TLING TLLING
TLI ...
He suddenly returned to his senses...
Why does Neko's excitement go from max to zero like that...?
END

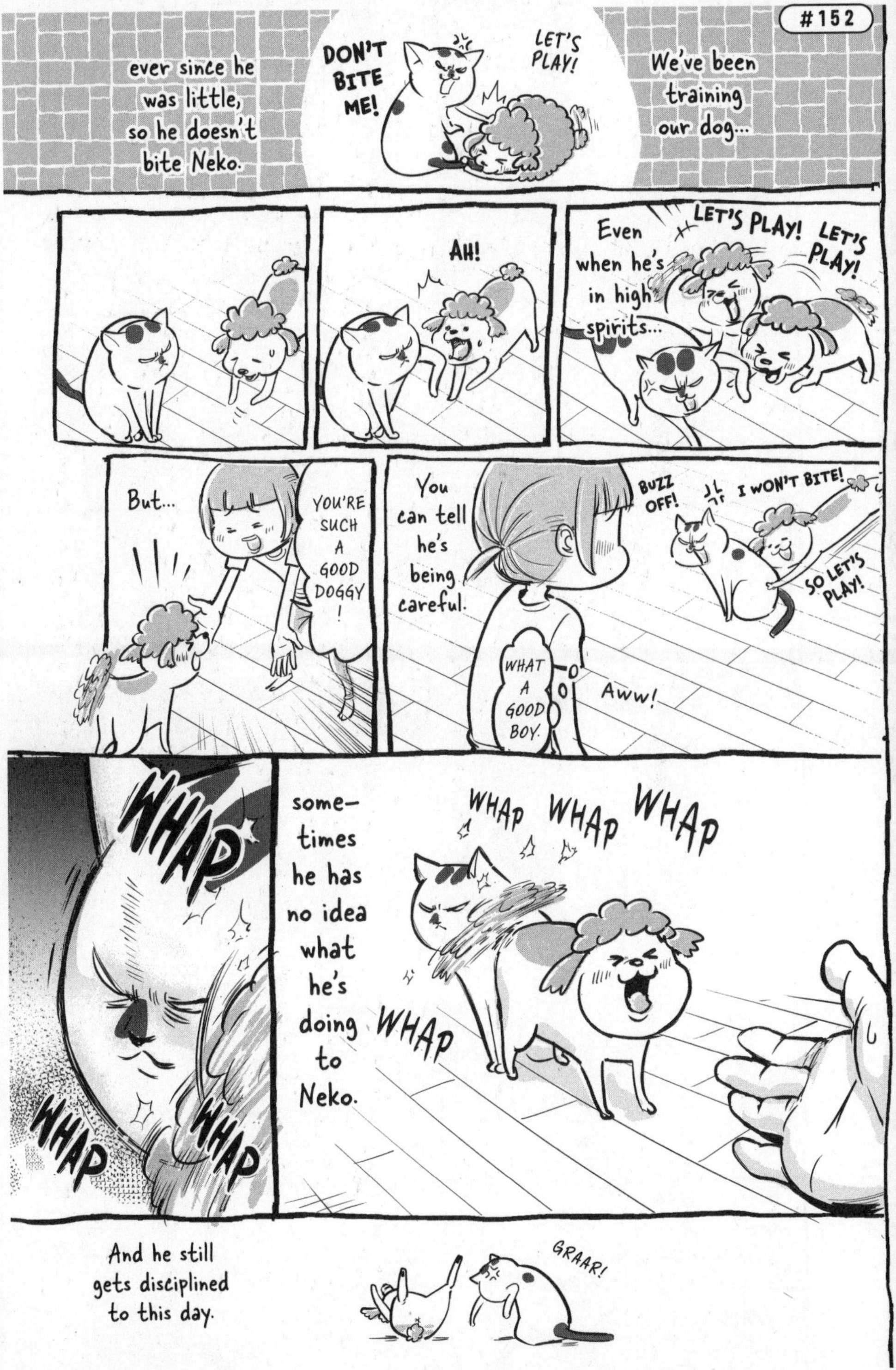
#152
We've been training our dog...
LET'S PLAY!
DON'T BITE ME!
ever since he was little, so he doesn't bite Neko.
Even when he's in high spirits...
LET'S PLAY!
LET'S PLAY!
AH!
You can tell he's being careful.
I WON'T BITE!
BUZZ OFF!
SO LET'S PLAY!
WHAT A GOOD BOY.
Aww!
But...
YOU'RE SUCH A GOOD DOGGY!
some-times he has no idea what he's doing to Neko.
WHAP WHAP WHAP
WHAP
WHAP
WHAP
WHAP
And he still gets disciplined to this day.
GRAAR!

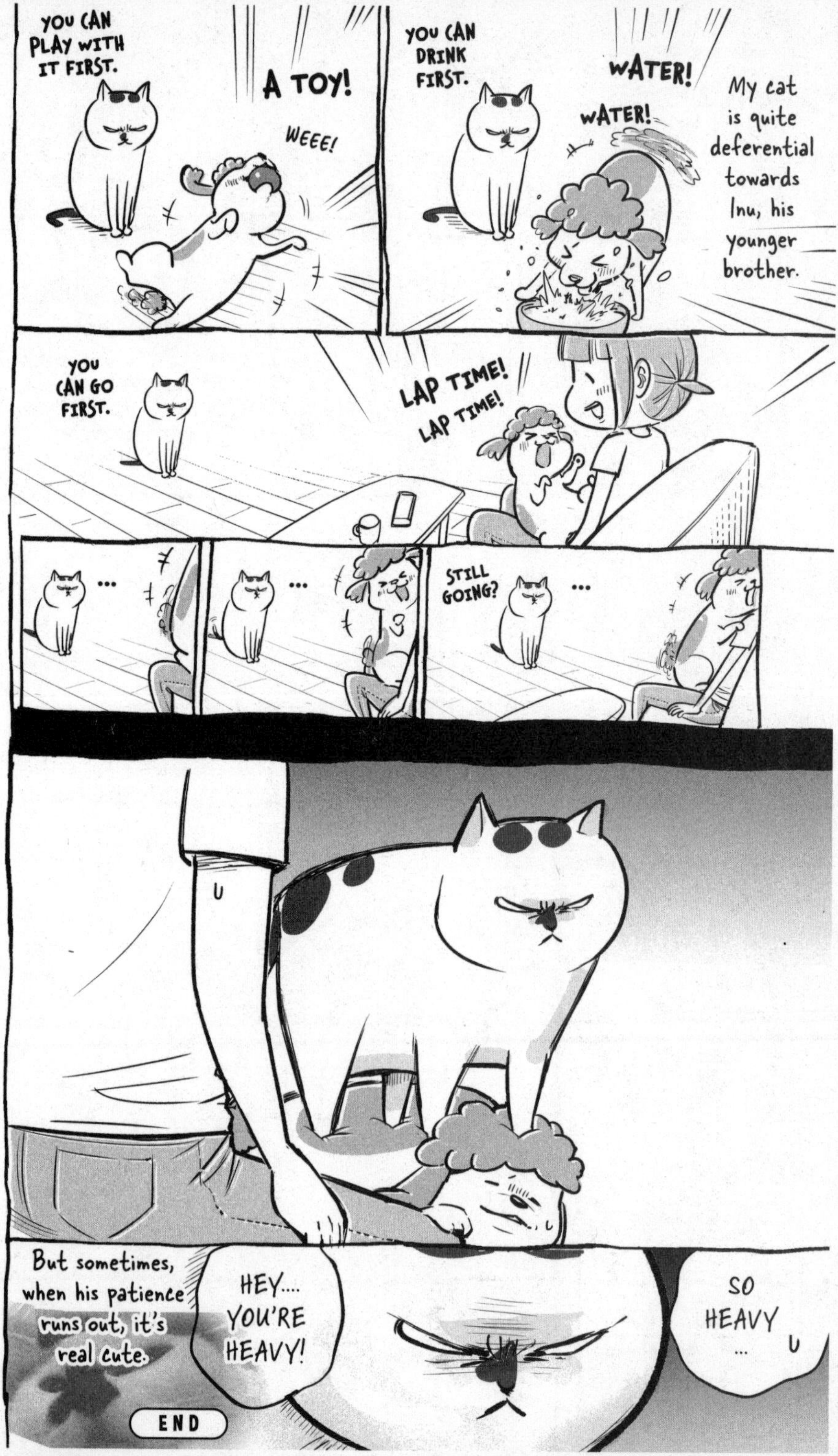
My cat is quite deferential towards Inu, his younger brother.
WATER!
YOU CAN DRINK FIRST.
WATER!
A TOY!
YOU CAN PLAY WITH IT FIRST.
WEEE!
LAP TIME! LAP TIME!
YOU CAN GO FIRST.
STILL GOING?
...
...
...
SO HEAVY ...
HEY.... YOU'RE HEAVY!
But sometimes, when his patience runs out, it's real cute.
END

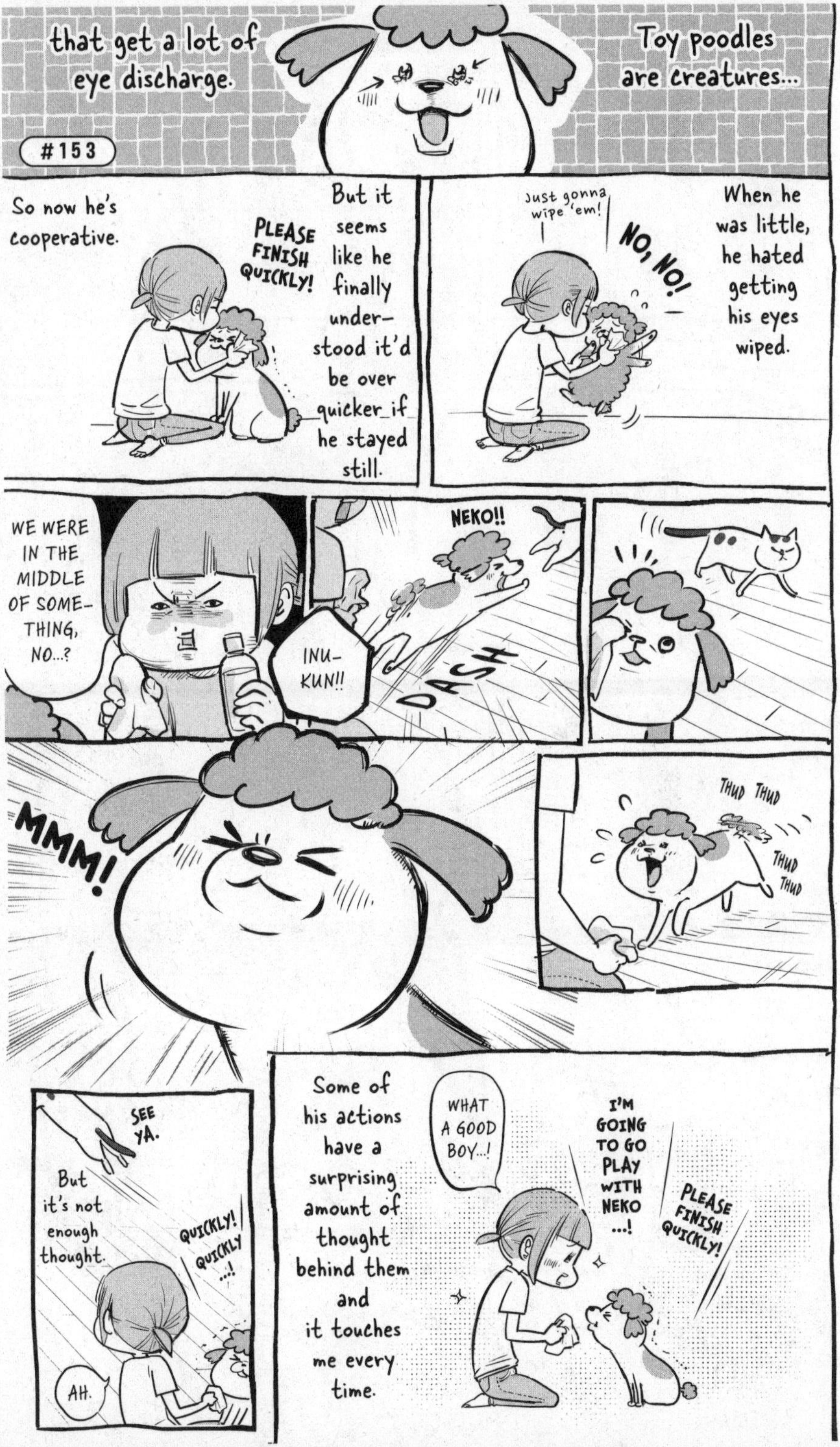
Toy poodles are creatures...
that get a lot of eye discharge.
#153
When he was little, he hated getting his eyes wiped.
Just gonna wipe 'em!
NO, NO!
But it seems like he finally under-stood it'd be over quicker if he stayed still.
PLEASE FINISH QUICKLY!
So now he's cooperative.
NEKO!!
DASH
INU-KUN!!
WE WERE IN THE MIDDLE OF SOME-THING, NO...?
THUD THUD
THUD THUD
MMM!
Some of his actions have a surprising amount of thought behind them and it touches me every time.
PLEASE FINISH QUICKLY!
I'M GOING TO GO PLAY WITH NEKO ...!
WHAT A GOOD BOY...!
SEE YA.
But it's not enough thought.
QUICKLY! QUICKLY ...!
AH.

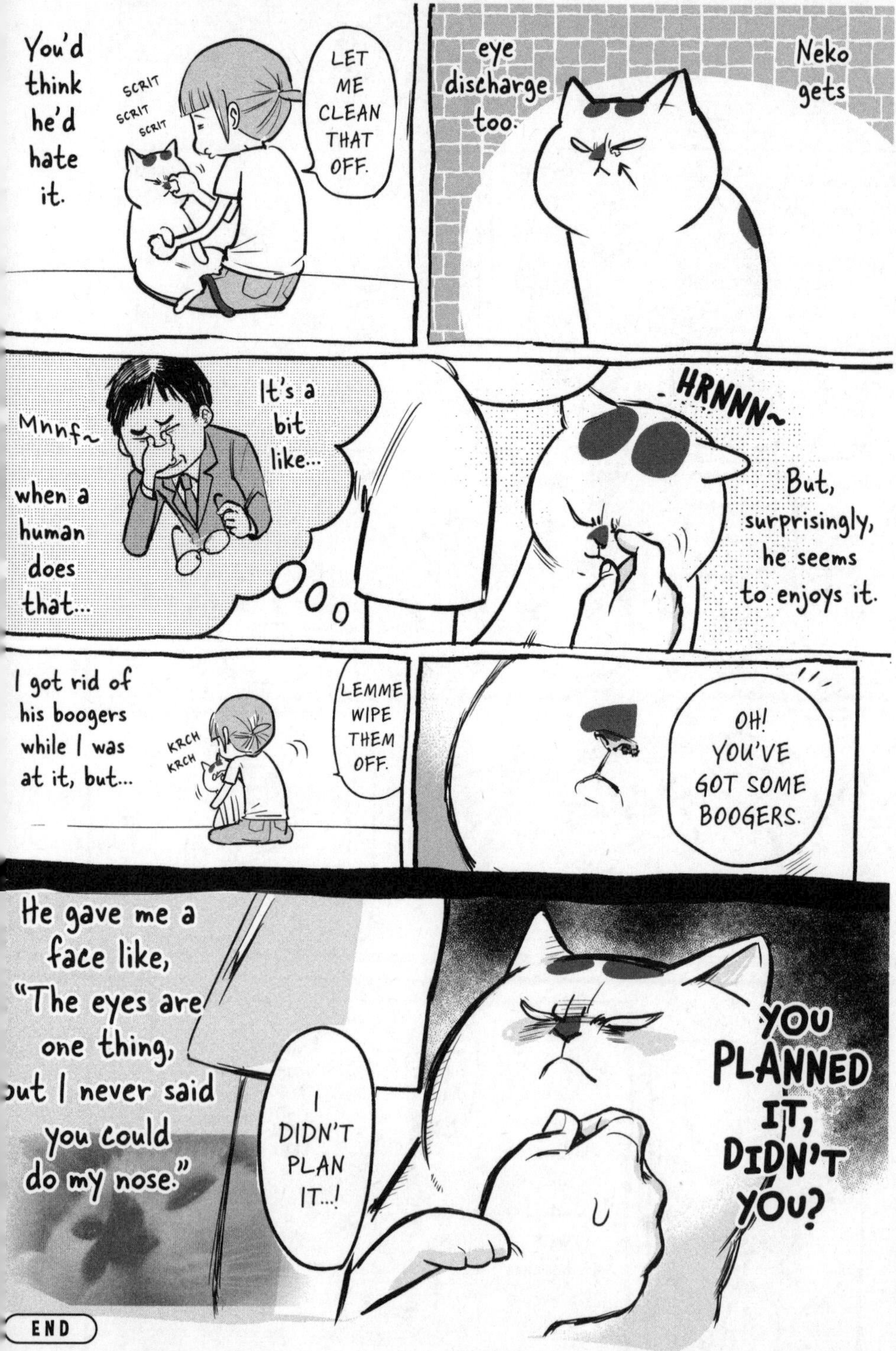
Neko gets
eye discharge too.
LET ME CLEAN THAT OFF.
SCRIT
SCRIT
SCRIT
You'd think he'd hate it.
HRNNN~
But, surprisingly, he seems to enjoys it.
It's a bit like...
Mnnf~
when a human does that...
OH! YOU'VE GOT SOME BOOGERS.
LEMME WIPE THEM OFF.
KRCH
KRCH
I got rid of his boogers while I was at it, but...
YOU PLANNED IT, DIDN'T YOU?
I DIDN'T PLAN IT...!
He gave me a face like, "The eyes are one thing, ut I never said you could do my nose."
END

"It's a yuzu!" "...Yuzu?"

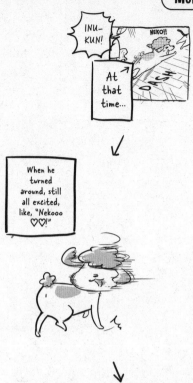

More About #153

NEKO!!
INU-KUN!
DASH
At that time...
When he turned around, still all excited, like, "Nekooo ♡♡!"
SORRY!
SORRY!
he had such a charming smile.
Humans are like this, too, sometimes.

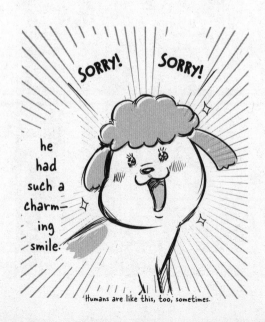

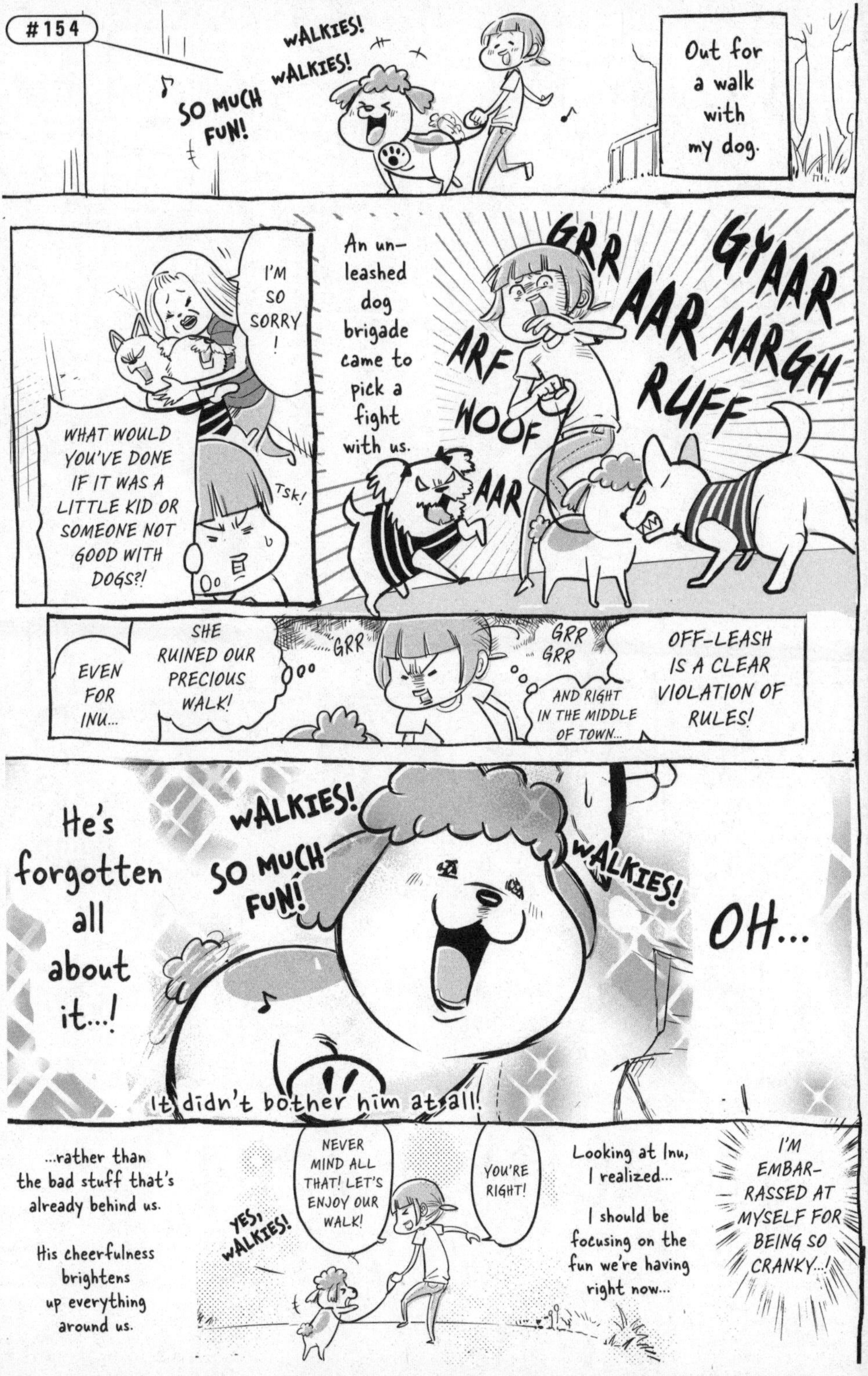
#154
Out for a walk with my dog.
WALKIES!
WALKIES!
SO MUCH FUN!
GYAAR
AAR AARGH
RUFF
GRR
An un-leashed dog brigade came to pick a fight with us.
ARF
WOOF
AAR
I'M SO SORRY!
WHAT WOULD YOU'VE DONE IF IT WAS A LITTLE KID OR SOMEONE NOT GOOD WITH DOGS?!
TSK!
OFF-LEASH IS A CLEAR VIOLATION OF RULES!
GRR GRR
AND RIGHT IN THE MIDDLE OF TOWN...
GRR
SHE RUINED OUR PRECIOUS WALK!
EVEN FOR INU...
OH...
WALKIES!
WALKIES!
He's forgotten all about it...!
SO MUCH FUN!
It didn't bother him at all.
I'M EMBAR-RASSED AT MYSELF FOR BEING SO CRANKY...!
Looking at Inu, I realized...
I should be focusing on the fun we're having right now...
YOU'RE RIGHT!
NEVER MIND ALL THAT! LET'S ENJOY OUR WALK!
YES, WALKIES!
...rather than the bad stuff that's already behind us.
His cheerfulness brightens up everything around us.

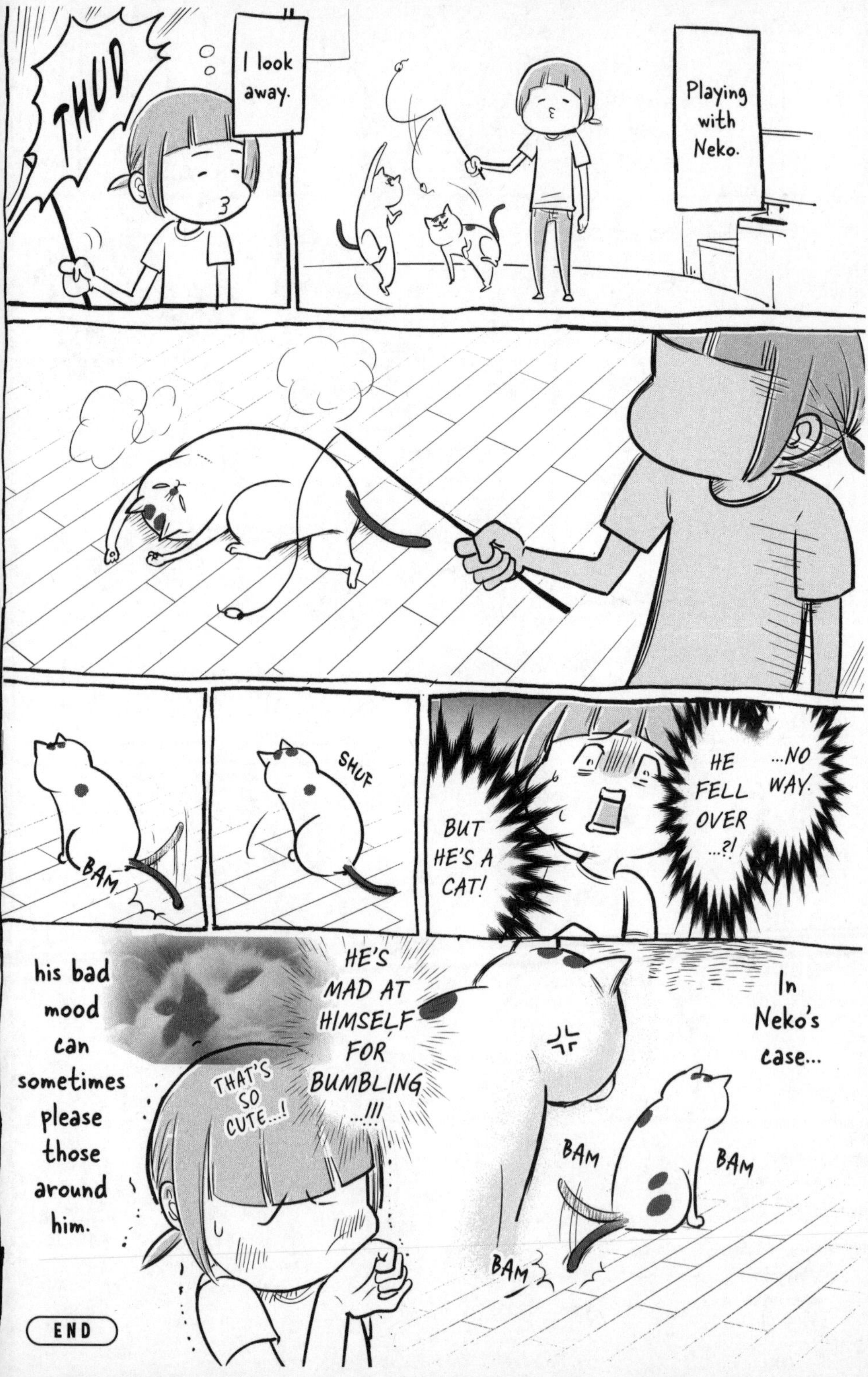
Playing with Neko.
I look away.
THUD
...NO WAY.
HE FELL OVER ...?!
BUT HE'S A CAT!
SHUF
BAM
In Neko's case...
BAM
BAM
BAM
HE'S MAD AT HIMSELF FOR BUMBLING ...!!!
THAT'S SO CUTE...!
his bad mood can sometimes please those around him.
END

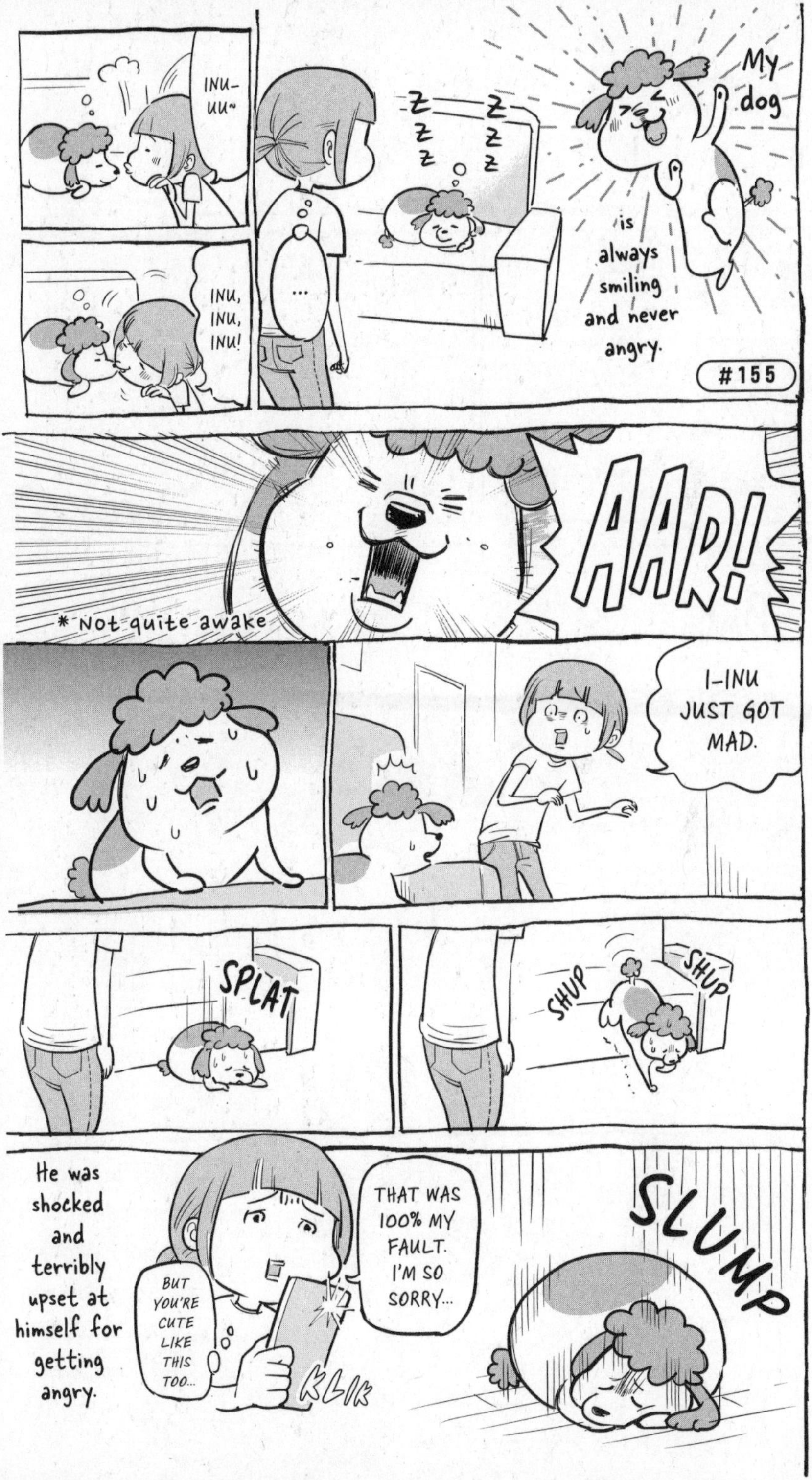
My dog
is always smiling and never angry.
#155
Z Z Z
Z Z Z
...
INU-UU~
INU, INU, INU!
AAR!
* Not quite awake
I-INU JUST GOT MAD.
SHUP
SHUP
SPLAT
SLUMP
THAT WAS 100% MY FAULT. I'M SO SORRY...
BUT YOU'RE CUTE LIKE THIS TOO...
KLIK
He was shocked and terribly upset at himself for getting angry.

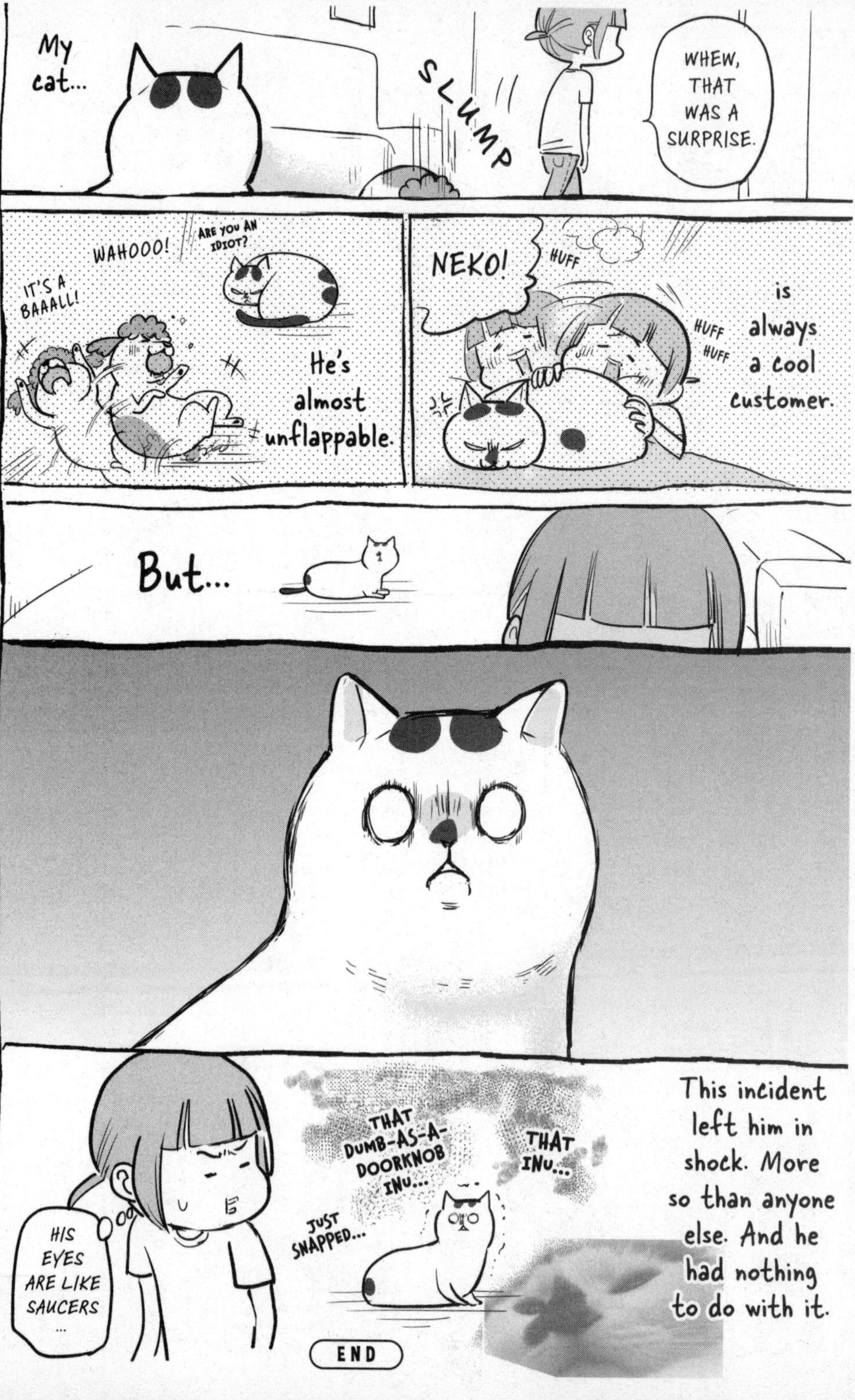
WHEW, THAT WAS A SURPRISE.
SLUMP
My cat...
HUFF
NEKO!
HUFF HUFF
is always a cool customer.
ARE YOU AN IDIOT?
WAHOOO!
IT'S A BAAALL!
He's almost unflappable.
But...
This incident left him in shock. More so than anyone else. And he had nothing to do with it.
THAT INU...
THAT DUMB-AS-A-DOORKNOB INU...
JUST SNAPPED...
HIS EYES ARE LIKE SAUCERS ...
END

#156

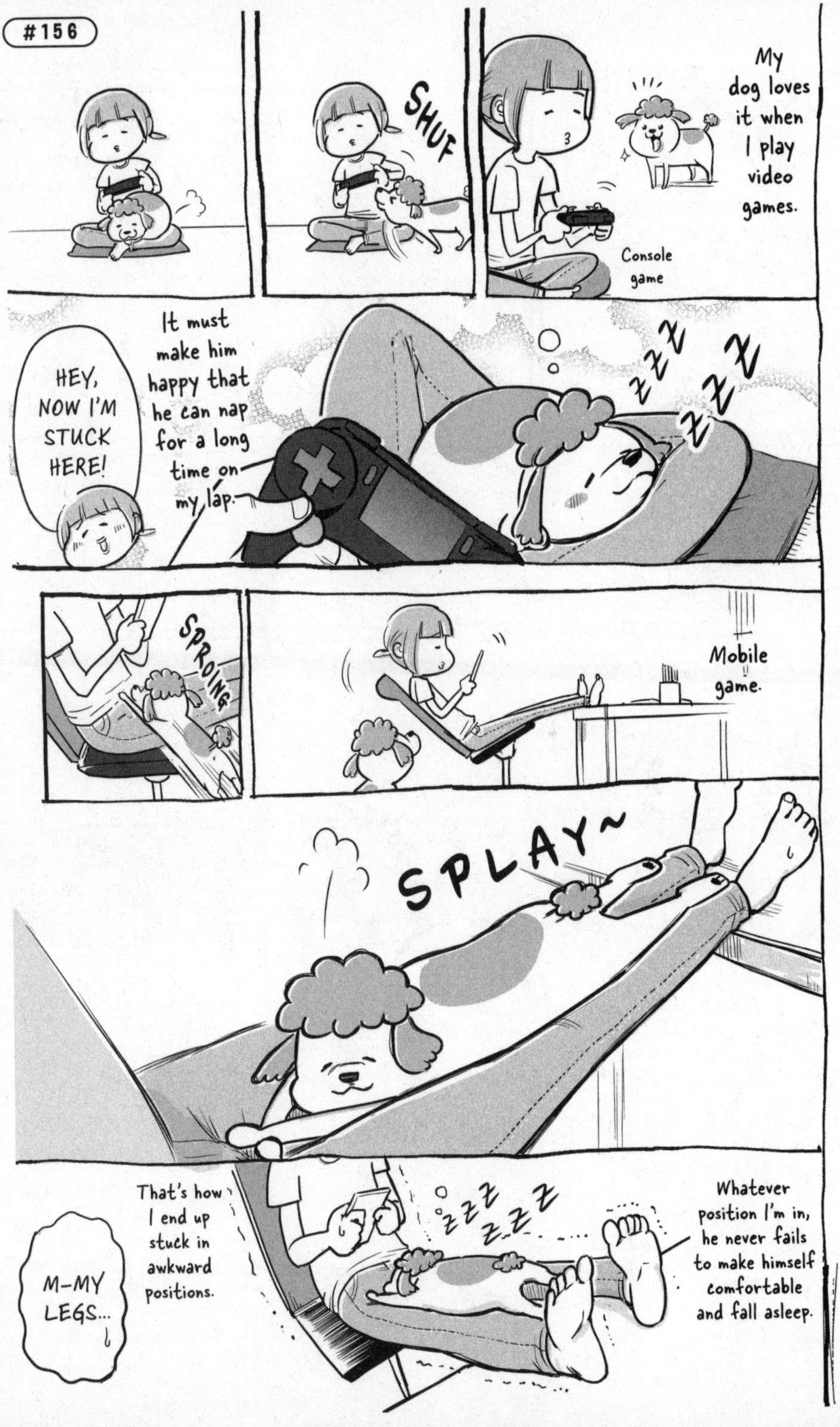

My dog loves it when I play video games.
Console game
SHUF
ZZZ
ZZZ
It must make him happy that he can nap for a long time on my lap.
HEY, NOW I'M STUCK HERE!
Mobile game.
SPROING
SPLAY~
Whatever position I'm in, he never fails to make himself comfortable and fall asleep.
ZZZ
ZZZ
That's how I end up stuck in awkward positions.
M-MY LEGS...

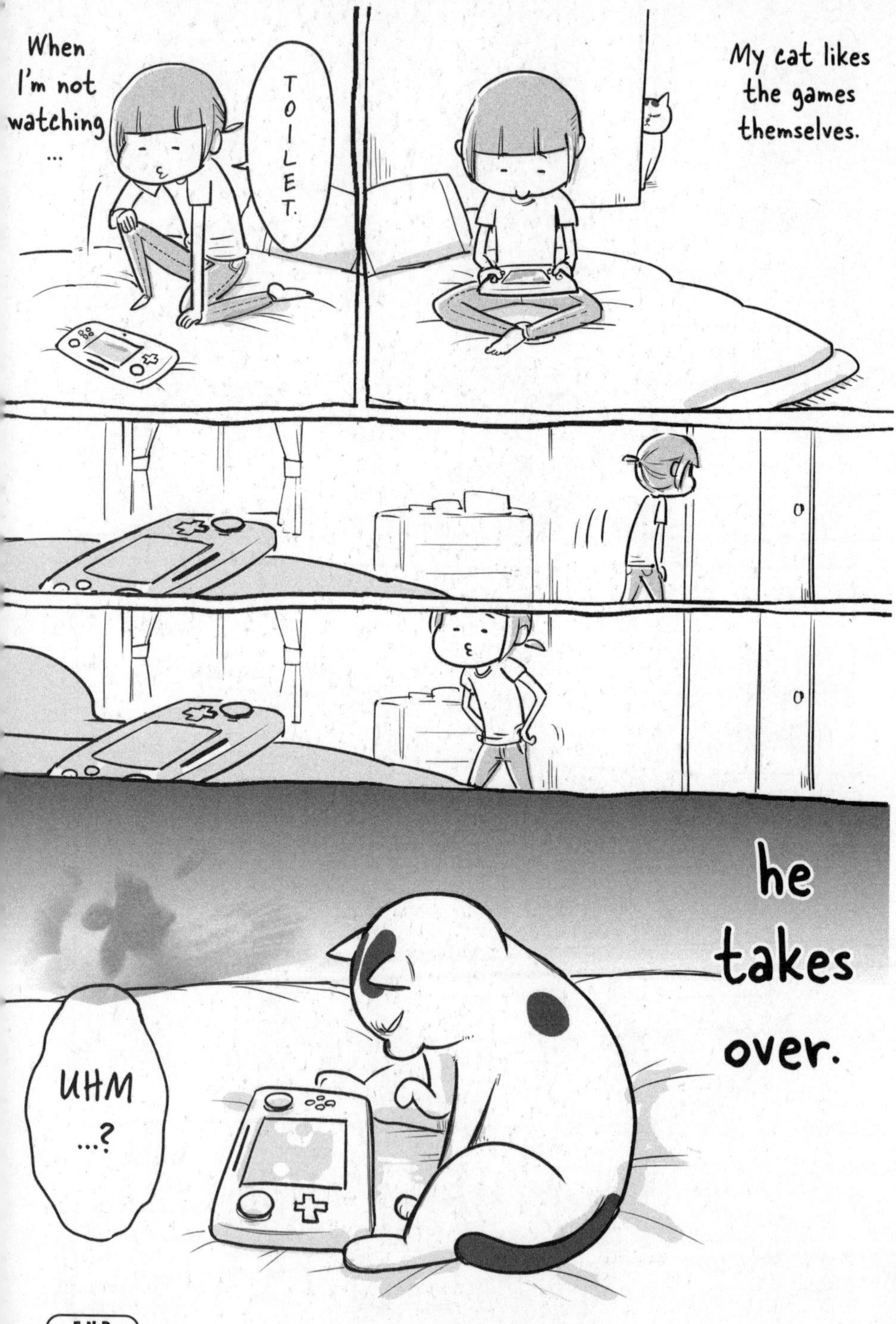
My cat likes the games themselves.
When I'm not watching ...
TOILET.
he takes over.
UHM ...?
END

Isn't it hard on your neck sleeping like that?

Newly-Drawn 4-Panel Strip

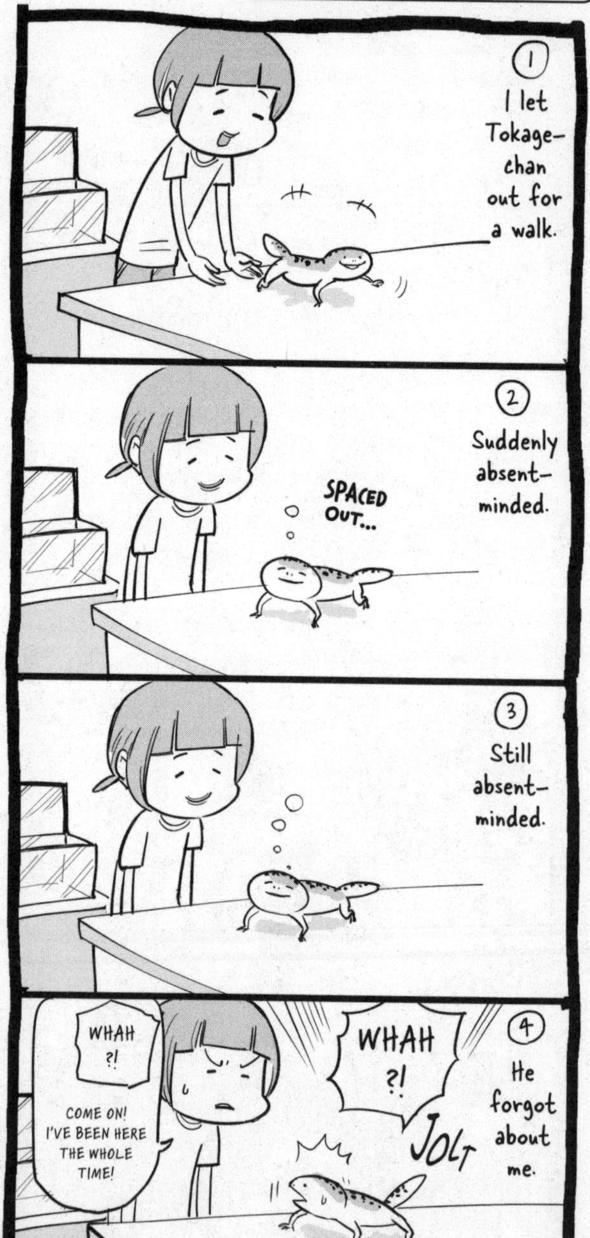

1
I let Tokage-chan out for a walk.
2
Suddenly absent-minded.
SPACED OUT...
3
Still absent-minded.
4
He forgot about me.
WHAH ?!
JOLT
WHAH ?!
COME ON! I'VE BEEN HERE THE WHOLE TIME!

Bonus

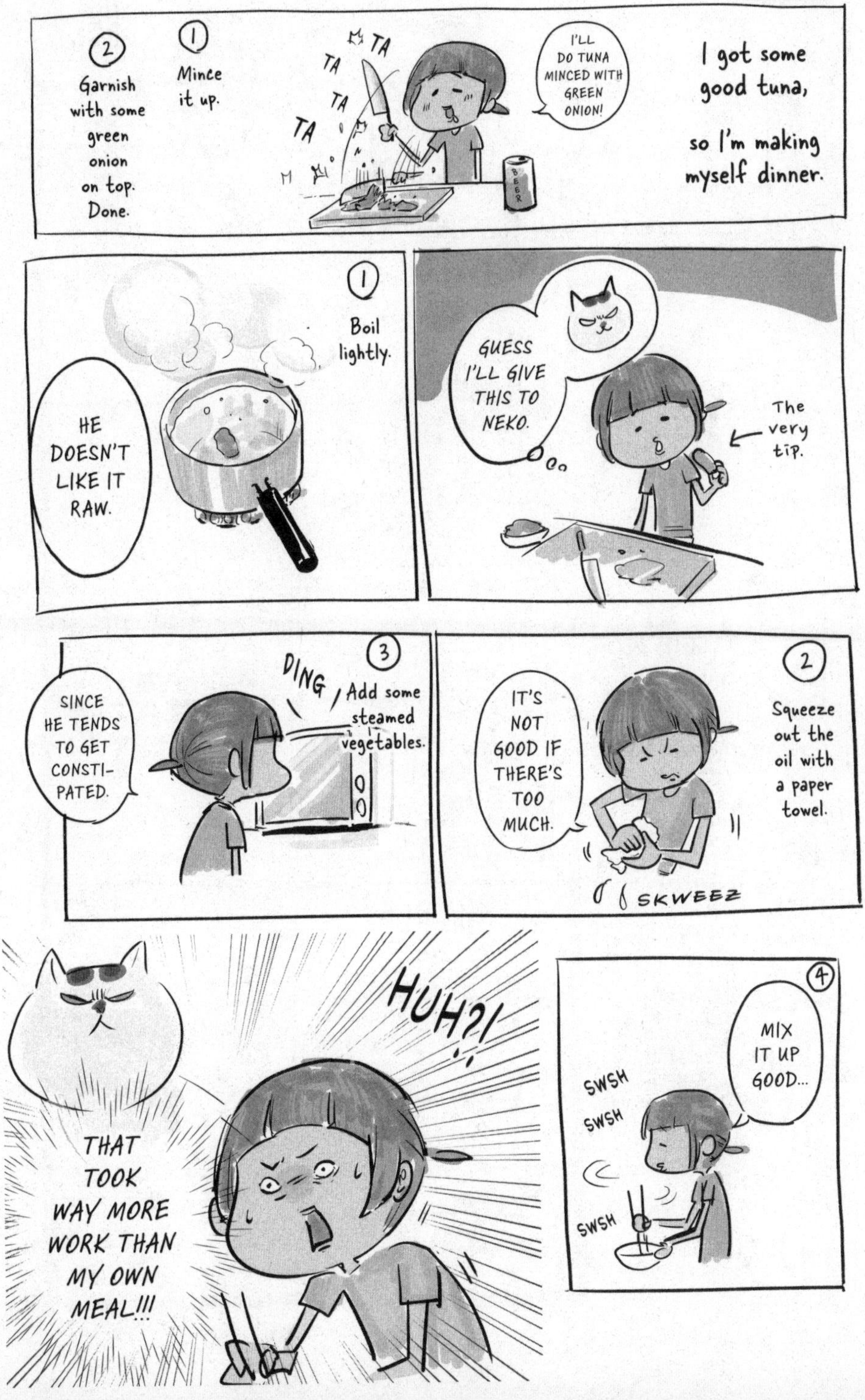
I got some good tuna,
so I'm making myself dinner.
I'LL DO TUNA MINCED WITH GREEN ONION!
BEER
TA
TA
TA
TA
1 Mince it up.
2 Garnish with some green onion on top. Done.
GUESS I'LL GIVE THIS TO NEKO.
The very tip.
1 Boil lightly.
HE DOESN'T LIKE IT RAW.
2 Squeeze out the oil with a paper towel.
IT'S NOT GOOD IF THERE'S TOO MUCH.
SKWEEZ
3 Add some steamed vegetables.
DING
SINCE HE TENDS TO GET CONSTI-PATED.
4
MIX IT UP GOOD...
SWSH
SWSH
SWSH
HUH?!
THAT TOOK WAY MORE WORK THAN MY OWN MEAL!!!

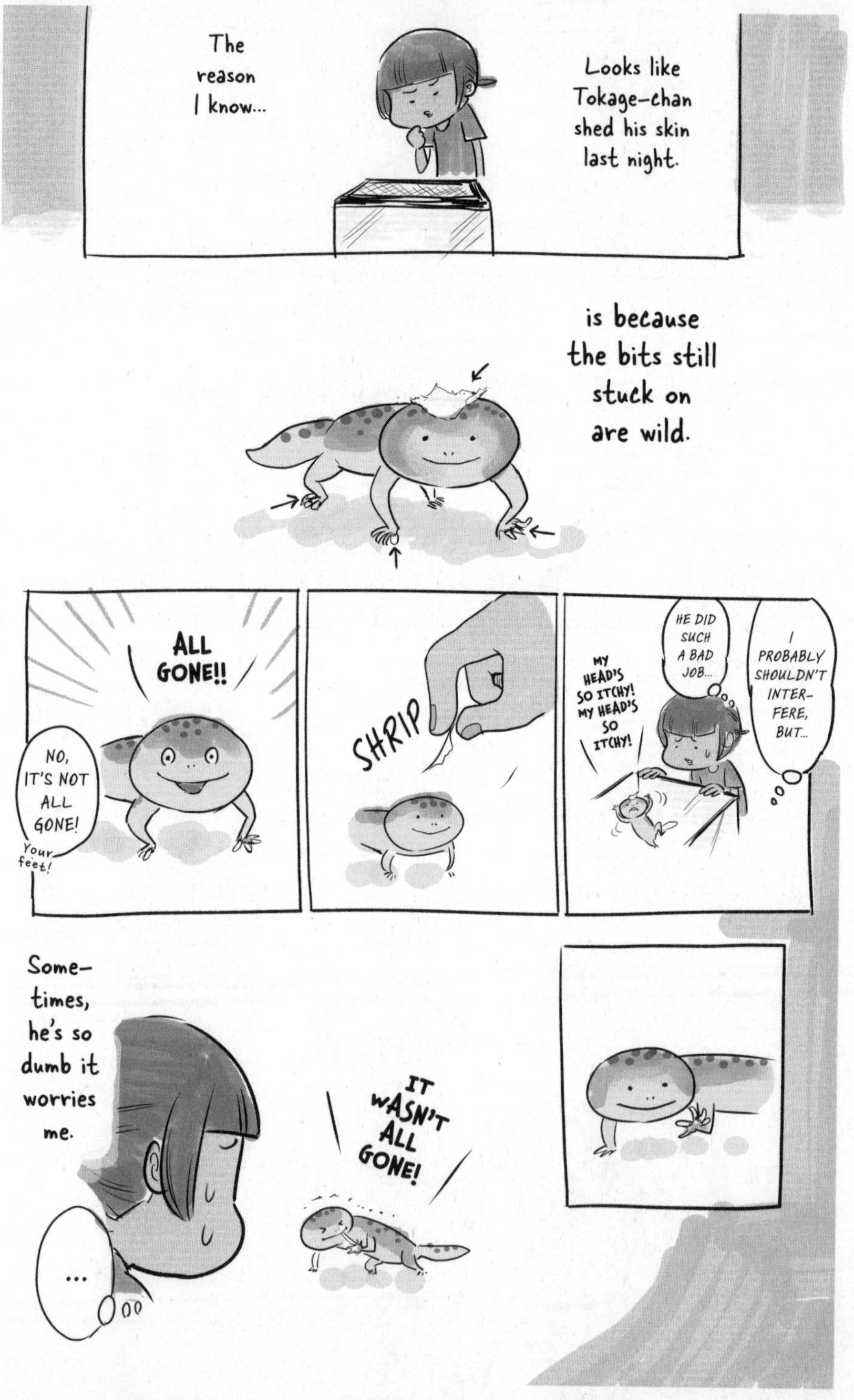
Looks like Tokage-chan shed his skin last night.
The reason I know...
is because the bits still stuck on are wild.
I PROBABLY SHOULDN'T INTER-FERE, BUT...
HE DID SUCH A BAD JOB...
MY HEAD'S SO ITCHY! MY HEAD'S SO ITCHY!
SHRIP
ALL GONE!!
NO, IT'S NOT ALL GONE!
Your feet!
IT WASN'T ALL GONE!
Some-times, he's so dumb it worries me.
...

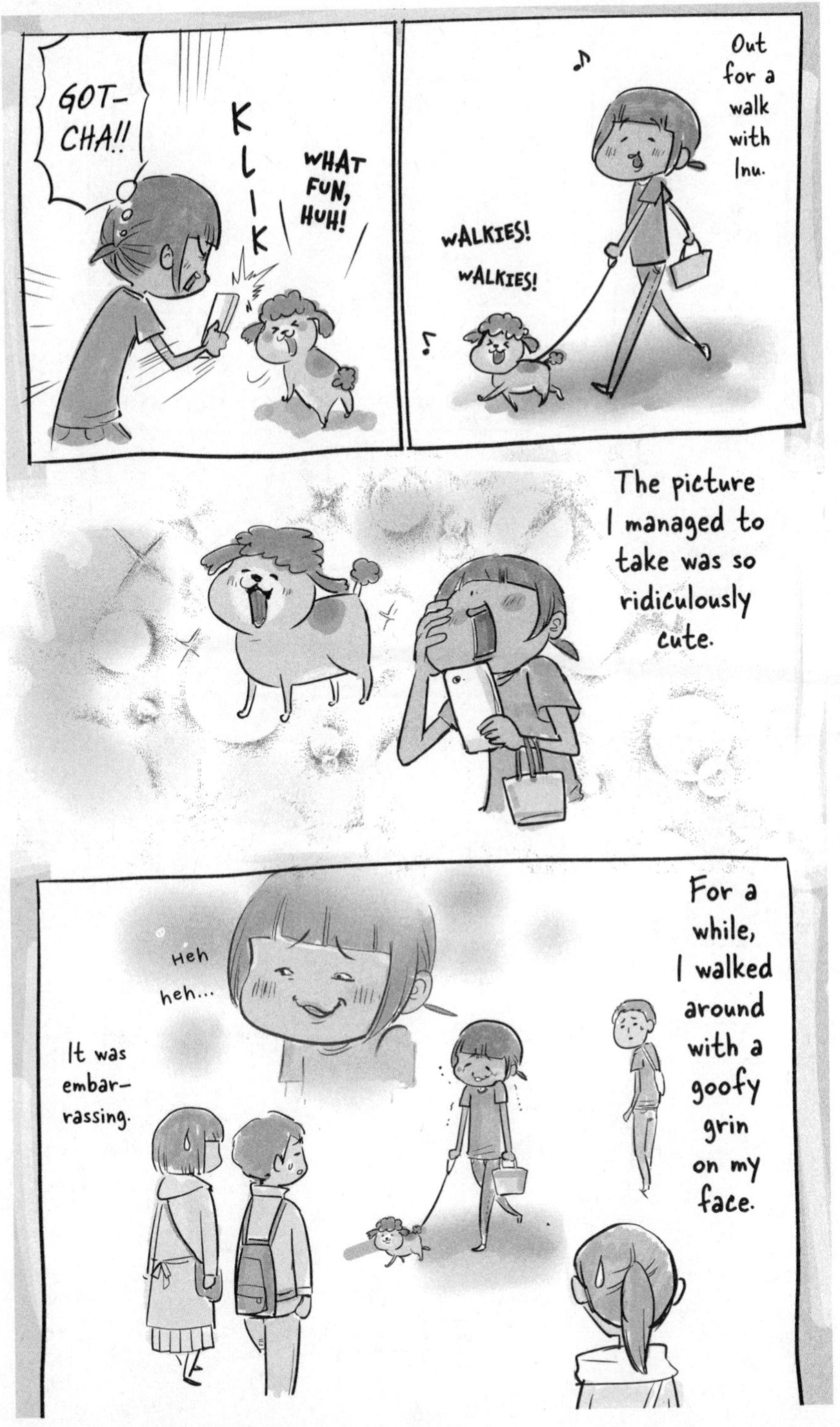
Out for a walk with Inu.
WALKIES!
WALKIES!
GOT-CHA!!
KLIK
WHAT FUN, HUH!
The picture I managed to take was so ridiculously cute.
For a while, I walked around with a goofy grin on my face.
Heh heh...
It was embarrassing.

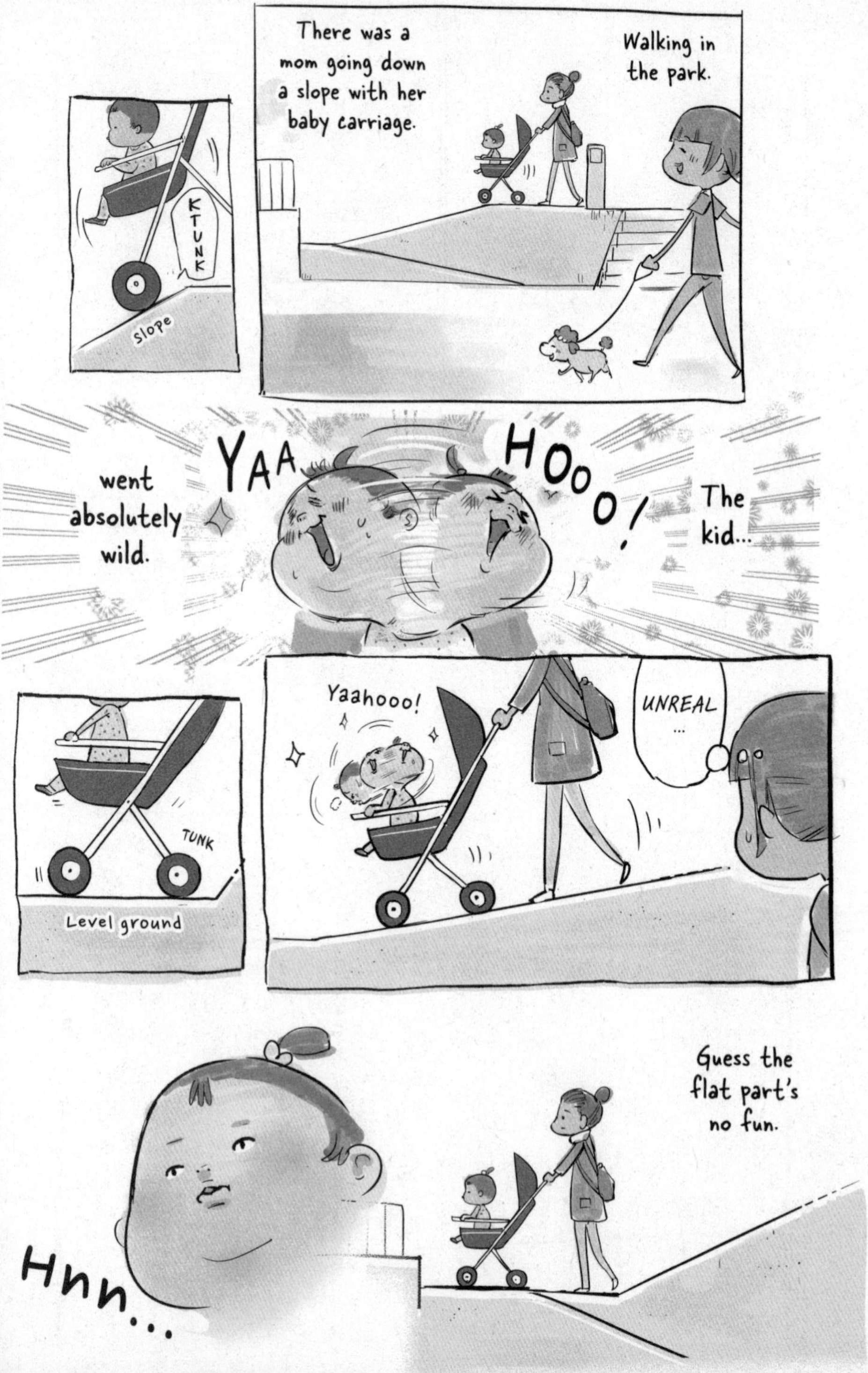
Walking in the park.
There was a mom going down a slope with her baby carriage.
KTUNK
Slope
The kid...
YAAHOOO!
went absolutely wild.
UNREAL...
Yaahooo!
TUNK
Level ground
Guess the flat part's no fun.
Hnn...

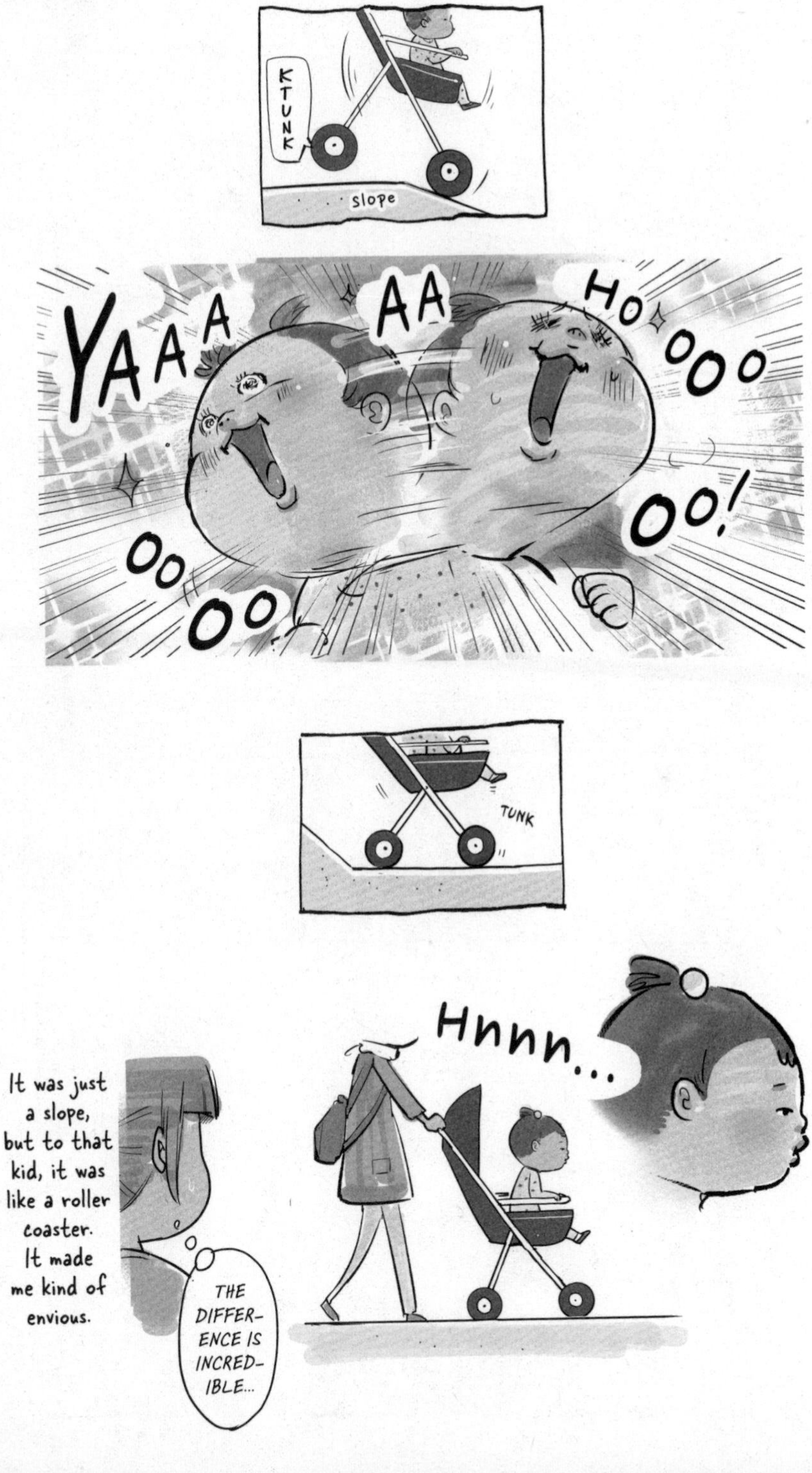
KTUNK
slope
HOOOO
AA
YAAA
OO!
OOOO
TUNK
Hnnn...
THE DIFFERENCE IS INCREDIBLE...
It was just a slope, but to that kid, it was like a roller coaster. It made me kind of envious.

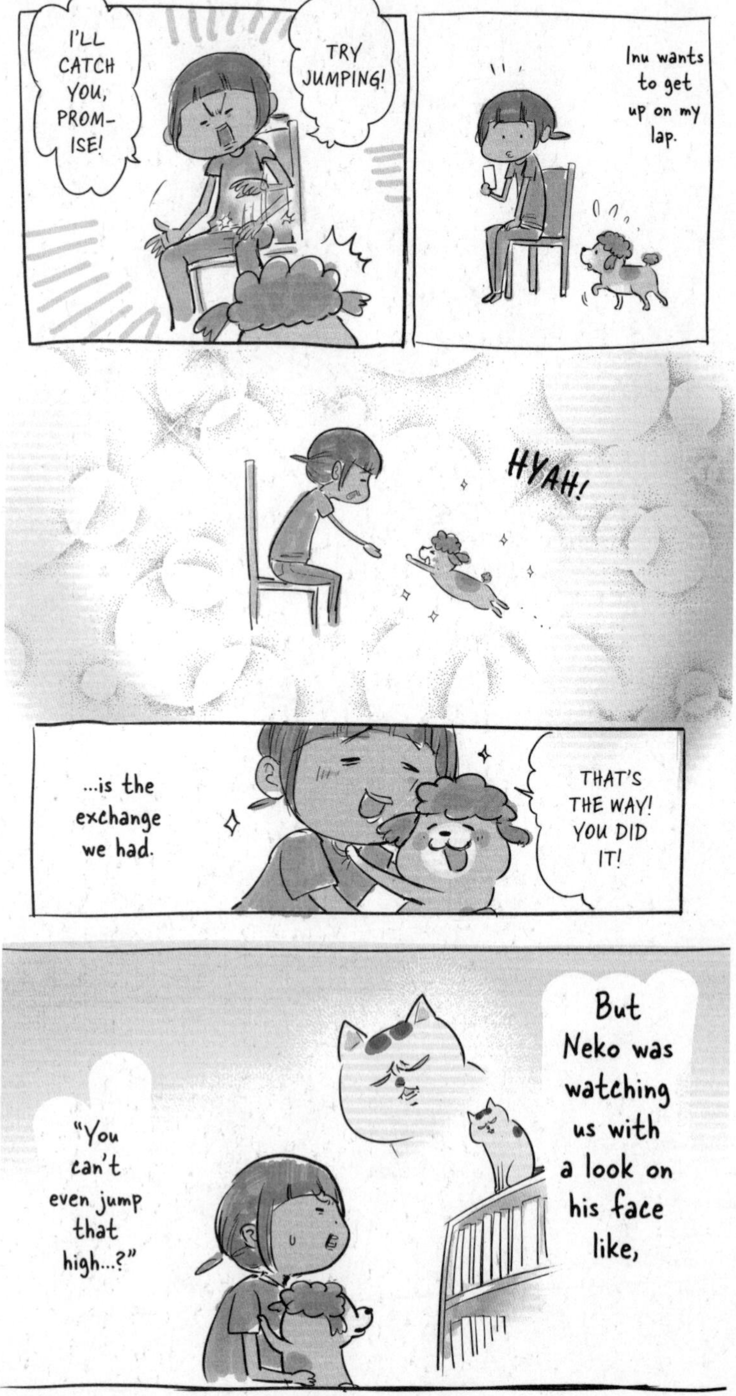
Inu wants to get up on my lap.
TRY JUMPING!
I'LL CATCH YOU, PROMISE!
HYAH!
THAT'S THE WAY! YOU DID IT!
...is the exchange we had.
But Neko was watching us with a look on his face like,
"You can't even jump that high...?"

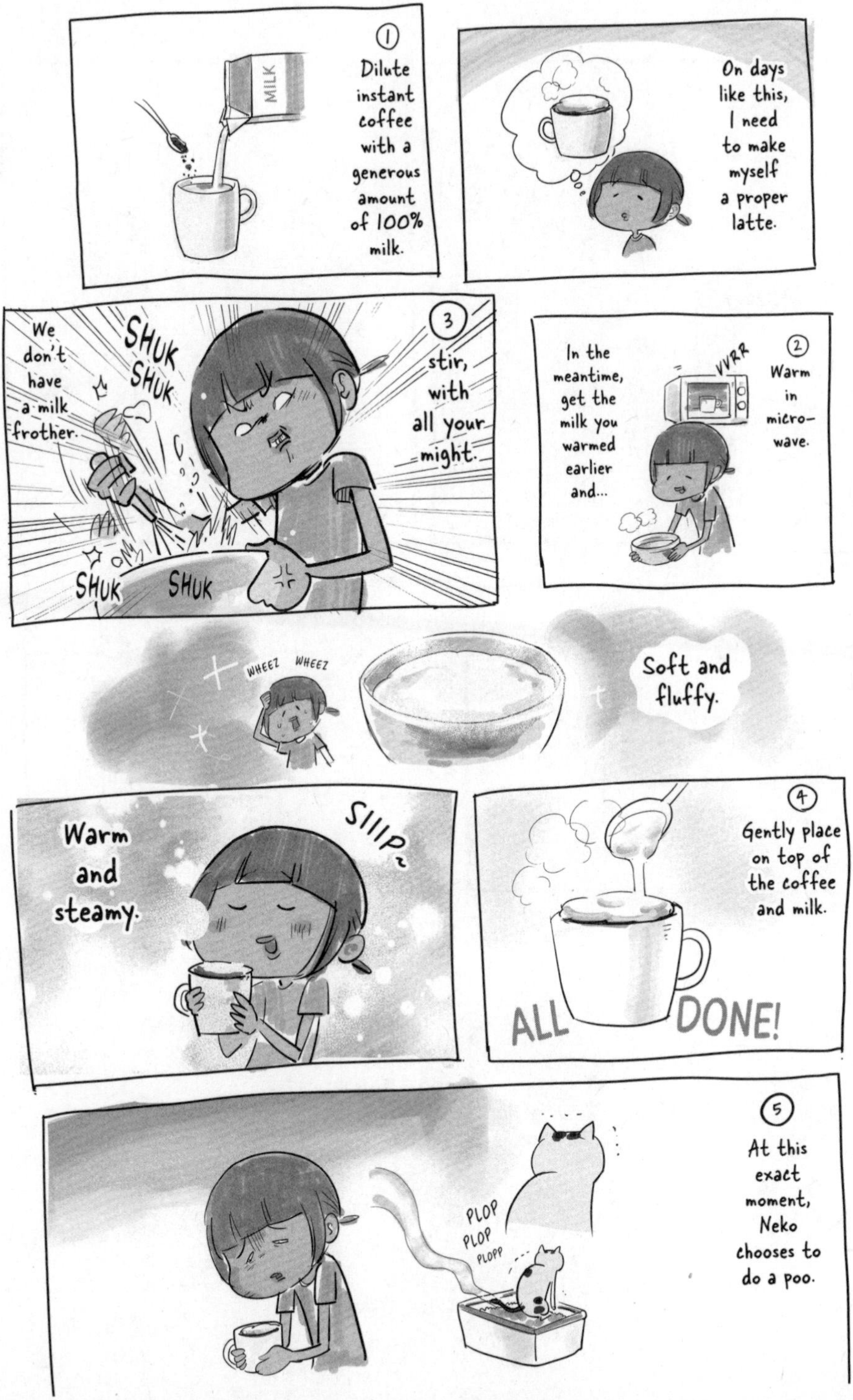
On days like this, I need to make myself a proper latte.
① Dilute instant coffee with a generous amount of 100% milk.
MILK
② Warm in micro-wave.
VVRR
In the meantime, get the milk you warmed earlier and...
③ stir, with all your might.
SHUK SHUK
We don't have a milk frother.
SHUK SHUK
Soft and fluffy.
WHEEZ WHEEZ
④ Gently place on top of the coffee and milk.
ALL DONE!
SIIIP
Warm and steamy.
⑤ At this exact moment, Neko chooses to do a poo.
PLOP PLOP PLOPP

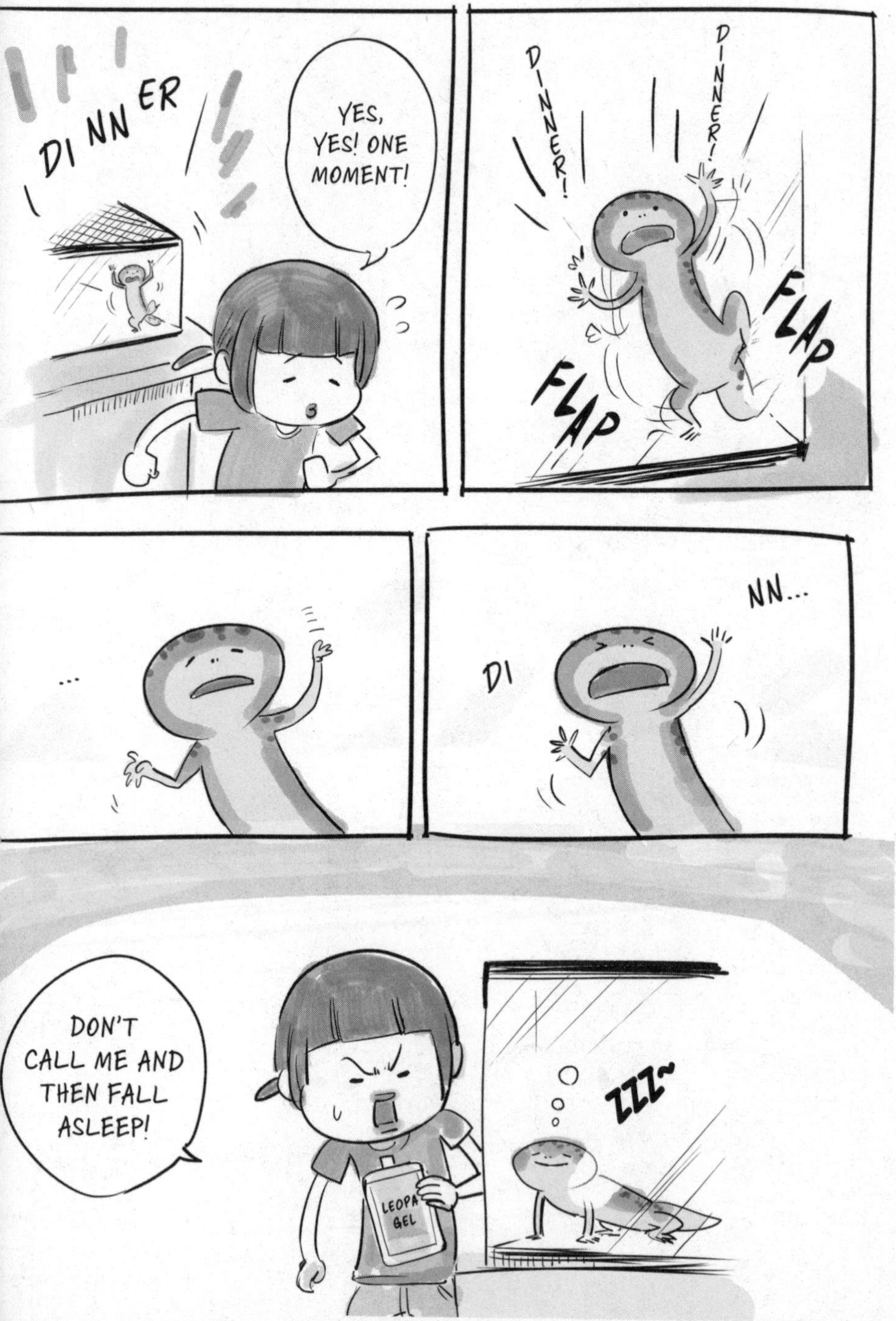
DINNER!
DINNER!
FLAP
FLAP
YES, YES! ONE MOMENT!
DI NN ER
NN...
DI
...
ZZZ~
DON'T CALL ME AND THEN FALL ASLEEP!
LEOPA GEL

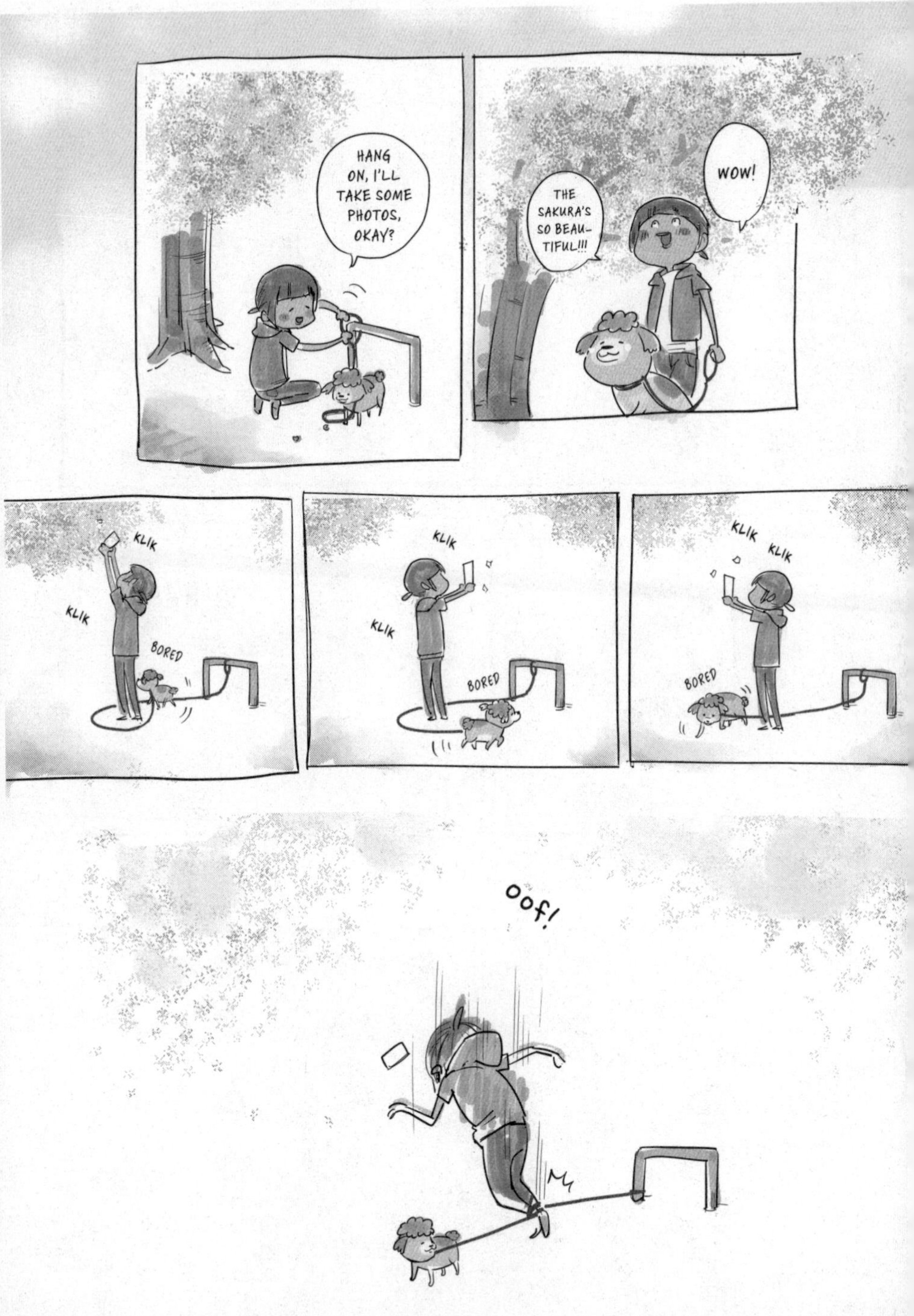
WOW!
THE SAKURA'S SO BEAU-TIFUL!!!
HANG ON, I'LL TAKE SOME PHOTOS, OKAY?
KLIK
KLIK
BORED
KLIK
KLIK
BORED
KLIK
KLIK
BORED
oof!

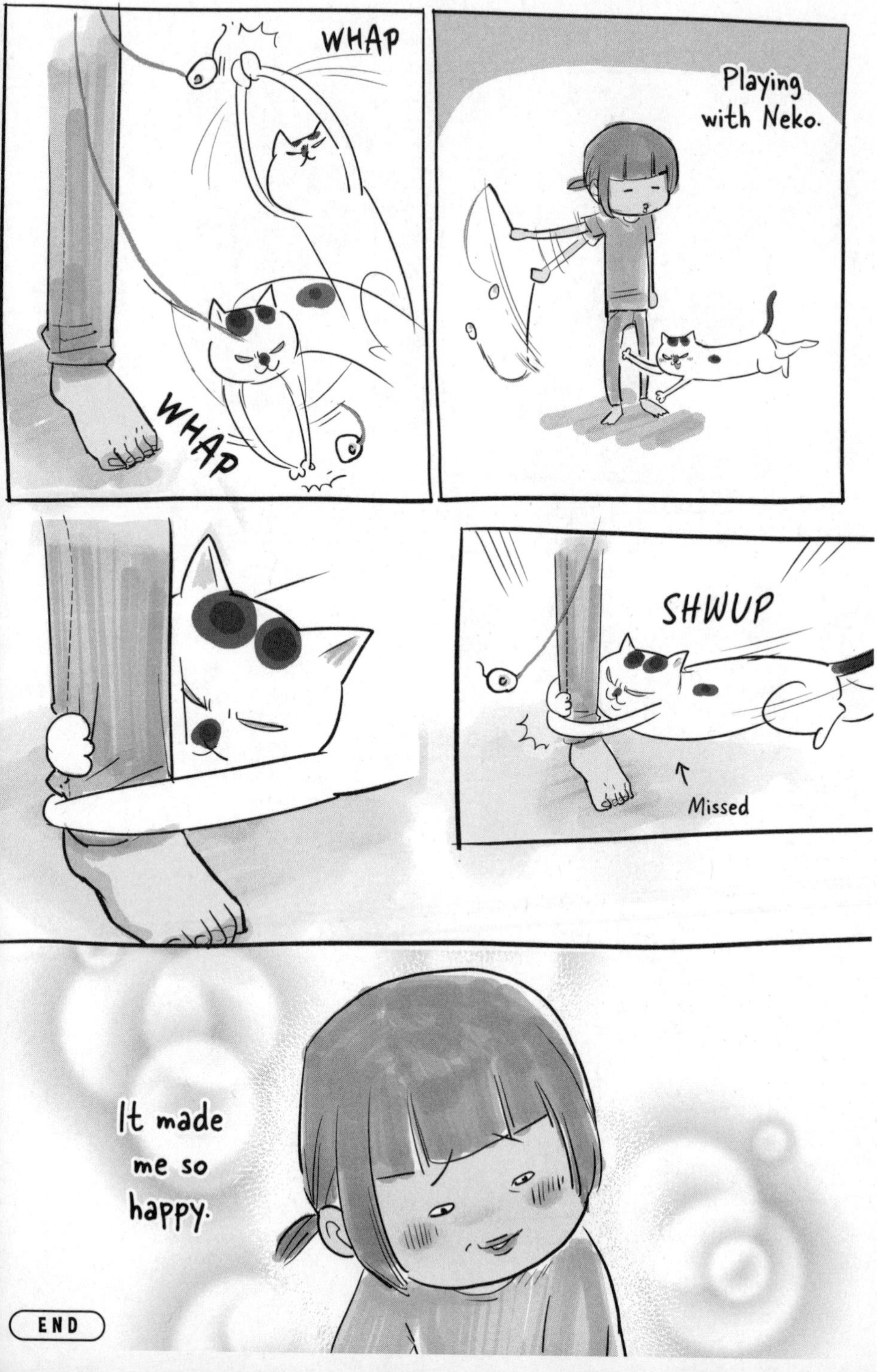
Playing with Neko.
WHAP
WHAP
SHWUP
Missed
It made me so happy.
END

Afterword

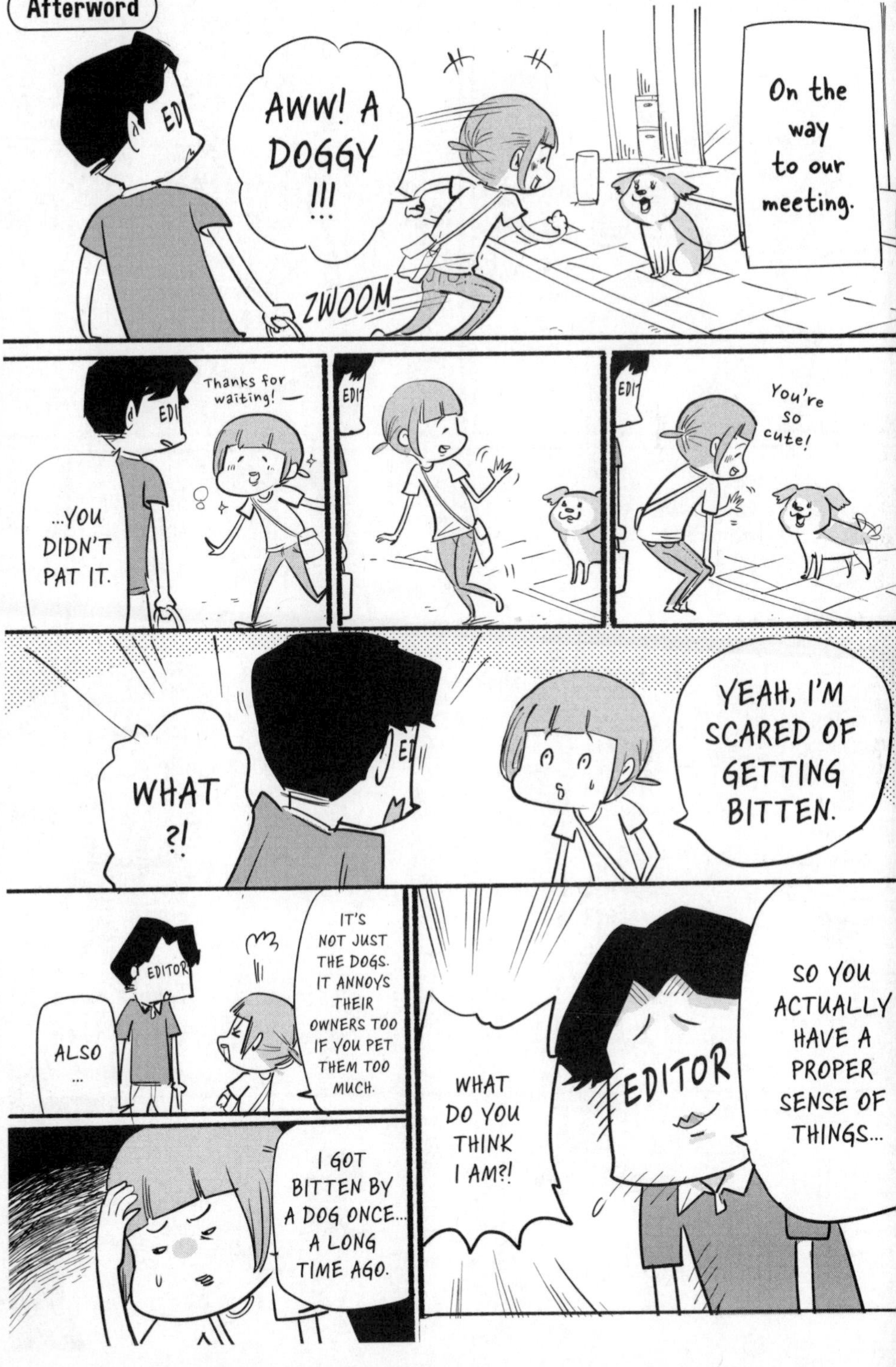

On the way to our meeting.
AWW! A DOGGY!!!
ZWOOM
You're so cute!
Thanks for waiting!
...YOU DIDN'T PAT IT.
YEAH, I'M SCARED OF GETTING BITTEN.
WHAT?!
SO YOU ACTUALLY HAVE A PROPER SENSE OF THINGS...
EDITOR
WHAT DO YOU THINK I AM?!
IT'S NOT JUST THE DOGS. IT ANNOYS THEIR OWNERS TOO IF YOU PET THEM TOO MUCH.
EDITOR
ALSO...
I GOT BITTEN BY A DOG ONCE... A LONG TIME AGO.

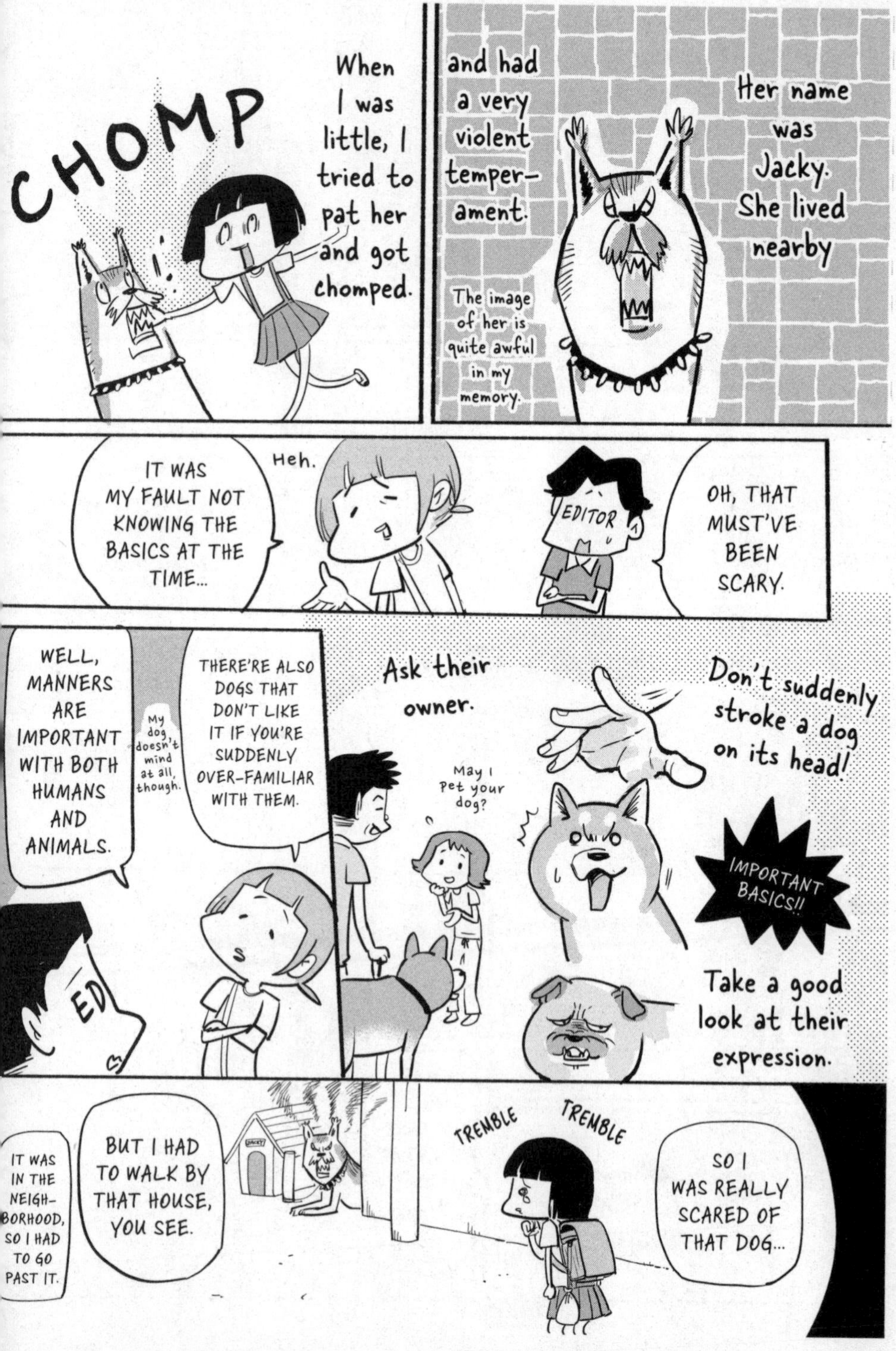
Her name was Jacky. She lived nearby
and had a very violent temper-ament.
The image of her is quite awful in my memory.
When I was little, I tried to pat her and got chomped.
CHOMP
OH, THAT MUST'VE BEEN SCARY.
EDITOR
Heh.
IT WAS MY FAULT NOT KNOWING THE BASICS AT THE TIME...
Don't suddenly stroke a dog on its head!
IMPORTANT BASICS!!
Ask their owner.
May I pet your dog?
Take a good look at their expression.
THERE'RE ALSO DOGS THAT DON'T LIKE IT IF YOU'RE SUDDENLY OVER-FAMILIAR WITH THEM.
My dog doesn't mind at all, though.
WELL, MANNERS ARE IMPORTANT WITH BOTH HUMANS AND ANIMALS.
ED
SO I WAS REALLY SCARED OF THAT DOG...
TREMBLE
TREMBLE
BUT I HAD TO WALK BY THAT HOUSE, YOU SEE.
IT WAS IN THE NEIGH-BORHOOD, SO I HAD TO GO PAST IT.

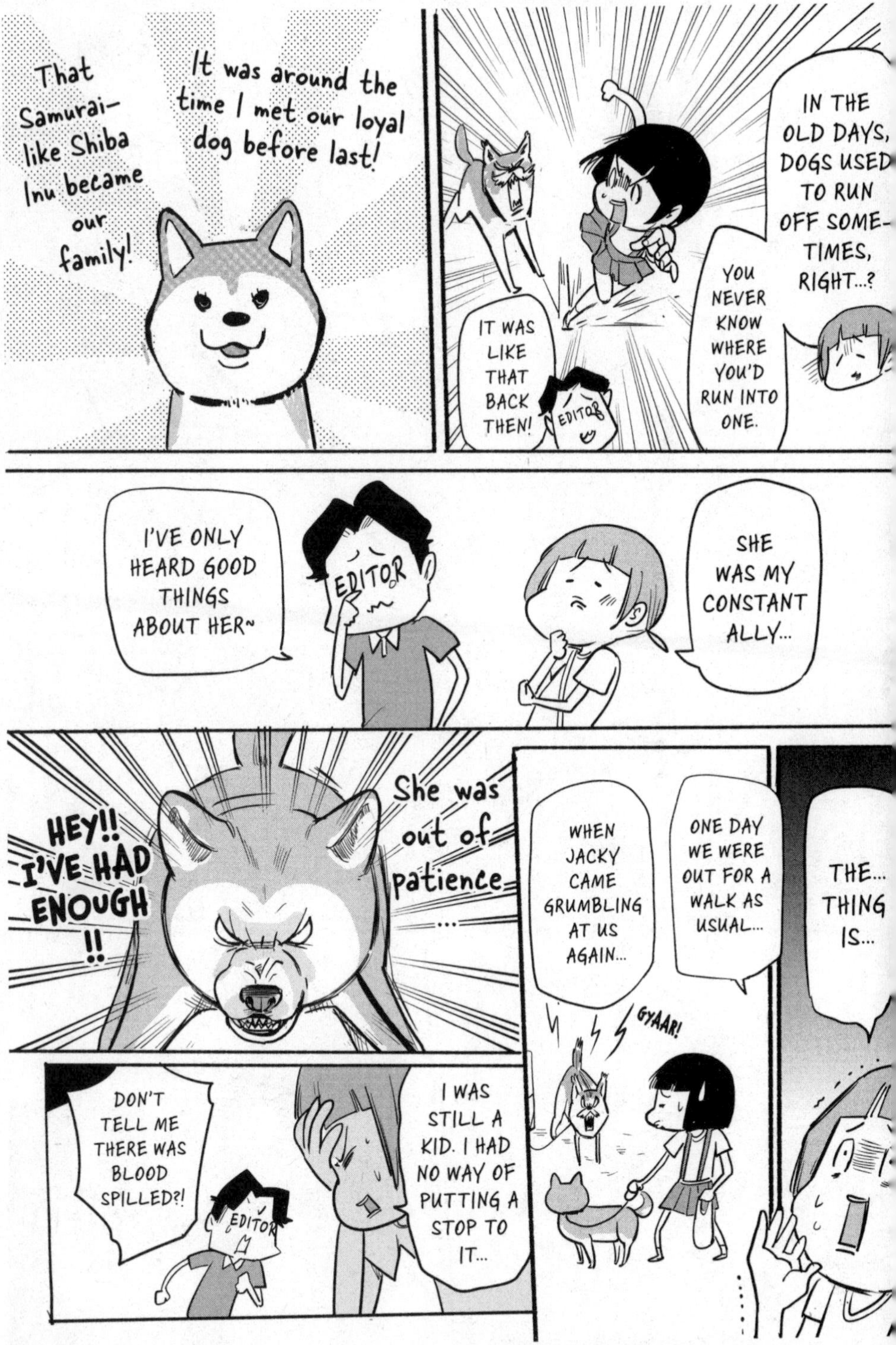
IN THE OLD DAYS, DOGS USED TO RUN OFF SOME-TIMES, RIGHT...?
YOU NEVER KNOW WHERE YOU'D RUN INTO ONE.
IT WAS LIKE THAT BACK THEN!
EDITOR
It was around the time I met our loyal dog before last!
That Samurai-like Shiba Inu became our family!
SHE WAS MY CONSTANT ALLY...
I'VE ONLY HEARD GOOD THINGS ABOUT HER~
EDITOR
THE... THING IS...
ONE DAY WE WERE OUT FOR A WALK AS USUAL...
WHEN JACKY CAME GRUMBLING AT US AGAIN...
GYAAR!
She was out of patience...
HEY!! I'VE HAD ENOUGH!!
I WAS STILL A KID. I HAD NO WAY OF PUTTING A STOP TO IT...
DON'T TELL ME THERE WAS BLOOD SPILLED?!
EDITOR

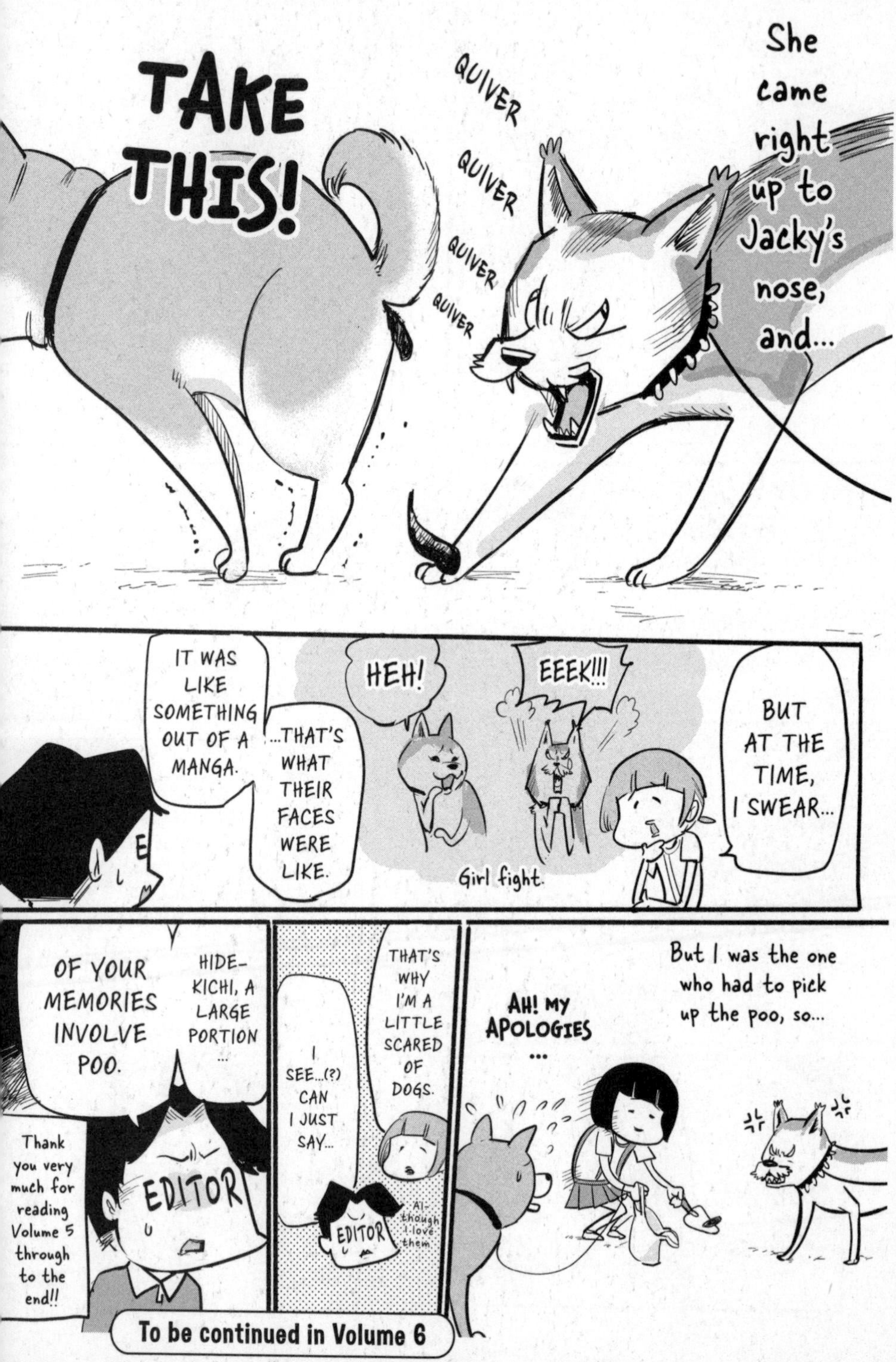
She came right up to Jacky's nose, and...
QUIVER
QUIVER
QUIVER
QUIVER
TAKE THIS!
BUT AT THE TIME, I SWEAR...
EEEK!!!
HEH!
Girl fight.
...THAT'S WHAT THEIR FACES WERE LIKE.
IT WAS LIKE SOMETHING OUT OF A MANGA.
But I was the one who had to pick up the poo, so...
AH! MY APOLOGIES...
THAT'S WHY I'M A LITTLE SCARED OF DOGS.
I SEE...(?) CAN I JUST SAY...
EDITOR
Although I love them.
HIDE-KICHI, A LARGE PORTION...
OF YOUR MEMORIES INVOLVE POO.
EDITOR
Thank you very much for reading Volume 5 through to the end!!
To be continued in Volume 6

 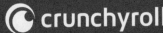

IS BEING SERIALIZED ON TWITTER! Information

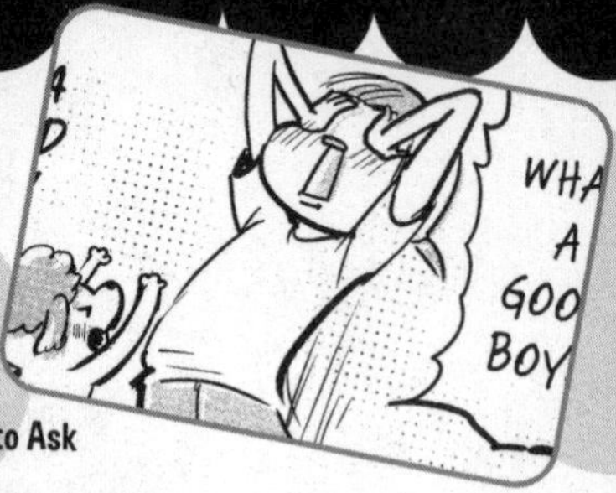
WHAT A GOOD BOY

VOLUME 5 EPISODE TITLES WHEN SERIALIZED ON TWITTER

#127	With a Dog AND a Cat,	It's Pretty Fun When You Try to Ask the Unreasonable
#128	〃	Your Personality Comes Out When You're Driving and Every Day is Fun
#129	〃	The Different Feelings of Summer are Fun
#130	〃	Getting a Glimpse of Their Hunting Instincts Makes Every Day Fun
#131	〃	Just Making Eye Contact Makes Every Day Fun
#132	〃	Their Sudden Human-Like Behaviors are Pretty Fun
#133	〃	Stubborn Exchanges Make Every Day Fun
#134	〃	Their Unexpected Expressions Make Every Day Fun
#135	〃	Their Toilet Habits Make Every Day Fun
#136	〃	Sudden Tummy Aches Can Be Tough and Fun
#137	〃	When They Have Conflicting Feelings, It Makes Every Day Fun
#138	〃	Changing Clothes for the Season is Somewhat Fun
#139	〃	You Learn About Life From Your Failures, So Every Day is Fun
#140	〃	Their Wildness When You Use Your Appliances Makes Every Day Fun
#141	〃	You Can Share Happiness and Warmth and Every Day is Fun

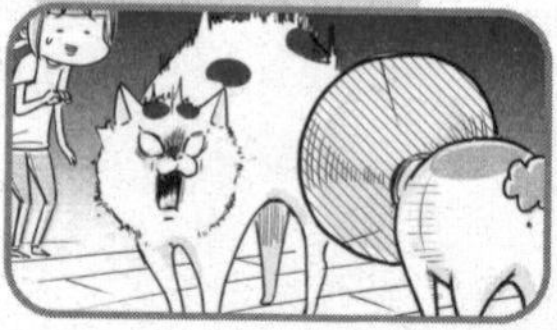

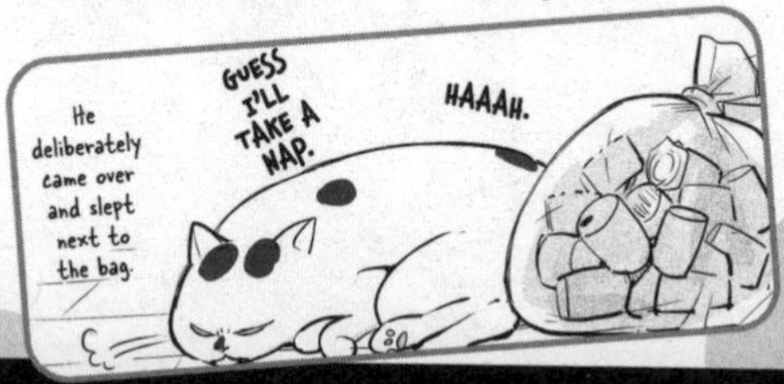
HAAAH.
GUESS I'LL TAKE A NAP.
He deliberately came over and slept next to the bag.

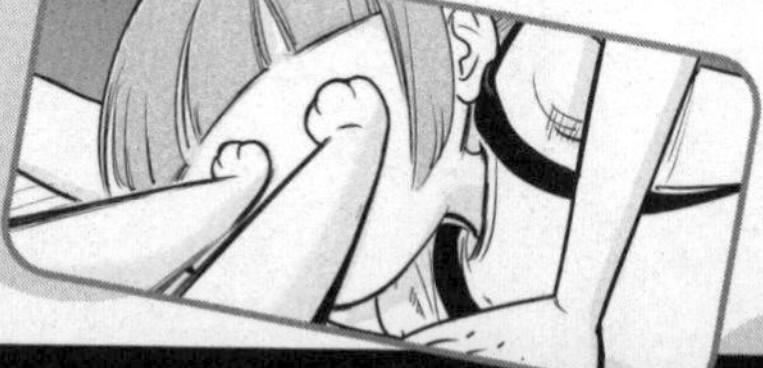

SUNDAY ☆ (AND TRYING NOT TO TAKE ANY WEEKS OFF!)

"WITH A DOG AND A CAT, EVERY DAY IS FUN"

Twitter @hidekiccan

APPEARING EVER

With a Dog AND a Cat, Every Day is Fun

HISTORY

?, ?, 2009

NEKO-SAMA IS BORN.

His face isn't scary!

Y-YOU SEEM KINDA LOW ENERGY HUH.
later became
That crazy limp kitten with no motivation
AH, NEKO, NOW ABOUT YOU...
I FOUND YOU CRYING IN A GUTTER.

Lovely from the very beginning!

APRIL 1, 2009

INU-KUN IS BORN.

OH...! THIS IS THE ONE WITH ALL THE FUR FROM BEFORE...
later became
That madly smiling puppy with the strange moves...
YOU WERE BORN ON APRIL 1ST.
Yup!
Yup!
YOU CAME FROM SHIGA PREFECTURE. DO YOU KNOW WHERE THAT IS?
Yup!
Yup!

FEBRUARY, 2017

FIRST TWEET

Matsumoto Hidekichi @hidekiccan

Whenever I open a bag of snacks, my dog comes over like, "Can I have some?" I've never given him any before, so I'm thinking, "Give up already." But I've figured it out. He's not thinking, "I've never gotten any before, so I'll give up." He's thinking, "Today may be the day I get some for the first time!" That's what he's living his life thinking. H-He is a sage... A dog sage!

The response was miraculous!

When I open a bag of snacks, my dog dashes over.
VWOOM
SNACKS
#1
CAN I HAVE SOME?
CAN I HAVE SOME?
NO... I'VE NEVER GIVEN YOU ANY EVEN ONCE BEFORE.
why... you...
GIVE UP ALREADY
No, wait!
AH!
He's...
He's not thinking, "I've never gotten any before, so I'll give up."
No...
"Today may be the day I get some for the first time!"
...is what he's living his life thinking.

IS YOUR BRAIN MADE OF FERTILIZER, SON?
WHAT YOU DO IS STEAL AND EAT IT AFTER THEY'RE FAST ASLEEP!
The next morning, Neko makes a swift attack and gobbles it all up.
Neko is truly scary.

JUNE, 2018

VOLUME 1 GOES ON SALE. GOES TO A SECOND PRINTING ON THE SAME DAY!

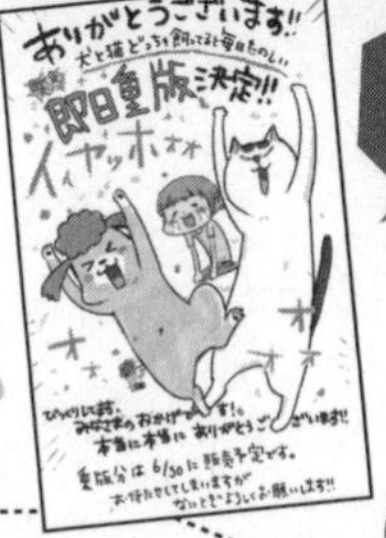

ありがとうございます!!
即日重版決定!!

It became a big deal!

OCTOBER, 2018

VOLUME 2 AS WELL AS A SPECIAL EDITION WITH A BONUS STICKY NOTE GO ON SALE AT THE SAME TIME.

This is now a famous product.

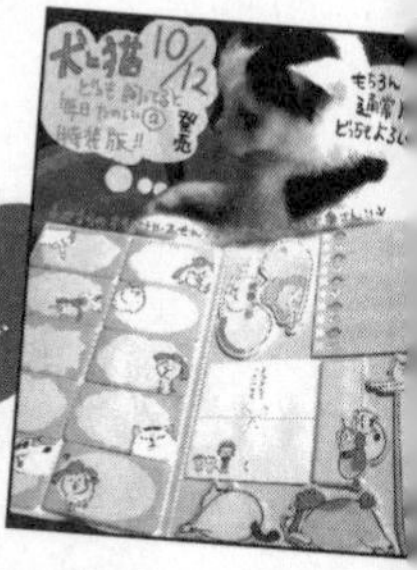

犬と猫

MAY, 2019

VOLUME 3, LIMITED EDITION WITH INU AND NEKO SOCKS SET.

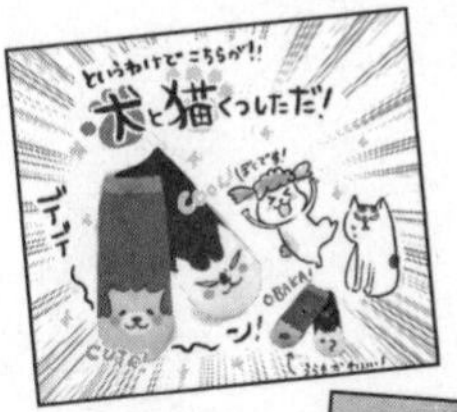

犬と猫くつしただ!

DECEMBER, 2019

VOLUME 4, LIMITED EDITION WITH HAPPY YELLOW COIN PURSE.

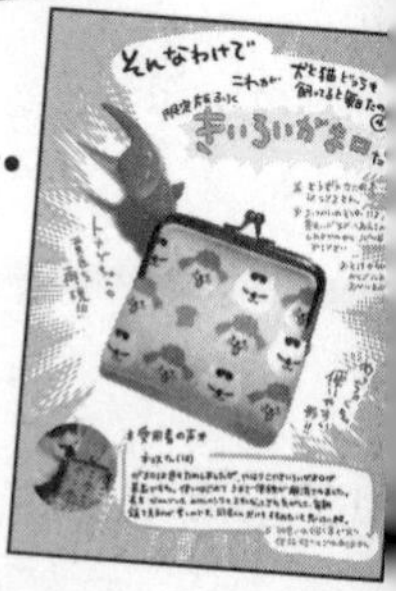

SEPTEMBER, 2020

VOLUME 5, LIMITED EDITION WITH BALLPOINT PEN THAT MOVES - THE KIND YOU OFTEN FIND AT SOUVENIR SHOPS.

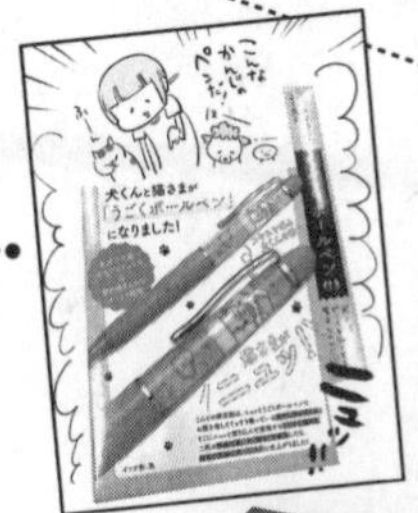

OCTOBER, 2020

TV ANIME BEGINS!

CAST

INU-KUN 🐾 KANA HANAZAWA

NEKO-SAMA 🐾 TOMOKAZU SUGITA

HIDEKICHI MATSUMOTO 🐾 MAI KANAZAWA

DIRECTOR 🐾 SEIJI KISHI

AVAILABLE ON CRUNCHYROLL.COM

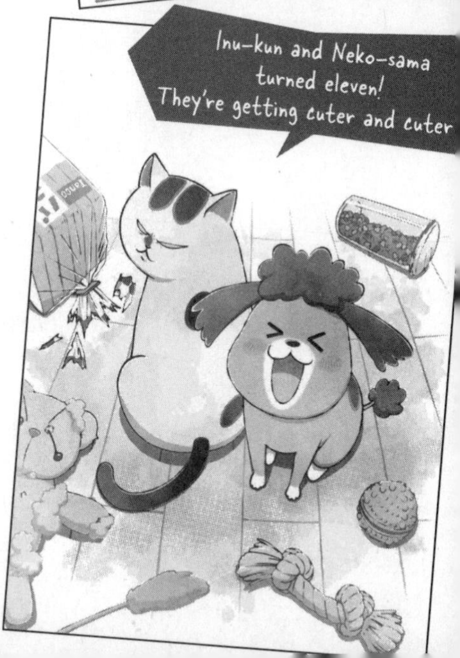

Inu-kun and Neko-sama turned eleven!
They're getting cuter and cuter

Chi returns to the US in a coloring book
featuring dozens of cute and furry illustrations from
award-winning cartoonist Konami Kanata.

Available Now!

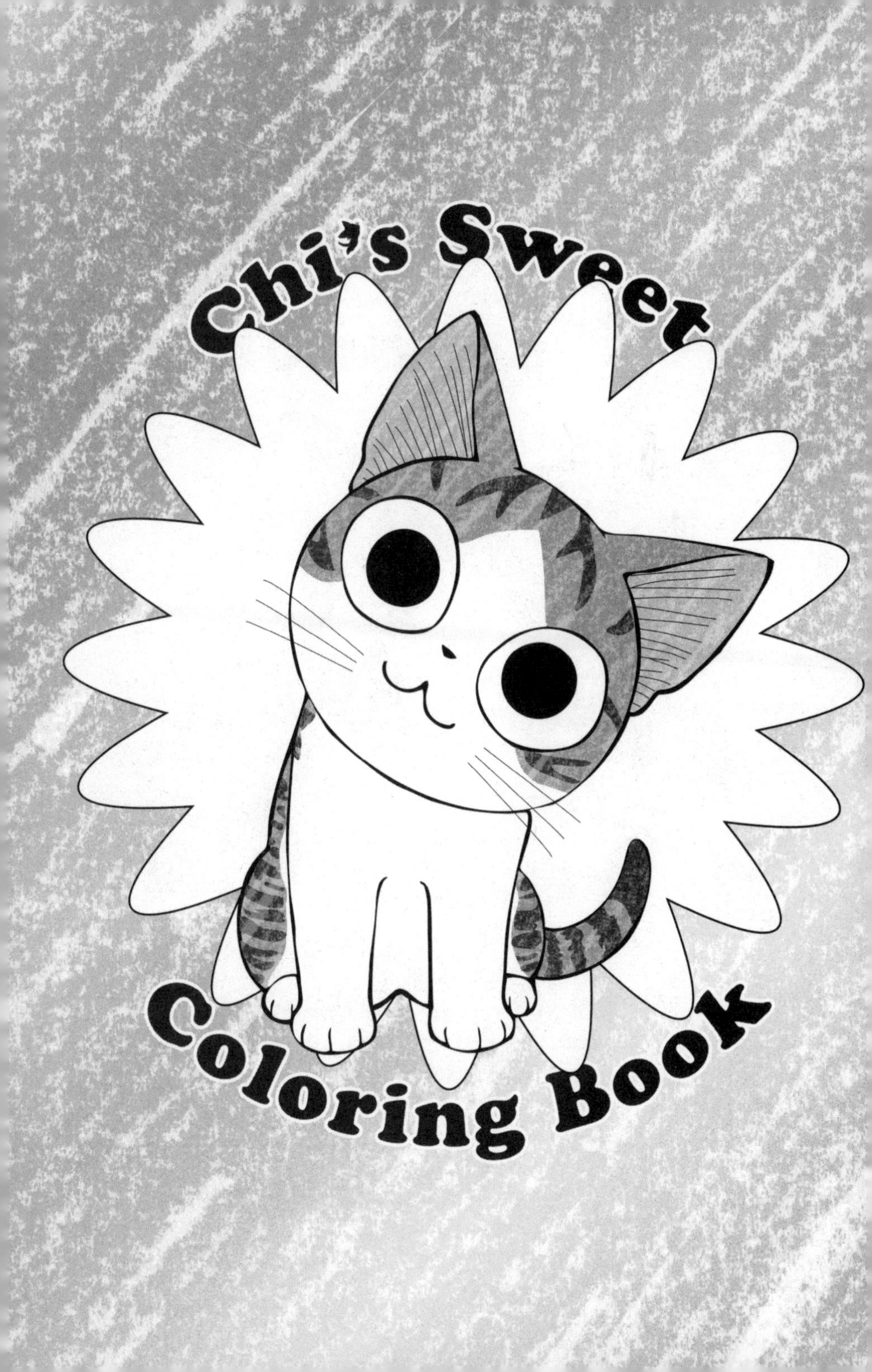
Chi's Sweet
Coloring Book

Chi's

Sweet Adventures

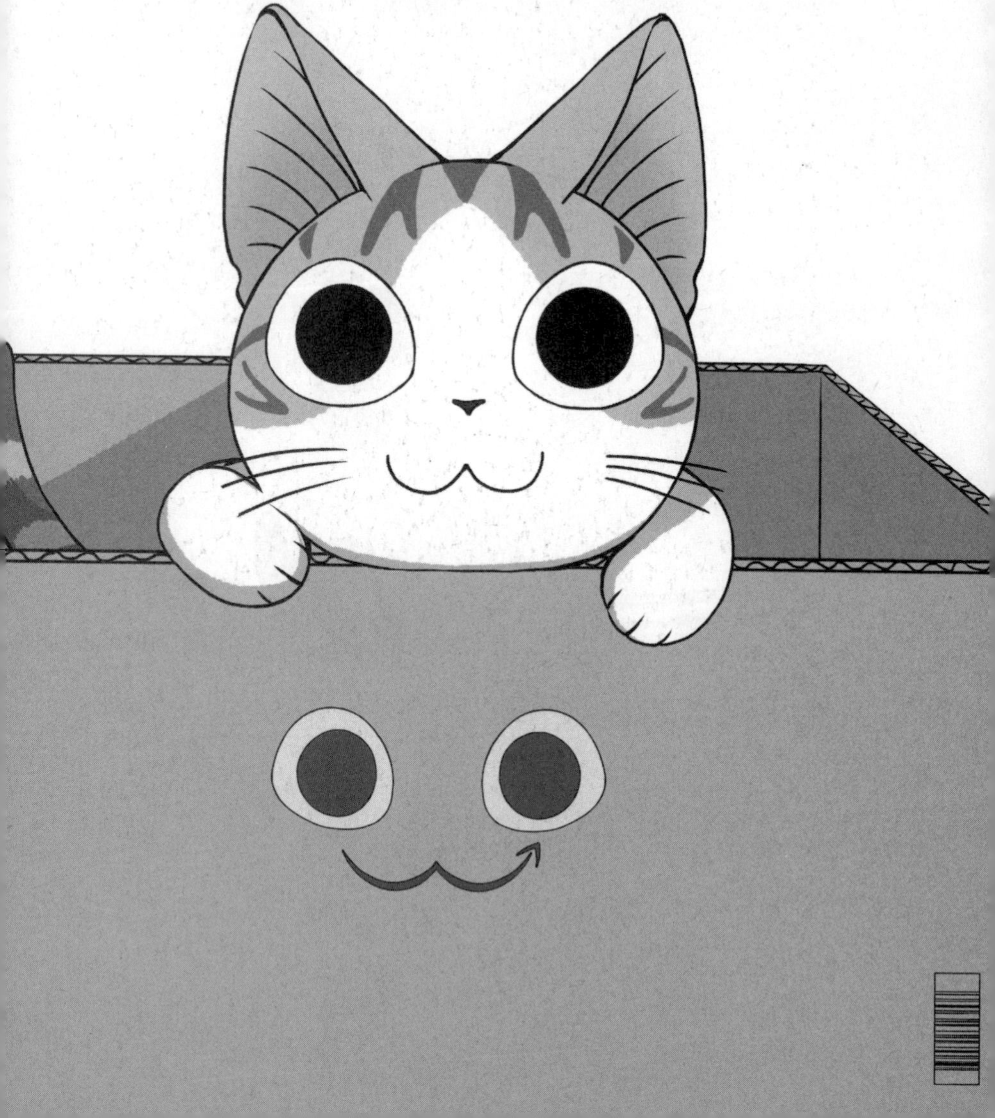

Created by Konami Kanata
Adapted by Kinoko Natsume

Chi is back! Manga's most famous cat
returns with a brand new series!
Chi's Sweet Adventures collects dozens
of new full-color kitty tales made
for readers of all ages!

Volumes 1-4
On Sale Now!

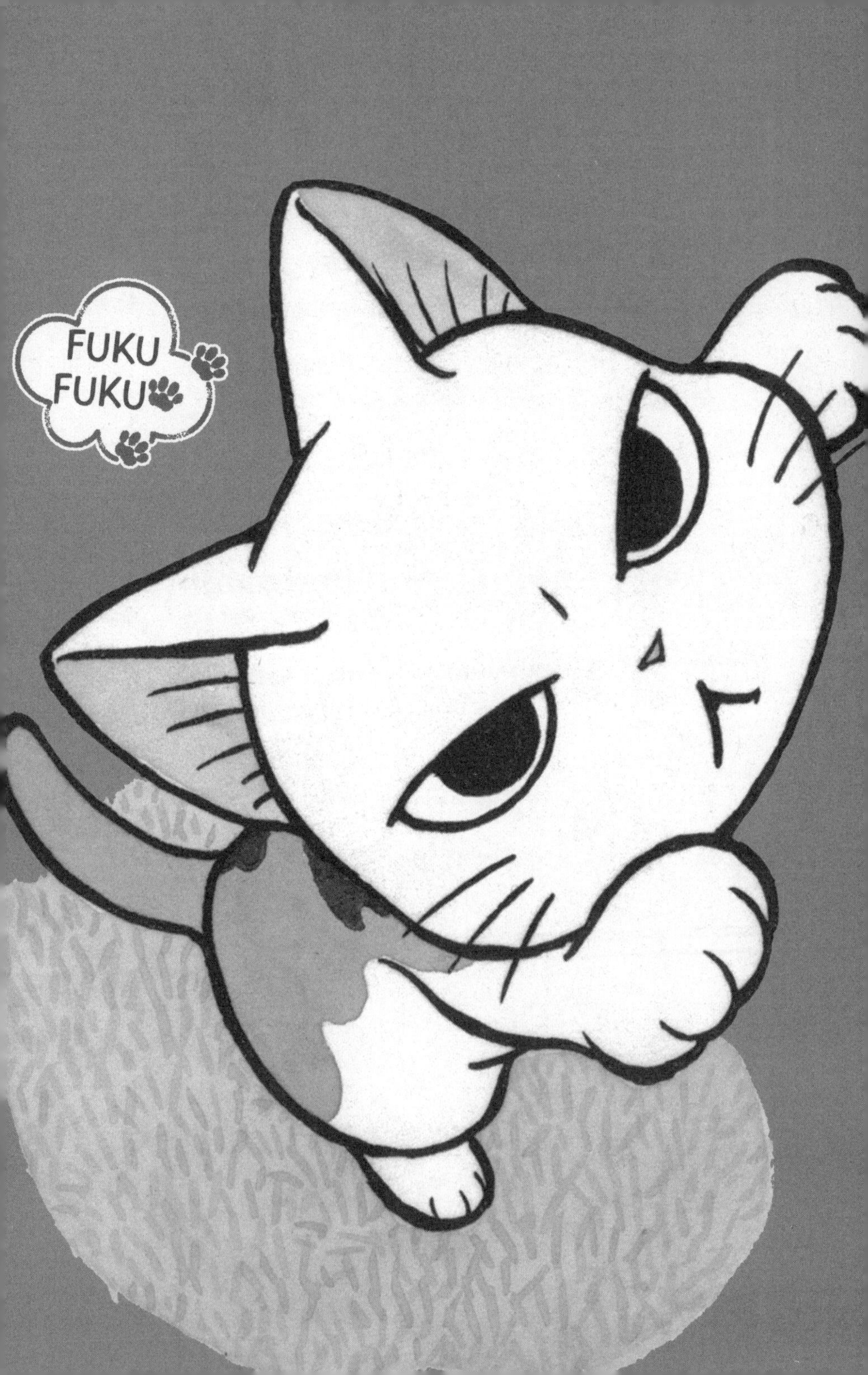
FUKU
FUKU

With a Dog AND a Cat, Every Day is Fun 5

A Vertical Comics Edition

Editor: Michelle Lin
Translation: Kumar Sivasubramanian
Production: Risa Cho
Eve Grandt
Alexandra Swanson (SKY Japan Inc.)

First published in Japan in 2020 by Kodansha, Ltd., Tokyo
Publication rights for this English edition arranged through Kodansha, Ltd., Tokyo
English language version produced by Vertical Comics, an imprint of Kodansha USA Publishing, LLC

Translation provided by Vertical Comics, 2021
Published by Kodansha USA Publishing, LLC, New York

Originally published in Japanese as *Inu to Neko Docchimo Katteru to Mainichi Tanoshii 5* by Kodansha, Ltd., 2020

This is a work of fiction.

ISBN: 978-1-64729-074-0

Manufactured in the United States of America

First Edition

Kodansha USA Publishing, LLC
451 Park Avenue South
7th Floor
New York, NY 10016
www.kodansha.us

Vertical books are distributed through Penguin-Random House Publisher Services.

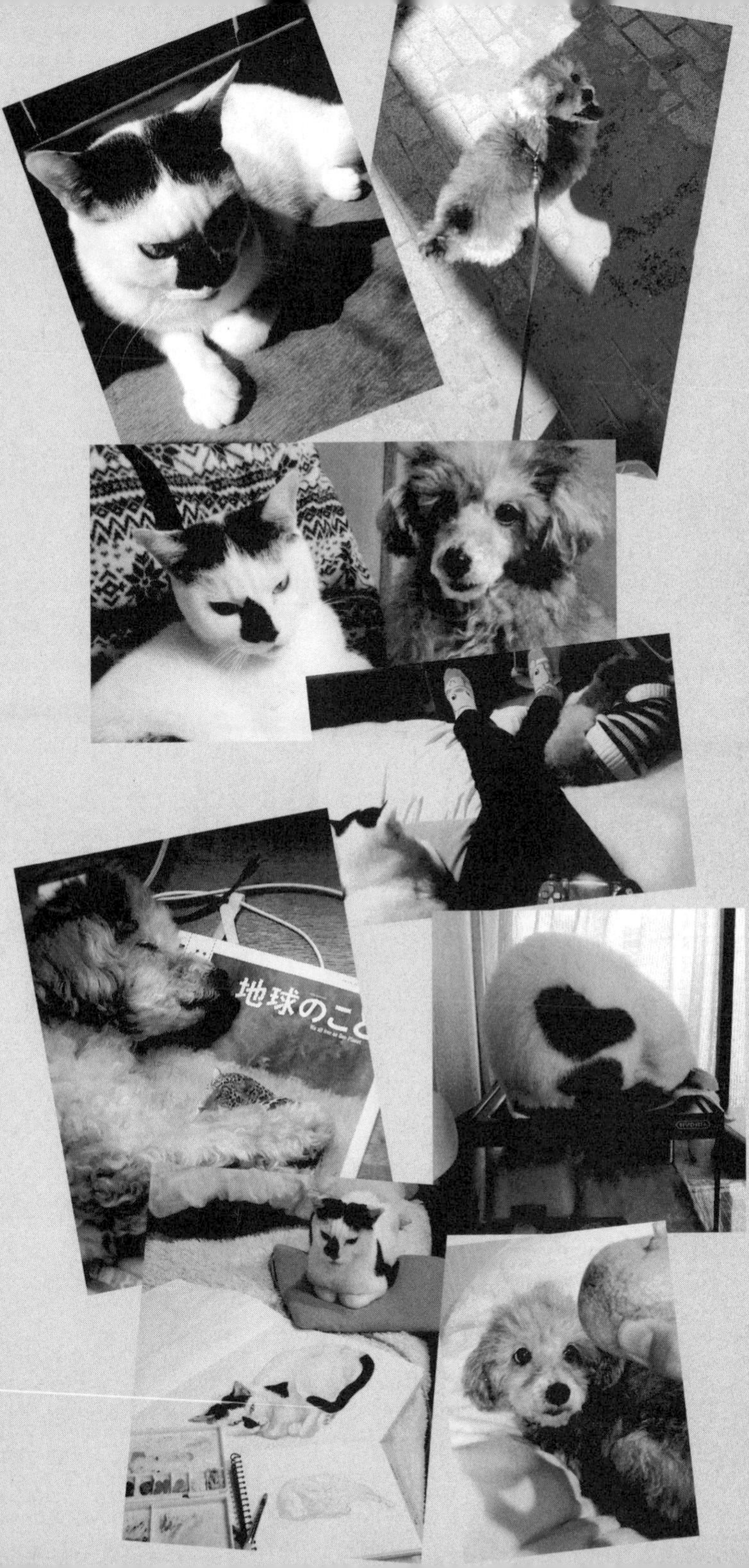
地球のこと

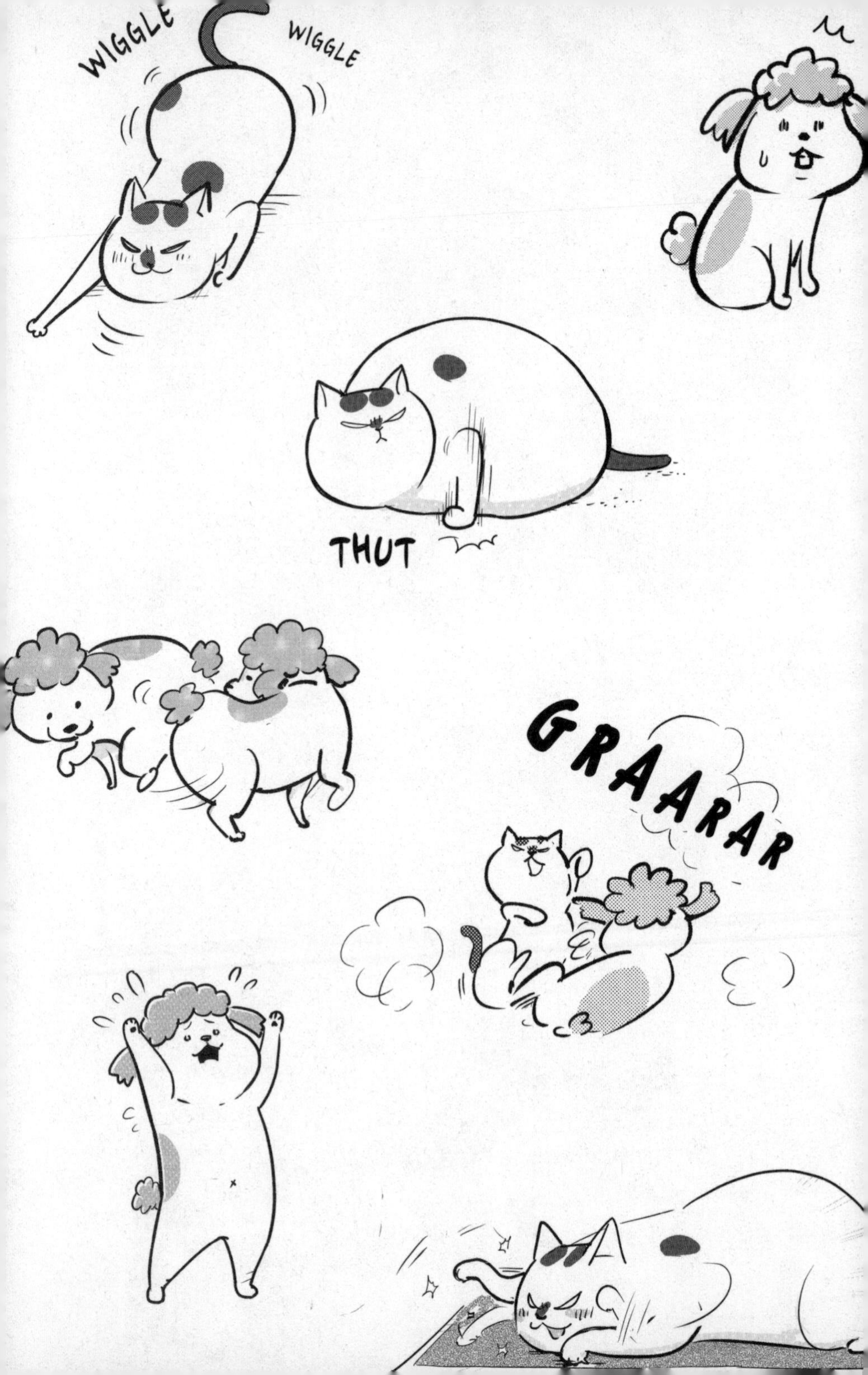
WIGGLE WIGGLE
THUT
GRAARAR